Illustrious Fife

LITERARY, HISTORICAL & ARCHITECTURAL
PATHWAYS & WALKS

By Duncan Glen

AKROS : *Kirkcaldy* : 1998

First Published 1998
AKROS PUBLICATIONS
33 Lady Nairn Avenue
Kirkcaldy, Fife, Scotland, UK

copyright © Duncan Glen 1998

Typeset by Emtext [Scotland]
Printed and bound in Scotland

A CIP Record for this book
is available from the British Library

ISBN 0 86142 087 X

Contents

Author's Preface

> My true self runs toward a Hill—
> More! O More! Visible.
> Theodore Roethke

As my wife can confirm, I have great difficulty in not wishing to find out what is to be seen not only from the top of a hill but also round the corner of a country road, or an unknown city street. This book is a good excuse for not only walking new roads but also revisiting ones I remember very well. Since I live, professionally, with Scottish literature I have given myself a pleasurable few months by linking literary works to many places to be found by rounding many a corner and walking many roads. I offer this journey to readers in the hope that some of my pleasure in travelling in Fife, a most splendid and diverse "kingdom" of people, landscapes, interesting buildings, history and literature, has rubbed off onto the words on these pages.

The Fife that I knew best, in the 1950s, as a cyclist and walker, radiated out from Markinch into the golden fringed county as it was when Glenrothes was a mere stripling around Woodside on the edge of the old burgh of Markinch with its elected Provost, Councillors and Baillies, and all the new roads created since the building of the Forth and Tay road bridges were quite beyond our imaginings. My travels in 1997 and 1998 have taken me further afield. I have aimed to introduce events of historical importance, men and women of consequence and interest, buildings of historical and/or architectural interest, and to quote from a wide range of literature. I have also included some of my own memories, sometimes built around my own poems on Fife, which are not always truly autobiographical.

DUNCAN GLEN, *Fife*, March 1998

Acknowledgements and Select Bibliography

The helpfulness of so many men and women that I met on my travels around Fife in 1997 and 1998 was a continuing pleasure. I am grateful to all those who spoke to me of their Fife memories and knowledge of its history. Others accepted my enquiring telephone calls with considerable patience. Some of these are friends over many years and some have written fine poetry. This is not an academic work that began with research in libraries but, as so often in the past, I am very grateful to the staffs of: the Scottish and Edinburgh Departments of the Central Library, Edinburgh; the Scottish Poetry Library, Edinburgh; the National Library of Scotland; and to Kirkcaldy Public Library which I have returned to with much pleasure, having been in it almost daily in the 1950s. I am only too well aware that there are many who know Fife and its history so much better than I do; my apologies to them and to all readers for errors of fact, or naming, which are solely my responsibility.

I am grateful to the authors of the many excellent brief histories and guides available in churches, historic buildings, mansions and Tourist Information Offices;

also the works written for Heritage and Civic Societies. There are also many histories of burghs, parishes and families but, this being an informal and personal work, I have not consulted many of these, or the biographies of famous individuals. What follows is: a very select list of the earlier standard works on Fife with a very few less formal works; a selection of specialist works; some of the current guide books that I found especially useful; and three anthologies of Scottish poetry. I have been unable to recommend an anthology of Scottish prose.

Sibbald, Sir Robert, *The History Ancient & Modern of the Sheriffdoms of Fife & Kinross*, 1710.
Millar, A.H., *Fife, Pictorial and Historical*, 2 Vols, 1895.
Wood, Rev. Walter, *The East Neuk of Fife*, second edition, 1887.
The Statistical Account of Scotland, 1791-1799, reprint of Fife parishes, 1978.
The New Statistical Account of Scotland, Vol.9, Fife, 1845.
The Third Statistical Account of Scotland, The County of Fife, edited by Alexander Smith, 1952.
Wilkie, J., *Bygone Fife: From Culross to St Andrews*, 1931.
Wilkie, J., *Bygone Fife: North of the Lomonds*, 1938.
Snoddy, T.G., *Afoot in Fife*, 1950.
Snoddy, T. G., *'Tween Forth and Tay*, 1969.

Bruce, Scott, *The Railways of Fife*, 1980.
Duckham, Baron F., *A History of the Scottish Coal Industry 1700-1815*, 1970.
Gifford, J., *The Buildings of Scotland: Fife*, 1988.
Jarrett, Tom, *St Andrews Golf Links: The First 600 Years*, 1995.
Pride, Glen L., *The Kingdom of Fife: An Illustrated Architectural Guide*, 1990.

Brown, Hamish, *Fife Coast: From the Forth Bridges to Leuchars by the Castles Coast and the East Neuk*, 1994.
Lamont-Brown, Raymond, *Discovering Fife*, 1988, latest reprint 1991.

Lindsay, Maurice, *History of Scottish Literature*, 1977 and later paperback edition.
Glen, Duncan, *The Poetry of the Scots*, 1991.

Lynch, Michael, *Scotland: A New History*, revised paperback edition 1992.
Mackie, J.D., *A History of Scotland*, 1964, revised and edited by Bruce Lenman and Geoffrey Parker, 1978, latest reprint 1991.
Mitchison, Rosalind, *A History of Scotland*, second edition, 1982.

The Oxford Book of Scottish Verse, edited by John MacQueen and Tom Scott, 1966, and various paperback editions.
The Penguin Book of Scottish Verse, edited by Tom Scott, 1970, and later editions.
The Poetry of Scotland: Gaelic, Scots and English 1380-1980, edited by Roderick Watson, 1995.

Forth and Tay Ferries & Bridges,
Tayport, Balmerino, Dairsie, Leuchars,
Guardbridge and via Strathtyrum
to St Andrews

THE OLD and illustrious Kingdom of Fife has the finest and most splendid approach roads of all the counties of the United Kingdom. It also has two great rail bridges—of Forth and Tay. Also, to these approaches by bridges over water, can be added the inland roads; that from Stirling comes along the foothills of the Ochils to Fife's own Lomond Hills; and that from Perth goes by Glenfarg to Abernethy. From the Kincardine Bridge there is an eye-opening view up river to Stirling and the Wallace Monument. From the rail and road bridges at Queensferry there is a view that takes in the historic isles of the Firth of Forth. It is difficult to choose between the view of the cantilevered rail bridge from the road bridge, and the elegant road bridge from the rail bridge. As for the bridges over the River Tay, as William McGonigal, master of great doggerel, wrote, "As for beauty thou art most lovely to be seen." The first rail bridge over the Tay dates from 1878 and the second from 1887. The famous, and functionally beautiful, rail bridge at Dalmeny and North Queensferry dates from 1890. The road bridge at Kincardine dates from 1936. The opening of the Forth Road Bridge in 1964 and the Tay Road Bridge in 1966 inaugurated a new era, ending the centuries-old ferries, diminishing the importance of the railway bridges and giving the new, or widened, roads a new significance in the old and often still fiercely-independent "Kingdom of Fife".

Before the railway and road bridges were built the ferries across the Forth were central to the routes taken by travellers through Fife, whether those going to make a career in Edinburgh or a monarch imposing a presence on the Kingdom or going hunting in the wood and hills of Falkland. The ferry at Queensferry was established as a free ferry in the eleventh century by the Saxon Queen Margaret, second wife of Malcolm III, Canmore, to provide transport across the Forth for pilgrims to the shrine of the saint at St Andrews; it remained important until the road bridge was opened in 1964. A ferry between North Berwick and Chapel Ness, near Elie, was established in the mid-twelfth century by the Celtic Duncan, Earl of Fife, to provide an alternative route for pilgrims to St Andrews, and later we have Earlsferry.

We have an early account of the ferry crossing from North Berwick to Elie, made in September 1586 by the great diarist Rev James Melville, professor in St Andrews and minister of Anstruther and nearby Kilrenny,

> We retourned the nearest way be the Ferrie of Northe Berwick, passing the quilk I was in the graittest perplexitie of ane that ever I was in my tyme befor, and haid the maist sudden and comfortable relief of my guid and gratius God and Father, to whase honour, as in all, I man record it. . . . We hoised seall with a lytle pirhe of east wind, and lainshed furthe till almaist the thrid of the passage was past, and

then it fell down dead calme. For rowing nather was ther eares meit, nor handes, the boott was sa heavie, the man auld, and the boyes young. In this mean tyme, the honest woman became sa seik with sic extremitie and preas of vomiting first, thereafter with swinings, that it was pitifull to behauld. Withe hir working, the bairn wackens, and becomes extream seik, being nane but myselff to curie tham, for Mr Robert Durie was rowing. This dreing for the space of thrie houres, in end I becam dead seik myselff, sa that then it becam a maist pitifull and lamentable spectakle, to sie a woman, a stranger, an honest mans wyff, com fra ham to pleasure me, to be with extream pres appeirand everie minut to giff upe the ghost; an infant of thrie halff yeirs auld spreauling in the awin excrements, and father, partlie for feir and cair of mynd, and partlie for fear seikness, lifting upe pitifull handes and eis to the heavines, voide of all erdlie confort or helpe of man.. . . . at last the Lord luiked mercifullie on, and send, about the sune going to, a thik ear from the Southeast, sa that, getting on the seall ther was upon hir, within an houre and a halff, quhilk was strange to our consideration, na wind blawing, we arryved within the Alie [Elie], and efter a maist weirisome and sair day, gat a comfortable nights ludging with a godlie lady in Carmury.

The "godlie lady" of Carmury was probably Catherine, widow of Paul Dishington of Ardross. The Dishingtons built a castle at Ardross, to which I shall return, but lived at Carmury for a time when the fortress had been ruined by some warfare. An earlier Dishington married a sister of King Robert I, the Bruce. Melville's hostess was a daughter of Walter Lundin and probably it was her brother, the Laird of Lundin, who escorted Melville on to St Andrews.

The once-important ferry at Pettycur near Kinghorn lost most of its trade in the early decades of the nineteenth century, but when James Boswell and Samuel Johnson crossed from Leith to Petttycur in 1773 it was still a major harbour. Pettycur still featured at the head of several milestones when I was cycling through the Howe of Fife in the 1950s but that was a tribute to the durability of the "stones" rather than an indication of Pettycur's importance. Sir Walter Scott put on record that when he visited Wemyss Castle on 18th June 1827 he "reached Pettycur about half-past one, crossed to Edinburgh, and so ended our little excursion." When Dr Samuel Johnson and Mr James Boswell landed at Pettycur a chaise awaited them which took them through Kinghorn, Kirkcaldy and Cupar to St Andrews. The often critical Johnson found,

> Though we were yet in the most populous part of Scotland, and at so small a distance from the capital, we met few passengers. The roads are neither rough nor dirty; and it affords a southern stranger a new kind of pleasure to travel so commodiously without the interruption of toll-gates. Where the bottom is rocky, as it seems commonly to be in Scotland, a smooth way is made indeed with great labour, but it never wants repair; and in these parts where adventitious materials are necessary, the ground once consolidated is rarely broken; for the inland commerce is not great, nor are heavy commodities often transported otherwise than by water. The carriages in common use are small carts, drawn each by one little horse; and a man seems to derive some degree of dignity and importance from the reputation of possessing a two-horse cart.

I find it difficult to remember that public road transport in Fife only began at the beginning of the nineteenth century when a coach service was offered from Newport, via

Kennoway, to Pettycur where passengers were left to book on a ferry. Soon, however, a through coach was running from Edinburgh to Dundee, taking a ferry from Newhaven to Pettycur, and another from Newport to Dundee. Kennoway became less important when the route was changed to go via New Inn. A new pier at Granton harbour was initially used by ferries crossing to Pettycur but soon Burntisland became more important. The ferry from Granton to Burntisland became a link to the first railway passenger service which ran from Burntisland to Cupar.

The construction of the line began at Kinghorn in 1846. The first trains ran on 17th September 1847 for invited guests and from Monday 20th September four trains ran daily between Burntisland and Cupar. The ferry crossing from Granton to Burntisland and transfer to the Cupar train was timetabled at forty minutes; the journey from Burntisland to Cupar at one hour fifteen minutes. Passengers who continued to Dundee by coach and ferry had to allow another one and a half hours. The time from Edinburgh to Dundee, given favourable crossings, was four hours, allowing day return journeys to be made by the fit and keen traveller. There were coach connections at a temporary station near Lindores to Perth, and from Auchtermuchty and Falkland to meet the trains at Falkland Road, and passengers could take a coach from Leslie to join a train at Markinch. In May 1848 the railway line was extended to Ferry-Port-on-Craig and soon there was a railway line, via the Granton-Burntisland ferry, through Fife to Perth. Some Perth-Edinburgh passengers preferred to avoid the six-mile sea crossing and took the competing Scottish Central Railway company's service which ran via Stirling, but Fife was opened up for travellers as never before.

The need for the ferry which took railway passengers over the Tay seemed to have ended when the first railway bridge over the Tay was officially opened for traffic in May 1878 but it collapsed on Sunday 28th December 1879 resulting in over sixty deaths. No one knows precisely how many died that gale-struck night; the police record lists 60 names but 75 tickets were counted at St Fort, the last stop before the bridge, and there was the crew of the train. The train was the 4.15pm from Edinburgh Waverley to Granton where the ferry was taken to Burntisland. The second train at Burntisland was due to leave at 5.27 stopping at fourteen stations and was due at Dundee about 7.15pm. There were five passenger coaches and the guard's van; engine no. 224 was driven by David Mitchell. One passenger got off at Leuchars where he expected to be met. Finding no-one there, he was about to rejoin the train when his transport arrived. There were no survivors.

The second rail bridge over the Tay was pronounced safe in July 1887 and this is the bridge still in use today. The need for passengers to use the ferry over the Forth ended with the building of the Forth Railway Bridge which was completed in 1890. The most popular poems on the Tay Bridge must be by William McGonigal,

> Beautiful new railway bridge of the silvery Tay
> With your strong brick piers and buttresses in so grand array;
> And your thirteen central girders, which seems to my eye
> Strong enough all windy storms to defy.
>
> And as I gaze on you my heart feels gay,
> Because thou art the greatest railway bridge of the present day
> And can be seen for miles away,
> From north, south, east, or west, of the Tay,
> On a beautiful and clear sunshiny day,

And ought to make the hearts of the Mars boys feel gay;
Because thine equal nowhere can be seen,
Only near by Dundee and the bonnie Magdalen Green.
* * *
And for beauty thou art most lovely to be seen,
As the train crosses oer thee with her cloud of steam
And you look well painted with the clour of marone,
And to find thy equal there is none;
Which, without fear of contradiction, I venture to say,
Because you are the longest railway bridge of the present day;
That now crosses oer a tidal river stream,
And the most handsome to be seen—
Near by Dundee and the bonnie Magdalen Green.

TTS Mars was a training ship for several hundred boys whose ages ranged from 12 to 16. It was moored off Woodhaven from 1869 to 1929. Until the mid-nineteenth century Woodhaven was more important than nearby Ferry-Port-on-Craig which became Newport. The equivalent of Pettycur on the Forth, Woodhaven was the ferry taken by Boswell and Johnson in 1773. It was the Englishman, not the Scot, who thought the fare too dear for such a short voyage across the Tay.

From the Tay Road Bridge, which is considerably lower than its counterpart at North Queensferry, the spans of the railway bridge seem to be made of delicate fretwork, and the ranks of houses in Newport make another varied pattern. Taking the road along the Tay to Tayport, the view over the estuary is not only of Dundee, and its Law, but also of the Perthshire hills and the well-grouped houses of Broughty Ferry.

In Tayport the tilting tower of the old Parish Church catches the eye, but my objective was the beautiful church with the emotive name of Our Lady Star of the Sea which stands on the western edge of the town, in Queen Street. Designed by Reginald Fairlie in 1938-39, this is one of the most beautiful modern buildings in Fife; certainly a classic of the 1930s. The clean-cut edges of the octagonal tower balance perfectly the simple shapes and proportions of the other walls. The white and smooth finish is masterly in its understatement. On the tower stands Hew Lorimer's equally restrained sculpture, "Our Lady". The simple lines of the prow of a wooden boat, from which the figures of mother and child rise, is so subtle as to almost assume abstract qualities. The child's head is showing some wear, but not the face, and that of the mother remains delicate and clean cut. The space around the church is mostly unadorned grass which excellently sets off Fairlie's masterpiece.

Along the Firth of Tay from Tayport is Balmerino. At the ruins of Balmerino Abbey we might be able to touch stones that were also touched by Queen Ermengarde de Beaumont and her son King Alexander II in the 1220s but I rather doubt it as their Cistercian Monastery has suffered from English burnings, Reformers' destructions, stone stealing by masonic farmers, and aimless polluting by thoughtless vandals. Thankfully today the remnants of the Abbey are in the care of the National Trust for Scotland. A minor road goes to Kilmany, which I have not seen since the A92 was made to take traffic to the Tay Road Bridge. When, from 1803 to 1815, Dr Thomas Chalmers, an important figure in the Disruption of the Church of Scotland, was minister in what had been a quiet village with an attractively simple church, he attracted many to the village to hear him preach. Another minor road goes from Kilmany to Cupar from where the A91 goes to St Andrews via Dairsie and Guardbridge.

When I went to Dairsie I took the no. 41 bus which runs from Dundee to Kirkcaldy via Newport, Balmullo, Dairsie, Cupar, Ceres and Kennoway. My destination was the old bridge over the Eden and St Mary's Old Parish Church. From the village of Dairsie it is about 1 mile to the church and, as two roads go to it, a circular route can be taken and in addition, from the bridge, roads go to both Pitscottie and Strathkinness.

My preference is for the most easterly of the minor roads that go from Dairsie to the bridge. From that road, initially the church looks quite low but, having passed under the railway bridge, gradually its true position in relation to the bridge and the castle behind it becomes clear. From below, near the bridge, the kirkyard seems to slope down quite dramatically and the old octagonal tower, with its unglazed windows, is enhanced by the many lichens on its spire. I favour corner belfries, and this one certainly achieves an unexpected harmony in relation to the tracery of the windows. Perhaps the buttresses between the windows help with this integration into a most pleasing merging of varied styles.

Down below the church, the three-arched medieval bridge over the Eden (c.1530) takes an enhancing curve and the road turns to climb steeply uphill along the tree-covered slopes behind which lie the uplands around Clatto Hill and Drumcarrow Craig. The bridge has been credited to Archbishop James Beaton. The church carries the date 1621 and the arms of Archbishop John Spottiswoode who had it built as a model for Episcopalian worship in Scotland. He may also have written his *History of the Church of Scotland,* 1655, in Dairsie Castle on this same hill. This is a history that is prelatical, but it was commissioned by King James VI with the command, "speak the truth, man, and spare not". The sight of Dairsie Castle was a major surprise of my journeys around Fife in 1997 and 1998. I went to Dairsie expecting to find a ruin; instead there stands a large and fully renovated castle. It is a private residence in which the owners, who restored it, have been living for some three years. I did not intrude upon them but, from the gateway, the restoration and rebuilding looked magnificent, and Historic Scotland seem to be pleased.

From Dairsie the A91 goes to Leuchars. When I came by rail in the 1940s from Lanarkshire to holiday in Fife we crossed the Forth by the famous cantilevered bridge and changed at Thornton Junction for a train to the coast, whether Leven or St Monans. One of the excitements of this holiday journey was in following the traditional custom of throwing pennies into the Forth as the train travelled across the bridge. Today we have wider roads but no railway station at Leven, any of the East Neuk villages or, *almost unbelievably*, at St Andrews which rail travellers reach by alighting at Leuchars and catching a bus or taxi to this town of university, golf and buildings heavy with history that attract many tourists.

The advantage of going via Leuchars, at least for travellers who have all day and nowhere particular to go, is that we can visit the strikingly distinctive Leuchars Church which has a history going back to the twelfth century. Such wayfarers may also discover one of these small-scale features which can remain in the memory more clearly than the grand prospect. A circular barn, a Georgian house topping a sloping pasture, an exotic thistle in a hedgerow, or an unassuming twisting drainage burn overhung with willows and lined with the first primroses of the year.

John Ruskin was at least half a Scot and he wrote of the Scottish word "mind" to remember, "In order that you may, in the Scottish sense, 'mind' anything, first there must be something to 'mind'—and then, the 'mind' to mind it." I am reluctant to attribute qualities to Scottishness or Scotland that are in reality rather commonplace in other countries, but Ruskin may at least be correct in seeing the song "Auld Lang Syne" as uniquely Scottish,

> Now it is the peculiar character of Scottish as distinct from all other scenery on a small scale in north Europe, to have these distinctively "mindable" features. One range of coteau by a French river is exactly like another; one turn of glen in the Black Forest is only the last turn re-turned; one sweep of Jura pasture and crag, the mere echo of the fields and crags of ten miles away. But in the whole course of Tweed, Teviot, Gala, Tay, Forth, and Clyde, there is perhaps scarcely a bend of ravine, or nook of valley, which would not be recognisable by its inhabitants from every other. And there is no other country in which the roots of memory are so entwined with the beauty of nature, instead of the pride of men; no other in which the song of "Auld lang syne" could have been written,—or Lady Nairne's ballad of "The Auld House".

> Oh, the auld house, the auld house,
>   What tho' the rooms were wee!
> Oh! kind hearts were dwelling there
>   And bairnies fu' o' glee;
> The wild rose and the jessamine
>   Still hang upon the wa',
> How mony cherish'd memories
>   Do they, sweet flowers, reca'!
>
> Oh, the auld laird, the auld laird,
>   Sae canty, kind, and crouse,
> How mony did he welcome to
>   His ain wee dear auld house!

Within Lady Nairne's sentimentality we are many a literary mile from the folk genius that, worldwide, we respond to in Robert Burns's version of "Auld Lang Syne".

The apse and chancel of the small Leuchars Parish Church, St Athernase, which stands high in the centre of the village, has been described as the "second finest piece of Norman work in the whole of Great Britain". Parts of the building may date from 1183 although it was dedicated by David Bernham, Bishop of St Andrews, in 1244. The nave is nineteenth-century and the original chancel and apse have also been restructured over the centuries. These alterations are complicated but without them the little kirk would lack some of what appeals to us today.

Alexander Henderson, a former regent in St Salvator's College, St Andrews, became minister of Leuchars in 1614 and remained there till 1638 when he was transferred to a highly-paid ministry in Edinburgh. Henderson is of special interest here because he was involved, as was Edinburgh advocate, Archibald Johnston of Wariston, in writing the National Covenant, which was signed on 28th February and 1st March 1638 in Greyfriars Church, Edinburgh. Wariston saw the 28th as "that glorious marriage day of the Kingdom with God". The mixing of the ideas of a razor-sharp minister and a diamond-bright lawyer produced a deceptively dull-looking cocktail of 5,000 revolutionary words out of which could be bubbled five more easily understood words—"For Christ's Crown and Covenant!". The highly-intelligent minister of Leuchars had other talents—he was clever with money. From Michael Lynch's *Scotland* I was surprised to learn of the new attitudes and wealth of ministers such as Henderson, who lent money to lairds in his Leuchars Parish and to nobles when he was in Edinburgh, and left a huge fortune–£23,000.

When the unique Glasgow Assembly of 1638 met in the Cathedral, Henderson was elected as its Moderator and Wariston as its Clerk. The Cathedral was crowded, the doors locked. In the context of its time, this was in a very a real sense a meeting of a Scottish parliament attended by ministers, elders representing presbyteries, burgh commissioners with lay assessors, lairds and noblemen who had signed the Covenant. The Bishops, fearing for their lives at the hands of the mob, defied the King and stayed safely away. The King's Commissioner was the Marquis of Hamilton who lost control and, failing to dissolve the Assembly, had to make an undignified exit. He wrote to the King, "Next Hell I hate this place". When Hamilton left, the Assembly had become illegal and an instrument of revolution. The Bishops were formally tried, excommunicated and Episcopacy abolished. A Revolution had been initiated and the King, and the Covananters, prepared for war.

Within Leuchars church are two memorial stones which have been removed from their original place on the chancel floor to be placed either side of the south door. The stones are of a subtle grey colour and obviously hard wearing. The right-hand stone is that of Dame Agnes Lyndsay, "Lady to William Bruce of Erlshall", who died in 1635 "of her age 68". The other stone commemorates Sir William Bruce, who built Earlshall tower, fought at Flodden, and as his stone states, without seeming fuss, he died in his 98th year, on 28th January 1584. Through his long life Sir William was in favour at the Courts of James IV, James V, Queen Mary and James VI. The man who fought at Flodden had lived to see James VI recognised as heir to the crown of England.

Earlshall Castle stands to the east of the village, and it may be that a hunting lodge of the Earls of Fife—the Erlis Hall—stood on this site. The Bruce family may have come here in 1495 and the building of the tower-house, from which today's Earlshall developed, has been credited to the long-lived Sir William Bruce and dates from the middle 1540s. Sir William's eldest son probably died before his father and it was his grandson, Sir Alexander, who began more building work. His initials, and those of his wife, Euphemam Leslie, granddaughter of the third Earl of Rothes, appear within the castle. He probably died within four years of the death of his grandfather and it was his son, another Sir William, who, with his second wife Dame Agnes Lyndsay, created the major part of Earlshall.

Sir William's first wife was Elizabeth Wood, a daughter of Sir Andrew Wood of Largo but, having giving Earlshall four sons, she died early. It is Sir William's second wife, Dame Agnes Lyndsay, whose tombstone is in Leuchars kirk and whose initials were featured beside those of W.B., who contributed to the interior design of the castle. Dame Agnes is of the family of Lyndsays of Kirkforthar, near Markinch, one of whom was the father of the historian, Robert Lyndsay of Pitscottie (c.1532-80). The particular glory of Earlshall lies in the painted ceiling of the Long Gallery commissioned by Sir William and Dame Agnes. The decorations on the wooden roof were armorial bearings, floral ornaments, and representations of birds and animals; all in grey, black and white distemper. Spaces were filled with proverbial sayings,

> Deal liberalye with neidful foike,
>   Deny nane of them al;
> For little thou knavest heir in this lyf
>   Quhat chance may the defal.

> A nice [fastidious] wyf and a back doore
> Oft maketh a rich man poore.

The death of Sir William's heir, Sir Andrew, is recorded by the diarist John Lamont, "1664, May 24. The old laird of Earlshall depairted out of this life att Earlshall, and was interred in the church of Leuchars the 27 of May in the evening". The next laird of Earlshall, Sir Andrew Bruce, became infamous in the history of the Covenanters as the "Fife Persecutor" who was in command of Lord Airlie's troop and Strachan's dragoons when they killed and mutilated Richard Cameron on Airds Moss. That same day he also captured David Hackston of Rathillet, one of the murderers of Archbishop James Sharp at Magus Muir.

> They stood prepared to die, a people doomed
> To death—old men, and youths, and simple maids.
>
> . . .
>
> For the horsemen of Earlshall around them were hovering,
> And their bridle-reins rang through the thin misty covering.

The son of the Persecutor, Robert Bruce, had no male heir and the castle and estate went to his daughter Helen. Her second husband, John Henderson of Fordell, near Inverkeithing, was clever enough to ensure that his family inherited, although soon there were other owners and the castle moved towards dereliction. New money came to Earlshall in 1891 when it was bought by Robert Mackenzie, a Dundee bleach merchant, who saw the opportunity for a restoration that would give him a castle with an authentic sixteenth-century appearance. The restoration of Earlshall by the young Robert Lorimer in the 1890s is part of a major success story. His Gate House of 1901 reveals his ability to copy, without exaggeration, the vernacular style of the old tower-castle. Today the saved and restored Earlshall is distinguished not by a hated Persecutor but by the restored painted ceiling of the Long Gallery and a fine garden with Lorimer's topiary lawn the most famous feature. The yews have been trimmed to shapes that have been seen as resembling chessmen although they are planted in the form of four saltires. At the end of the topiary lawn is a gateway with an inscription that modifies only very slightly lines from Shakespeare's Greenwood song in *As You like It,* "Here shall ye see / No enemy / But winter and rough weather." As Lorimer wrote, "Such surprises—little gardens within the garden, the 'months' garden, the herb garden, the yew alley. The kitchen garden too—and this nothing to be ashamed of, to be smothered away from the house, but made delightful by its laying out. Great interesting walls of shaven grass, on either side borders of brightest flowers backed by low espaliers hanging shining apples, and within these espaliers again the gardener has his kingdom . . . ."

Earlshall was one of several grand houses bought by the Nairn family, linoleum manufacturers in Kirkcaldy. Sir Michael Nairn bought it in 1926, and is said to have given it as a wedding present to his daughter, Rachel, on her marriage to Major Arthur Purvis. Mrs Purvis died in 1981 and two years later the Baxter family moved in; Mrs Baxter was to show a particular interest in the gardens which, like the castle, were open to the public until their recent acquisition by a business company.

Parallel to the modern bridge over the Eden at Guardbridge are the stumps of pillars of what I take to have been the railway bridge, but here, also, is a six-arched medieval bridge which carries the initials of Archbishop James Beaton. His contribution may be repairs and alterations and the credit for the original structure of "Le gair brig" should probably be given to Bishop Henry Wardlaw who founded St Andrews University. The name Guardbridge may, like many another place-name, not be what it seems. In 1685 it was referred to as "The Gair Bridge". The guard part may be a progression from "gair" which is Scots for a green strip or patch of ground and a triangular piece of cloth. The river Eden certainly takes sharp turns here.

From Guardbridge the A91 can give quick access to St Andrews, although when the Open Championship is being played on the Old Course progress can be slower even than some professionals who walk its fairways. A glimpse of the entrance to the grand mansion of Strathtyrum can delay me without the excuse of a tailback. The gateposts have been cleaned recently, and a new nameplate put up, but they give access to a fine Georgian building which is still owned by the Cheape family who, since 1782, have been significant in the history of the Old Course. A bunker on the famous Road Hole which was known as the Corner of the Dyke was renamed Cheape's bunker to honour the family who then owned the links. In 1986 Mrs Gladys Cheape sold land to the Links Trust and a new course, the Strathtyrum, was built on part of these acres and opened in 1993. Today the entrance to Strathtyrum faces a new golf course, but it was its nearness to the Old and New Courses that made it attractive to John Blackwood, famous Edinburgh publisher. For the last twenty years of his life Blackwood (1818-79) spent every summer and autumn with his family at Strathtyrum, which he rented.

In his excellent, and very readable, history of the first 600 years of *St Andrews Golf Links,* Tom Jarrett relates how, following a dinner given by John Blackwood on 10th August 1869, two cousins and future captains of the Royal and Ancient Golf Club, Sir Alexander Kinloch and Mr Robert Dalzell, went onto the links to what is today the 15th hole, to restore a bunker that Tom Morris, great champion golfer and Custodian of the Links, had filled in. The two formally-dressed diners left a piece of paper in the restored bunker with the name Sutherland on it. A. G. Sutherland, an Edinburgh lawyer, had been campaigning to have the bunker restored and he was blamed for the restoration—and a famous bunker was named after him.

John Blackwood is the second youngest son of William Blackwood, the founder of Blackwoods. In 1845 he became the third editor of the famous *Blackwood's Magazine* and succeeded his brother Robert as head of the firm in 1852. Among the many famous writers John published, the name of George Eliot stands out and, amongst Scottish authors, there is the hugely prolific Margaret Oliphant. One of her works is the first two volumes of a history of the publishing house of William Blackwood and his sons. Mrs Oliphant died in 1897, soon after correcting the proofs of the second volume.

Whilst at Strathtyrum, John Blackwood visited Edinburgh two or three times a week, and had parcels of manuscripts and proofs sent to him on other days. In the mornings Blackwood worked as a publisher in the library at Strathtyrum; in the afternoons he played golf. To this country house, on the edge of St Andrews, came many famous writers of the time, Charles Kingsley, Charles Reade, J. A. Froude, but the best known today is Anthony Trollope who outlived Blackwood by three years. Mrs Oliphant came to the house, and worked hard although, as John Blackwood's daughter wrote, "She worked early and she worked late, and yet there was no time in the day when she could not be seen . . . Down in the morning in time for the golfers' early breakfast, she would wait about and see them off, and talk and work with the ladies of the party, and then steal quietly away to her room to do a morning's work . . . in the quiet hush of the night I believe some of her best work was done."

2

St Andrews:
Many a Writer

ANDREW LANG, once famous for his *Fairy Books,* came to St Andrews as a student in 1860. He went on to Glasgow University and won a Snell Exhibition to Balliol College, Oxford, where he became a Fellow of Merton College. Amongst Lang's many dozens of works is a history *St Andrews,* 1893, and he retained a genuine liking for the small grey town on the Forth, writing in his "Almae matres",

> St Andrews by the northern sea,
> A haunted town it is to me!
> A little city, worn and gray,
> The gray North Ocean girds it round;
> And o'er the rocks, and up the bay,
> The long sea-rollers surge and sound;
> And still the thin and biting spray
> Drives down the melancholy street,
> And still endure, and still decay,
> Towers that the salt winds vainly beat.
> Ghost-like and shadowy they stand
> Dim-mirrored in the wet sea-sand.

Lang's poem is also of Oxford 1865 but,

> All these hath Oxford: all are dear,
> But dearer far the little town,
> The drifting surf, the wintry year,
> The college of the scarlet gown,
> St Andrews by the northern sea,
> That is a haunted town to me!

There is a monument to Lang in St Salvator's Collegiate Church in North Street where I have a fanatasy that John Knox's pulpit is pricking my conscience at emphasising above Lang's fairybooks over his more "serious" work as an anthropologist with his *Myth, Ritual and Religion* (1887) almost still readable. As to his poetry, he did not have the core of it in his intelligent but uninspired imagination; this despite his wife editing four volumes of *Poetical Works,* 1923.

Today St Andrews University is endowed with two well-known and highly-regarded poets within the School of English; Professor Douglas Dunn and Professor Robert Crawford. Douglas Dunn was born in Renfrewshire in 1942 and attended Hull University where he worked as a librarian in the time of Philip Larkin. Robert Crawford was born in Lanarkshire in 1959 and indeed attended the same West Coats Junior School in Cambuslang as I did some twenty-five years earlier. Following school at Hutcheson's

Grammar and a first degree at Glasgow University he, like Andrew Lang, was a Snell Exhibitioner at Balliol College, Oxford.

From 1947 to 1968 Douglas Young, poet, classical scholar, political activist for Scottish independence in both the Labour Party and the Scottish National Party, lectured in St Andrews, living in Tayport. Long refused a chair at St Andrews, Young went first to McMaster University in Canada and then to the University of North Carolina where he was Professor of Greek, and where he died in 1973. Tall, bearded, generous, kind and one of the last of the genuine characters of Scottish academic life, Douglas Young is best known for a cruelly witty short poem that is very true to a certain characteristic of the Scots and their humour. Entitled "Last Lauch", it may tell a fictional story but one which I like to think of in relation to the Youngs' home in Tayport although, if I remember aright, many will have read it on a stone set into a pedestrian area of Glenrothes,

> The Minister said it wald dee,
> the cypress buss I plantit.
> But the buss grew till a tree,
>   naething dauntit.
>
> It's growan stark and heich,
> derk and straucht and sinister,
> kirkyairdie-like and dreich.
>   But whaur's the Minister?

Tom Scott, who spent most of his working life in Edinburgh, is another poet who lived for a time in St Andrews. Out of these youthful years the poet was able to write an impressive sequence of poems entitled "Auld Sanct-Aundreans", with that entitled "Brand the Builder" an exceptionally fine work which includes these most-descriptive lines of the scene as Brand, master builder, leaves his yard,

> When scrawnie craws flap in the shell-green licht
> Towards yon bane-bare rickle o trees
> That heeze
> Up on the knowe abuin the toun,
> And the red goun
> Is happan mony a student frae the snell nor-easter,

The red gowns are not in evidence these days but as ever,

> Doun by the sea
> Murns the white swaw owre the wrack ayebydanlie.

There is a sadness in these slow-paced syllables as there is in these lines from Andrew Lang's "St Andrews Bay at Night",

> When all is done, when all the tale is told,
> And the grey sea-wave echoes as of old

16

George Bruce was born in Fraserburgh in 1909 and knows the North Sea very well, as he also does St Andrews of which he writes in "A Gateway to the Sea (1)",

> Pause stranger at the porch: nothing beyond
> This framing arch of stone, but scattered rocks
> And sea and these on the low beach
> Original to the cataclysm and the dark.

And in "St Andrews, June, 1946" Bruce enables us to envisage both historical and living town,

> Old tales, old customs and old men's dreams
> Obscure this town. Memories abound.
> In the mild misted air, and in the sharp air
> Toga and gown walk the pier.
> The past sleeps in the stones.

But the complexities with which George Bruce ends "A Gateway to the Sea (1)" move optimistically into a new day,

> Under the touch the guardian stone remains
> Holding memory, reproving desire, securing hope
> In the stop of water, in the lull of night
> Before dawn kindles a new day.

Another poet who has lived in St Andrews for many years is Lillias Forbes. Mrs Forbes is a daughter of F. G. Scott, the composer who set many Scots poems to music, including the early lyrics of Hugh MacDiarmid. Mrs Forbes' first husband was Erik Chisholm the composer and her second, John Forbes, was an accomplished professional musician who had worked as a young man in Tullis Russell's paper mills at Markinch. Lillias Forbes writes often of the Borders but in "Birds Talking" we are given a glimpse of North Street, St Andrews,

> But this clamorous talk
> Deafening down the chimneys of North Street
> As you and I sit quiet for chit and chat
> Around midmorning—
> How it awakes again the sleeping syllables;
> Our infant lisp of cradled innocence.
> Now, all but speech-tethered
> With too long living
> We have near forgotten this other tongue—
> Rise up then for a riotous brave Scots birl
> And some parley with these gulls on the chimney-tops
> In a gabble of shout and skirl!

The skirl of the Scots language can be impressively heard in Douglas Young's translation of Paul Valéry's "Le Cimietière marin" which begins,

> This lown riggin-side, whaur whyte doos gang,
> quhidders amang the pines, the graves amang;
> thonder perjink midday compounds frae fires

the sea, the sea, that's aye begun anew.
Braw guerdon eftir musandry to view
canny and lang the verra Gods' lown lires.

lown: quiet   riggin-side: roof   doos: pigeons   quidders: palpitates   perjink: precise
guerdon: recompense   musardry: meditation   lown lires: calm surfaces

In 1963 the Welsh poet R. S. Thomas included Douglas Young's "The Kirkyaird by the Sea" in his *The Penguin Book of Religious Verse* where he also printed Edwin Muir's "The Incarnate One" which begins,

The windless northern surge, the sea-gull's scream,
And Calvin's kirk crowning the barren brae;
I think of Giotto, the Tuscan shepherd's dream,
Christ, man and creature in their inner day,
How could our race betray
The Image, and the Incarnate One unmake,
Who chose this form and fashion for our sake?

In the late 1920s Edwin Muir wrote *John Knox: Portrait of a Calvinist* and, not long after the publication of that notable book, in August 1935, the Muirs came to live in St Andrews at Castlelea, East Scores. Their house is a semi-detached villa with bay windows which may date from the last decade of the nineteenth century. The house looks over the open sea with the castle a little to the east. On the ruined castle, the Muirs could see, today, the fish-tailed weather-vein glinting as if of purest gold when the sun shines. The sound of the sea can be heard, even on the most calm days, as it breaks on the rocks beyond the small sandy bay. Whilst living in St Andrews, Edwin Muir, an eminent critic as well as a poet, was mostly ignored by those of the gown. There is some irony in that today some members of staff of the School of English have rooms in Kennedy Hall, which stands only a few yards eastwards from Castlelea. Muir had written about St Andrews Castle in his novel *The Three Brothers* which was published in 1931. It is likely that it was in St Andrews that Muir wrote his poem "Scotland 1941" where he also expresses a view of the Calvinist inheritance of Scotland,

The busy corn-fields and the haunted holms,
The green road winding up the ferny brae.
But Knox and Melville clapped their preaching palms
And bundled all the harvesters away,
Hoodicrow Peden in the blighted corn
Hacked with his rusty beak the starving haulms.
Out of that desolation we were born.

G. S. Fraser, another exiled literary and academic Scot, wrote of Muir in his poem "Meditation of a Patriot",

St Andrews soothes that critic at her breast
Whose polished verse ne'er gave his soul release.

We learn from Willa Muir's *Belonging*, 1968, that, far from soothing Muir, living in St Andrews led to what Mrs Muir described as "the uncharacteristic acerbity of Edwin's remarks about Scotland" in *Scott and Scotland*, 1936. George Fraser may have been correct in suggesting that Muir's poems did not release him from his tensions and anxieties but perhaps writing those on Scotland did partially soothe him after the slights he endured in the repressed, class-conscious and provincial St Andrews of the 1930s. Something close to bitterness can also be seen in several of Muir's Scottish poems including "Scotland 1941".

The Muirs were not quite as isolated as Willa suggested as they had their own, rather cliqueish, group of friends. These included John Tonge, and James H. Whyte, a rich American who owned the Abbey Bookshop in St Andrews from where he published the influential quarterly, *The Modern Scot*. Also, friends came to holiday in St Andrews. These included Francis George Scott, the composer, who came with his family in three successive years and they were welcomed by the Muirs at their somewhat esoteric parties. Nevertheless, the Muirs willingly left St Andrews in the Spring of 1942 for Edinburgh where Edwin took up a post with the British Council.

Andrew Melville, whom Edwin Muir linked to John Knox as a suppresive force, was certainly an influential intellectual of the Reformation. He was educated at St Andrews, Paris, and also at Geneva where he was taught by Theodore de Bèze, who had succeeded Calvin. Dr Melville became Principal of Glasgow University and in 1580 returned to St Andrews as the influential Principal of St Mary's College which was founded by Archbishop James Beaton who would have been most antagonistic to Melville's educational aims. We can see St Mary's College as a sixteenth-century "think tank" created by Melville to shape the policy of the Reformers in the reign of James VI.

Andrew Melville's confrontations with King James VI are famous, as is his description of the king as "God's sillie [weak] vassall". The most dramatic source for this undiplomatic description is the diary of Rev James Melville, nephew of the great protagonist. The date is 1596 and those who went to see the King in Falkland were Andro Melvill, Patrick Galloway, James Nicolsone, and the diarist. Initially it was the younger Melville who addressed the King in a "smooth manner" but James "crabbotlie" interrupted him and Melville was about to reply diplomatically when, he writes,

Mr Andro doucht nocht [could not] abyd it, bot brak af upon the King in sa zealus, powerfull, and unresistable a maner, that whowbeit the King used his authoritie in maist crabbit and colerik maner, yit Mr Andro bure him down, and outtered the Commission as from the mightie God, calling the King bot, "God's sillie (weak) vassall;" and, taking him be the slieve, says this in effect, throw mickle hat reasoning and manie interruptions: "Sir, we will humblie reverence your Majestie alwayes, namelie in publict, but sen we have this occasioun to be with your Majestie in privat, and the treuthe is, ye ar brought in extream danger bathe of your lyff and croun, and with yow the countrey and Kirk of Christ is lyk to wrak, for nocht telling yow the treuthe, and giffen of yow a faithfull counsall, we mon discharge our dewtie thairin, or els be trators bathe to Christ and yow! And, thairfor, Sir, as divers tymes befor, sa now again, I mon tell yow thair is twa Kings and twa Kingdomes in Scotland. Thair is Chryst Jesus the King, and his kingdom the Kirk, whase subject King James the Saxt is, and of whase kingdome nocht a king, nor a lord, nor a heid, but a member!

There even the bravest or most foolhardy of men might have stopped but not Mr Andro Melvill who, as reported by his nephew, continued,

And they whome Chryst hes callit and commandit to watch over his Kirk, and governe his spirituall kingdome, hes sufficient powar of him, and authoritie sa to do, bathe togidder and severalie, the quhilk na Christian King nor Prince sould controll and discharge, but fortifie and assist, utherweyes nocht faithfull subjects nor members of Chryst.

When a General Assembly was held in Dundee in 1598, Melville was excluded on the technicality that he was not a "pastor" but only a "doctor"—an academic! In 1611, safely in England and, as he boasted, ruling Scotland with his pen, King James VI, vassall of the Lord, finally banished his thrawn, learned and brave protagonist to France.

Religious capitals tend to follow the political powers. The Viking threat led to a withdrawal from Iona in 807 with the relics of St Columba being divided some fifty years later when Dunkeld was becoming an important religious centre. The early small church at Kinrimund, later Kilrymont (to be renamed St Andrews), may have been established by a Pictish king with the Gaelic name of Óengus. This church was dedicated to a then not significant saint in Scotland—St Andrew. The replacement of St Columba by St Andrew as the sole patron saint of Scotland was gradual, as was the establishment of the town as the ecclesiastical capital with its shrine to St Andrew; its college, or university, followed as the first in the land. There were many pilgrims to the shrine of St Andrew whilst the town was still known as Kilrymont and the influence of Queen Margaret increased this traffic. The medieval pilgrims who approached St Andrews from the coast were given a magnificent prospect of their journey's climax, and today the view from the Anstruther Road is one of sparkling sea and towers and spires and, for returning golfers, a reminder of triumphs and tragedies on the courses of this their Mecca. We can identify the Tower of St Salvator's Collegiate Church and the ruins of the Cathedral are enhanced by the tall square tower of St Rule's Church and, below the blue heat-haze, the famous links await the faithful of golf.

Forbes Macgregor mischievously suggested that St Rule's could be a phonetic rendering of the Celtic St Riaghal which was mistakenly Latinised into St Regulus. The tall, square tower, with its two-light windows, is eleventh century and well preserved but the small choir is roofless and the remainder of this small church has quite gone. Work began on the adjoining and magnificent Cathedral in 1160 and the completed building was consecrated in 1318 by Bishop William Lamberton, with King Robert, the Bruce, present, as were seven Bishops, fifteen Abbots and other spiritual and temporal leaders. Remembering the words of John Knox, "ding doun the nests and the craws will flee awa", the Reformers were to strip the Cathedral and leave it to the forces of nature which were very considerably assisted by the grasping hands of those who took the stones for use on buildings in the town.

Inside the roofless choir building of St Rule's is the memorial of Robert Chambers which informs that he was born in Peebles in 1802 and died in St Andrews in 1871. He first came to St Andrews in 1842 and, in 1863, built a house which still stands in The Scores near the Martyrs' Monument within sight of the first tee of the Old Course. Robert and his brother, William, founded the Edinburgh publishing company of W. & R. Chambers which contributed to the extension of education through their encyclopaedias and other works aimed at the newly literate. His memorial informs that Robert is the author of *Traditions of Edinburgh* but he also compiled *The Popular Rhymes of Scotland* which includes this one,

> Blaw the wind as it likes,
> There's beild about Pitmilly dikes.

The road from St Andrews to Crail makes a very sharp turn at Pitmilly, as it also does at nearby Boarhills, and so there was always beild, shelter, at one part of it or another, as the walls face to each of the cardinal points (of the compass). Cardinal David Beaton's mother was a Monypenny of Kinkell who were also of Pitmilly where there were Monypennys for over six-and-a-half centuries. Interestingly, the laird of Pitmilly was accused of giving support to the Cardinal's murderers, as was his daughter Janet Monypenny.

The University of St Andrews has a history that goes back to 1412 when Bishop Henry Wardlaw gave university privileges to a school founded in 1410. Papal recognition came in 1413. St Salvator's College, in North Street, was founded in 1450 by Bishop James Kennedy and the Collegiate Church, the Gate and the tenement (no. 75 North Street) are mid-fifteenth century. The Collegiate Church has been reduced to a basic nave and apse, and even the magnificent tomb of Bishop Kennedy has suffered damage, but the tower and spire do remain as dramatic features of the town. Also, the vaulted gateway in the tower forms a splendid entrance to the College quadrangle. No. 79 has a plaque that informs passers-by that James Crichton (1560-1582), who was called "Admirable", lived there whilst a student. He became the hero of J. M. Barrie's play, "The Admirable Crichton". Crichton was a pupil of George Buchanan and, when achieving some fame in Italy, was described by Aldus Manutius, the great Venetian printer, as "athlete, scholar, and linguist." Sir Thomas Urquhart, another "Wandering Scot", wrote of Crichton's exploits in *Discovery of a Most Exquisite Jewel*, 1652. The epithet "admirable" was first given to him by John Johnston in 1603 in *Heroes Scoti*. Johnston was Professor of Theology at St Andrews from 1593 till his death in 1611. It is interesting that in his epigram on King Malcolm III, Canmore, Johnston does not mention the saintly Queen Margaret.

William Dunbar, the great poet of the court of King James IV, could have been a student at St Andrews. Certainly a man of that name appears in the Register of St Andrews as that of a Determinant or Batchelor of Arts in 1477 and as a Master of Arts two years later and his dates make it possible that he is the poet. Very little is certain in what has been written on Dunbar's life but he does begin a poem, "To the King" by invoking St Salvatour,

> Sanct Salvatour! Send silver sorrow;
> It grevis me both evin and morrow,
> Chasing fra me all cheritie;
> It makis me all blythness to borrow;
> My paneful purs so prikillis me.
>
> Quhen I wald blythlie ballattis breif,
> Lasgour thairto givis me no leif;
> War nocht gud howp my hairt uphie,
> My verry corpis for cair wald cleif;
> My paneful purs so prikillis me.
>
> . . .
>
> I haif inquyrit in mony a place,
> For help and confort in this cace,
> And all men sayis, My Lord, that ye
> Can best remeid for this malice,
> That with sic panis prikillis me.

The great poet was as brave in facing James IV as was Andrew Melville three monarchs on. Dunbar was possibly something of a manic-depressive, and not free of paranoid tendencies, but his poetry leaves us in no doubt that he was never properly valued at the court of the much-admired King James IV.

The other great poet of James IV's reign is Gavin Douglas but, unlike William Dunbar, he belonged to a powerful family, that of the Red Earls of Douglas, and Douglas achieved positions of power at Court and in the Church. He conducted a vigorous campaign for the top ecclesiastical job of Archbishop of St Andrews but had to ungraciously accept being Bishop of Dunkeld. Gavin Douglas was a son of "Bell-the-Cat", otherwise Archibald Douglas, 5th Earl of Angus, who has been said to be illiterate. His son, graduating M.A. at St Andrews in 1494, is one of the most learned of the auld makars. In his literary works Douglas is a true humanist son of the Italian Renaissance. He is best known for his superb translation of Virgil's *Aeneid* to which he added magnificent Prologues, including that of the seventh on winter which includes this chilling cameo,

> The dew droppis congelit on stubble and rind
> And sharp hailstanis mortfundit of kind
> Hopping on the thak and on the causey by.
> The schot I closit, and drew inwart in hie,
> Chiverand for cauld, the seasoune was so snell,
> Schup with hait flambe to fleme the freesing fell.

> rind: bush   mortfundit: cold as death   of kind: by nature   thak: thatch
> causey: street   in hie: in haste   Schup: tried, shaped   fleme: banish

Having completed his translation of Virgil just as the death of King James IV at the battle of Flodden transformed the power structure of the Kingdom, Douglas thereafter largely devoted himself to the vile politics of his time which were many a bloody sword-length from any civilised humanism. When in 1520 the followers of the rival earls, Douglas and Hamilton, faced each other on the High Street of Edinburgh (known as the "Clear the Causeway" affray), it was Gavin Douglas who approached Archbishop James Beaton, who had his house in Blackfriars Wynd, to suggest a diplomatic withdrawal of both forces but Beaton pled ignorance and, with a thump of his chest, swore that his conscience was clear. Hearing the chain-mail rattling below the clerical robes Douglas said, "My lord, methinks your conscience clatters" [tells tales]. Beaton favoured the Hamiltons because of their support for the Catholic French party but he also had family ties to them.

When I came to spend a day in St Andrews in the 1950s my fondness for Bell Street had more to do with the second-hand bookshop there than any interest in the aesthetic appeal of a Georgian Street. Today I still like to go along Bell Street on my way from South Street to Market Street where, as is to be expected, the Mercat Cross once stood. The Cross was removed as early as the eighteenth century but we can see where it stood by a cobbled cross in the road. Unlike a good few Fife burghs, St Andrews has also lost its Tolbooth. What it has gained, in Market Street, is a memorial fountain, of 1880, to the novelist Major George John Whyte-Melville (1821-78). The fountain has three basins, fourteen feet in diameter. One of the basins has a marble medallion portrait of the Major and a tablet beside the portrait informs, "This fountain is erected by many friends, rich and poor, to the beloved memory of George John Whyte-Melville of Mount Melville, Bennochy and Strathkinness; born 19th July 1821; died 5th december 1878, from an accident in the hunting-field near Tetbury, Gloucestershire. His writings delighted; his conversation charmed and instructed; his life was an example to all who enjoyed his friendship, and who mourn his untimely end." Today we might ask, "Who is he, and what did he write?"

George Whyte-Melville was one of the novelists entertained by John Blackwood at Strathtyrum. His most-read novels were on hunting although he also wrote a fictional work on *The Queen's Maries*. His life is a classic example of the anglicised Scottish gentleman of the nineteenth century. He was born near St Andrews at Strathkinness, educated at Eton and served in the 93rd Highlanders and the Coldstream Guards. He lived the life of a country gentleman with many days spent in the hunting field, but he also wrote twenty-eight novels. In a far corner of the graveyard of St Andrews Cathedral there is a Gothic shrine to members of the Whyte-Melville family. Soon the words on this ornate memorial will have become quite unreadable and those on the fountain are also showing signs of wear. In the kirkyard of Kirkcaldy's Parish Church is the grave of Robert Whyt of Pourin who was the first provost of Kirkcaldy and died in 1667. As very successful merchants the Whytes bought part of the Abbotshall estate and all of Bennochy. The mansion of Mount Melville, near St Andrews, was built by General George Melville of Strathkinness, who was related to the Melvilles of Carnbee which is north-east of Kellie Law. The General died without children and the estate passed to his cousin, John Whyte of Bennochy (1755-1813) who added the Melville name to his own. The novelist is a grandson of this Whyte-Melville. Near Abbotshall Church, behind Kirkcaldy railway station, runs Whyte Melville Road. When the novelist's father died the Mount Melville estate passed to James H. Balfour-Melville. In the 1890s the owner of Bennochy was Viscountess Masserene and Ferrad, daughter of Major George Whyte-Melville.

Although St Andrews lacks a University printing press of real distinction, the burgh did house the typefounder Alexander Wilson (1714-86) and he cut and cast founts of type for Robert and Andrew Foulis, the great scholarly printers of Glasgow, who are worthy to be named alongside other great European printers such as Aldus Manutius, Froben and Estienne who achieved excellence as editors, printers, publishers and booksellers. The scholarly ambitions of the Foulis brothers can be seen in their attitude to proof-reading. Each book was proof-read six times; three times in their own office, three times by the two university professors they employed as editors. They published near enough 700 books and pamphlets and their *Homer* (1756-8) and *Paradise Lost* of 1770, printed using Alexander Wilson's types, remain masterpieces of Scottish printing.

Alongside the typefaces of Wilson we can put that other great and, indeed, unique creation of the old royal burgh—the Old Course. Rather, as has been said, it is a product of nature, modified and nurtured by man and the animals he grazed on it. Those who do not know the history of Scottish golf quite understandably assume that the Old Course is owned by the Royal and Ancient Golf Club, which is the international authority for golf, but the old links are common land owned by the Local Authority and, as authorised by an Act of Parliament, a St Andrews Links Trust and a St Andrews Links Management Committee are responsible for running the links. Local people have the right to cheaper green fees and special rights in relation to playing times on the Old Course. Annually the Royal and Ancient Golf Club pays a lump sum to the Trust which allows its members free golf on the courses and preferential starting times on certain days on the Old and New Courses.

There have been golfers in St Andrews since at least the late fifteenth century and The Society of St Andrews Golfers dates from 1754. It became the Royal and Ancient Golf

Club in 1834, with patronage from King William. The building of the first phase of the famous clubhouse started in 1853, one year after the opening of Leuchars railway station. The emotive Swilken Bridge was made not for golfers but as a pack bridge for seventeenth or eighteenth century importers who had landed goods at the old port on the Eden's Estuary. I stood within yards of the bridge when Arnold Palmer took his leave of the Open Championship from it. The "modern" Old and New Courses were created by Tom Morris (1821-1908) who won the Open Championship four times. His son, Tommy, won the Championship four times and a triple sequence of wins gave him ownership of the Championship Belt. Tommy died in 1875 age 24 and has a memorial in the Cathedral Graveyard which I tend to make a detour to see, and also the stone below it of his father. Tommy's memorial looks rustic, but it was designed by John Binny, an Edinburgh sculptor. The young golfer is shown in bas relief, three-quarters life size, wearing a Scotch cap, and posed as he would be before playing a golf shot.

Looking from the links over the clubhouse of the Royal and Ancient Golf Club the little grey town looks peacefully idyllic with its grouping of low buildings and high towers and spires. I like walking by the Old Course, as I do along North Street to go through the gateway to the quadrangle of St Salvator's, with its not-over-manicured lawn and nineteenth-century buildings. The courtyard of St Mary's College, with its more varied groupings of buildings, including those of the sixteenth century, has a more obvious appeal. To walk down Gregory Place, alongside the Cathedral wall, against a wintry gale is invigorating and to come out onto the terrace, to look over the sea wall down to a stormy sea, is to add high visual drama to physical pleasure. My most pleasing memories of St Andrews, however, are in summertime and of walking through the ruined cathedral to a gate that gives access to the same terrace that allows, not a stormy winter view, but a peaceful panoramic prospect round the bay and over the rippling blue sea with the seabirds rising and falling in the rising currents of a warm summer breeze. But my poem "St Andrews Town" has a critical edge,

> "St Andrews town may look right gawsy,
> Nae grass will grow upon her cawsey"—Robert Fergusson
>
> The tounsfolk still walk gress-free streets wi pride
> though some would notice noses in the air and plummy voices.
> In term-time there's the bonus o mony a bricht reid goun
> and mair loud voices frae the South.
> There are ither fremmit voices and colourt claes in summer time
> wi visitors in toon for the golf even if it's but ae roond
> to say they've done it on the sacred turf.
>
> The Old Course may not be much to look at to the likes o me
> but there's a fine view to be had frae the heichts o St Rule's Touer
> lookin oot to the herbour and the cauld grey sea
> or doon to the foonds o the aince-prood Cathedral.
> There are mony tourists walkin the shaven weys
> aroond the auld stanes. There's a neat wee shed
> whaur postcards and illustratit books can be bocht
> on thae stumps left frae an amputatit buildin.
>
> Here it's near aw gress.

24

The quotation from Robert Fergusson at the head of my poem is from his satirical poem "To the Principal and Professors of the University of St Andrews, on their Superb Treat to Dr Samuel Johnson" in which the poet suggests an alternative very Scottish menu to set before the man who had famously referred in his *Dictionary* to oatmeal as the diet of horses in England but of the people in Scotland,

> *Imprimis,* then, a haggis fat,
> Weel tottled in a seything pat,
> Wi' spice and ingans weel ca'd thro',
> Had help'd to gust the stirrah's mow,
> And plac'd itsel in truncher clean
> Before the gilpy's glowrin een.
> *Secundo*, then a gude sheep's head
> Whase hide was singit, never flead,
> And four black trotters cled wi' girsle,
> Bedown his throat had learned to hirsle.
> What think ye neist, o' gude fat brose
> To clag his ribs? A dainty dose!
> And white and bloody puddins routh,
> To gar the Doctor skirl, O Drouth!
> Whan he cou'd never houp to merit
> A cordial o' reaming claret,
> But thraw his nose, and brize and pegh
> O'er the contents o' sma ale quegh:
> Then let his wisdom girn and snarl
> O'er a weel-tostit girdle farl,
> An' learn, that maugre o' his wame,
> Ill bairns are ay best heard at hame.

tottled: boiled   seythingg pat: nearly-boiling pot   ingans: onions
gust the stirrah's mow: please his palate
truncher: wooden platter   gilpy's glowerin een: rascal's scowling eyes
singit, never flead: singed never flayed   girsle: gristle
hirstle: move as with a rustling noise   brose: oatmeal mixed with boiling water
glag: stick to   routh: abundance   gar: make   drouth: thirst
reaming: overflowing   pugh: pant   quegh: quaich, small shallow cup
girn: grimace, snarl   girdle farl: quarter of an oatcake, baked on a girdle
that maugre o' his wame: that spite of his stomach

In Johnson's *A Journey to the Western Islands* we are given a view of St Andrews in August 1773 by a traveller who carried with him the conceit that, like his fellow Englishmen, he walked by a middle road. When Johnson and Boswell arrived in St Andrews "at an hour somewhat late" they found that, "by the interposition of some invisible friend, lodgings had been provided for us at the house of one of the professors, whose easy civility quickly made us forget that we were strangers; and in the whole time of our stay we were gratified by every mode of kindness, and entertained with all the elegance of lettered hospitality."

> . . . The change of religion in Scotland, eager and vehement as it was, raised an epidemical enthusiasm, compounded of sullen scrupulousness and warlike ferocity, which, in a people whom idleness resigned to their own thoughts, and who, conversing only with each other, suffered no dilution of their zeal from the gradual flux of new

opinions, was long transmitted in its full strength from the old to the young, but by trade and intercourse with England, is now visibly abating, and giving way too fast to that laxity of practice and indifference of opinion, in which men, not sufficiently instructed to find the middle point, too easily shelter themselves from rigour and constraint. The city of St Andrews, when it lost its archiepiscopal preeminence, gradually decayed: One of its streets is now lost; and in those that remain, there is the silence and solitude of inactive indigence and gloomy depopulation.

. . . Having now seen whatever this ancient city offered to our curiosity, we left it with good wishes, having reason to be highly pleased with the attention that was paid us. But whoever surveys the world must see many things that give him pain. The kindness of the professors did not contribute to abate the uneasy remembrance of a university declining, a college alienated, and a church profaned and hastening to the ground.

It was ten years before the visit of Boswell and Johnson to St Andrews when Robert Fergusson, aged fourteen, came to the United College of St Salvator and St Leonard in the University of St Andrews in the winter of 1764. The town was in at least as bad a condition as when the two tourists were entertained "with all the elegance of lettered hospitality". It was mostly a slum alongside the overgrown and rubbish-covered ruins of the former Episcopal magnificence. Many of the one thousand houses were roofless and St Leonard's College, where George Buchanan had been Principal, had been left to nature, allowing the chapel to ruin and the lecture rooms to be used to store hay. The number of ale houses exceeded forty. The harbour was near enough destitute of ships.

Fergusson had a bursary and bursars lodged in a building on the north side of the quadrangle of St Salvator's. The non-bursars were usually in lodgings—bunks in St Andrews—and with a caring bunkwife they could be more comfortable than the boys in the college where they were two to a room with a box-bed, table and an inefficient fire best left unlit to avoid the suffocating smoke; warmth was achieved by plaid and gloves.

In his fourth session Fergusson "majored" in Natural Philosophy under Professor William Wilkie who took an interest in the bursary student. Wilkie had a farm near St Andrews in the parish of Cameron through which today's A915 passes, and he took Fergusson there and also to visit the minister of Anstruther. In his own time Wilkie was famous for his long poem, written over many years in English, *The Epigoniad,* based on the fourth book of the *Iliad* and this brought him the title of "the Scottish Homer". As might be anticipated, Wilkie achieved more when he wrote in Scots, his mother-tongue, which he used for high intellectual debate in Edinburgh and St Andrews. Certainly his fable in Scots "The Hare and the Partan" remains readable. This is one of the poems that the professor paid Fergusson to copy, and so added to the future poet's knowledge of Scottish literature. Something of the flow of Wilkie's fable can be seen from its first verse,

> A hare, ae morning, chanc'd to see
> A partan creepin on a lee;
> A fishwife wha was early oot
> Had drapt the creature thereaboot.
> Mawkin bumbas'd and drighted sair
> To see a thing but hide and hair,
> Which if it stur'd not might be taen
> For naething ither than a stane:

partan: crab   mawkin: hare   bumbas'd: startled
stur'd stirred   taen: taken

Fergusson's second "Eclogue" is to the memory of Dr Wilkie and, in addition to paying tribute to his professor's literary work, the young poet acknowledges, as befits a pastoral dialogue, Wilkie's importance as a remarkable agriculturist who greatly improved the working of his farm and pioneered potato crops in Fife,

> Ye saw yoursell how weel his *mailin* thrave,
> Ay better faugh'd an' snodit than the lave;
> Lang had the *thristles* an' the *dockans* been
> In use to wag their taps upo' the green,
> Whare now his bonny riggs delight the view,
> An' thrivin hedges drink the caller dew.

mailin: farm holding   faugh'd: furrowed   snodit: in good order
lave: the remainder   riggs: fields   caller: fresh

As a boy in Lanarkshire I was often in what was then the small dairy-farming village of East Kilbride and natives of the village would point out with some pride the cottage of Kate Dalrymple, by then not "far across the muir" but within the village and surrounded by many other houses. In Fife, however, there are those who believe that this heroine of William Watt's comic poem had her cottage in Cameron parish close to the burn of the same name and that later she lived in St Andrews. Who knows, perhaps she was a product of the poet's imagination and lived wherever suited him.

> In a wee cot-house far across the muir,
> Where peeweeps, plovers, and whaups cry dreary,
> There lived an auld maid for mony lang years,
> Wham ne'er a wooer did e'er ca' "Dearie".
> A lanely lass was Kate Dalrymple,
> A thrifty quean was Kate Dalrymple;
> Nae music, exceptin' the clear burnie's wimple,
> Wae heard round the dwellin' o' Kate Dalrymple.

As was customary at that time, Robert Fergusson left the university without taking a degree but whilst there he developed a talent for satirising the regents or professors. Later he wrote an "Elegy, On the Death of Mr David Gregory, late Professor of Mathematics in the University of St Andrews", and another "Elegy on John Hogg, Late Porter to the University of St Andrews"; the latter gives us a glimpse of student life, at least as lived by bursars, in the 1760s,

> On einings cauld wi' glee we'd trudge
> To heat our shins in Johnny's lodge;
> The de'il ane thought his bum to budge
>   Wi' siller on us:
> To claw het pints we'd never grudge
>   O' *molationos.*
>
> Say ye, red gowns! That aften here
> Hae toasted bakes to Kattie's beer,
> Gin e'er thir days hae had their peer,
>   Sae blyth, sae daft;
> You'll ne'er again in life's career
>   Sit ha'f sae saft.

Kate was the shrewd and careful John Hogg's winsome wife to whom he left both houses and land. Fergusson had a very few years of other saft seats in Edinburgh before dying on 17th October 1774, aged twenty-four years and one month, in the Edinburgh Bedlam. Robert Burns was to write in a copy of the second edition of Fergusson's *Poems,*

> O thou, my elder brother in Misfortune,
> By far my elder Brother in the muse,
> With tears I pity thy unhappy fate!
> Why is the Bard unfitted for the world,
> Yet has so keen a relish of its pleasures?

Fergusson's longest and in many respects finest poem is on his native city, "Auld Reikie" which ends with a view of the capital from Fife which he would have seen especially well from the watch tower of Rev James Melville's manse in Anstruther, a small room at the top of the building with a southerly view,

> Reikie, farewell! I ne'er cou'd part
> Wi' thee but wi' a dowy heart;
> Aft frae the Fifan coast I've seen
> Thee tow'ring on thy summit green;
> So glowr the saints when first is given,
> A fav'rite keek o' glore and heaven;
> On earth nae mair they bend their ein,
> But quick assume angelic mein;
> So I on Fife wad glowr no more,
> But gallop'd to Edina's shore.

> dowy: gloomy   glowr: look stern
> keek: glimpse   glore: glory   ein: eyes

Today it is difficult to think of Edinburgh on a "green summit" but the Pentlands do act as a superb backdrop to the city. Also, the cloud of smoke, or reek, that hung over Edinburgh has gone. On a day when the light makes the city of Edinburgh almost invisible, with the islands giving the Forth a loch-like aspect, these hills merge into Arthur's Seat to assume a profile and form a panorama that is truly highland. Many visitors to Fife who look over to Edinburgh are surprised to have the black mass, that sits low down and often almost merged into the background, identified as Edinburgh Castle which from Princes Street is seen as towering over the city. The view of Fife from the Castle is very fine but it is matched by the view from Kirkcaldy of sea, islands, Edinburgh city with Arthur's Seat, and the crags; all crowned by an ever-changing sky and enhanced by the northern light which outlines the varied line and masses of the Pentland hills. This must be one of the most under-appreciated of Scottish views. On some winter days, when the dark cloud-cover breaks above the sea and the sun descends in vibrant slanting beams, the dramatic position of the castle at the topmost point of the long sloping ridge of the old town, with its various spires, can be appreciated from Fife's shore.

In the 1770s Robert Fergusson saw St Andrews as not only a town "right gawsy" where no grass was allowed to grow on the streets for Dr Johnson's visit; but, "Nor wa'-flowers of a yellow dye,/Glour dowy o'er her ruins high." John Ruskin saw the ruins of St

Andrews Cathedral as "those rent skeletons of pierced wall through which our sea winds moan and murmur." Many of today's visitors to St Andrews, myself amongst them, regard these ruins as pleasingly emotive, but probably Fergusson did not see them any more pleasurably than did Samuel Johnson who asked, "where is the pleasure of preserving such mournful memorials?" Certainly, having satirised the provincialism of Johnson and imposed on the good Doctor what he would be likely to regard as revolting food, Fergusson, who to some has appeared unsympathetic to Fife, reveals a confidence that allows him to be truthful in describing the poverty then to be seen not only in Fife but in Scotland generally,

> Ah! willawins, for Scotland now,
> Whan she maun stap ilk birky's mow
> Wi' eistacks, grown as 'tware in pet
> In foreign land, or green-house het,
> When cog o' brose an' cutty spoon
> Is a' oor cottar childer's boon,
> Wha thro' the week, till Sunday's speal,
> Toil for pease-clods an' gude lang kail.

> willawins: alas   birky's: fellow's   eistacks: dainties   cog: wooden dish
> brose: oatmeal mixed with boiling water   het: hot
> cutty spoon: short-handled spoon   speal: holiday
> pease-clods: coarse rolls of pease meal   kail: colewort

The situation of the peasantry may not have been much better in the twelfth century but the town of St Andrews was certainly not then in a state of decline. When work began in the 1160s on the new cathedral one of the aims of the powerful clergy was to give St Andrews a building that was the largest and grandest in the land. When completed it measured 168 feet across its transepts and 357ft long. This length compares with Glasgow's 285ft; Dunfermline's 268ft and Elgin's 263ft. It took some 160 years to complete the cathedral. The ruins we have are a preserved indictment of the destructive forces that rapidly swept through Scotland at the Reformation. Against this physical wrecking we can set the creative and democratic forces of the new religious humanism that the Reformers released, even if that was not their intention.

Before following the actions of the Reformers in St Andrews, I would turn to Robert Lyndsay of Pitscottie for a most admirable description of a joyful and regal time in St Andrews, and indeed royal Scotland, in June 1538 when King James V welcomed his new Queen, Mary of Guise, to Scotland. On 1st January King James V married Madeleine, the delicate third daughter of Francis I of France. The wedding took place with great royal pomp in the Cathedral of Notre-Dame. The King and Queen returned to Scotland where Sir David Lyndsay prepared a celebratory pageant. The new Queen died only a few weeks after coming to Scotland where public mourning was worn for the first time. The King did not delay in finding a new wife, Mary of Guise-Lorraine, a widow, who was married to James in Paris by proxy. The story of the Queen's arrival in Scotland is well told by Lyndsay of Pitscottie,

> the quen landit in Scotland the viij day of Juin . . . in ane place callit Fywisness besyde
> Ballcome [inland from Fife Ness], quhair scho remanit quhill horse come to hir. Bot
> the kingis grace was in Sanctandrois for the tyme witht money of his nobilietie
> waittand upoun hir hame comming. Then he sieand scho was landit in sic ane pairt, he
> raid fourtht him self to meit hir. Than the kingis grace and the hail lordis baitht

29

spirituall and temporall, money barrouns, lairdis and genyillmen quho was convenit at St androis ffor the tyme in thair best array raid and ressavit the quens grace witht great honouris and mirrenes witht great treumph and blythness of phrassis and playis maid to hit at hir hame comming. And first scho was ressavit at the New Abbey yeit. Upoun the eist syde thair was maid to hir trieumphant frais [pageant] be Schir David Lyndsay of the Mont, lyoun harrot, qhilk caussit ane great clude to come out of the heivens done abone the yeit quhair the quene come in, and oppin in two halffis instantlie and thair appeirit ane fair lady maist lyk ane angell havand the keyis of haill Scotland in hir handis deliverand thame unto the quens grace in signe and takin that all the heartis of Scottland was opnit to the ressaving of hir grace; witht certane wriesuns and exortatiouns maid by the same Schir David Lyndsay into the quens grace instructioun quilk teichit hir to serve her god, obey hir husband, and keep hir body clene according to godis will and commandement. This beand done, the quen was ressavit into hir palice and luging quhilk was callit the New Innes and was weill decoirit againe hir comming, with all necessariss perteinand to ane quen and thair scho ludgit that night, quhill on the morne at ten hours scho passit to the abbay kirk and thair scho saw money ane lustie lord and barrone and gentillmen landit all weill arayit in thair abullyementis againe hir comming; also the bischopis, abbotis, pryouris, monkis, freiris and chanounis regular maid great solemnitie in the abbay kirk witht messes [masses] songis and playin on the organis. This being done, the king ressavit the quen in his palice to the dinner quhair thair was great mirth schallmes draught trumpattis and weir [war] trumpattis witht playing and phrassis [farces] efter denner quhill tyme of supper. On the morne the quen passit throw the toune and visitit all the kirkis and colledgis and the universietie within the toun, that is to say scho vessit the blak freirs, the greyfreirs, the auld coledge and the new colledge and Sanct Leonardis, the paroche kirk and the Lady kirk of heuche, to wit. Scho was convoyit be the provost of the toune and honest burgessis thairof.

The King and Queen remained in St Andrews for, Pitscottie relates, "the space of fourtie dayis with great merrienes and game and justing and ryoting at the listis, archorie, huntting and halking, witht singing and danceing, menstrelling and playing, witht uther princlie game and pastyme according to king and quein." The royal cavalcade then left for Cupar, where they dined, before going on to Falkland where they remained "in the hunting of the fallow deir sex or aught dayis." In Stirling they were received in both town and castle with "great merrienes and pastyme", and in Linlithgow also, where they remained a day or two in the Palace, before cavalcading to Edinburgh,

> quhair thair the king and the quen was weill ressavit witht great treumph in the castell and toun and in the palice and thair he was honestlie and richlie propynit witht the provost and communitie of the toun baitht witht spyce and wyne gold and sillver and also greit triumph phraisses maid and playis unto the queins grace on the expenssis of the said toun. . . . And sa lyke wyse in Dundie and Sanct Johnstoun everie ane of thame according to thair nobilietie ressavit thair quene and maistres as it become thame to do.

A little over three years later James failed to meet Henry VIII at York and, having made this great effort to travel north of the Trent, the English King was enraged by his nephew's insulting behaviour. An English invasion went badly and the Scottish response resulted in the rout at Solway Moss. The two sons of King James had already died and he was disappointed to learn on his death bed of the birth of a daughter, Mary, whose tragedy unfolded with the Reformation, and whose son was to take the Scottish court south to London. Both events diminished life in St Andrews and the second that in all Scotland.

As the arrogance of John Knox and the bravery of Andrew Melville distinguishes them, so George Buchanan, at least in his later involvement with Mary, Queen of Scots, is marked by his blatant duplicity. The violence of Buchanan was that of a scholar and propagandist who abused truth for personal and political ends. In his own time Buchanan was recognised as an important Latinist in Europe and a major intellectual of the Scottish Reformation. The complexities of his character equal those of his pupil King James VI. Despite his Reformist views he was also tutor to Queen Mary whom initially he admired but later, after the murder of Darnley, he devoted much effort to writing vituperative and scurrilous pamphlets against her, including this passage which has the Queen rushing to make a great journey to Jedworth on learning of Bothwell's injuries, when he knew very well that she was already there for the Jedburgh assizes,

> She heard of Bothwell's wounds, whereupon she flingeth away in haste like a mad woman, by great journeys in post, in the sharp time of winter, first to Melrose, then to Jedworth. There, though she heard news of his life, yet her affectioun, impatient of delay, could not temper itself, but neids she must bewray her outragious lust, and in an inconvenient time of the year, despising all discomodities of the way and weather, and all dangers of thieffis, she betook herself hedlong in hir journey, with sic company as na man of any honest degree wald haif adventured his life and his goods amang them.

This is the man who had dedicated his Latin paraphrases of the Psalms to the Queen with an epigram in Latin which tells of a queen who, to use a prose translation by Vivian Nutton, "excelled the brave in merit, the old in virtue, men in courage, and your family in noble manners". Not that such dedications can be taken too seriously.

Educated at the Universities of Paris and St Andrews, Buchanan was taught at the latter by John Mair (or Major), historian and philosopher who, having established a European reputation in Paris, returned to Scotland to become Provost of St Salvator's College in 1534. With further European experience behind him, Buchanan was appointed by James V as tutor to one of his natural sons. His rough satire attacking Cardinal Beaton, *Franciscanu*, led to his fleeing into exile where he became Professor of Latin at Bordeaux and of Philosophy at Coimbra in Portugal. He returned to Scotland in 1560 and in 1566 he became Principal of St Leonard's College in St Andrews. Unlike Knox, Buchanan was not a preacher but his vituperative abilities with the pen were of an order of viciousness that age did not diminish. He died in 1582 having contributed to the Scottish Reformation a hard-edged intellectualism, some good Latin poetry and four interesting plays, one of which was translated by Robert Garioch and published in 1959. Buchanan is buried in Greyfriars Kirkyard, Edinburgh.

Sir James Melville of Halhill (1535-1617), who remained loyal to Queen Mary, wrote in his diaries a shrewd paragraph on the character of Buchanan,

> Mester George was a stoik philosopher, and loked not far before the hand; a man of notable qualites for his learnying and knawlege in Latin poesie, mekle maid accompt of in other contrees, plaisant in company, rehersing at all occasions moralities schort and fecfull, wherof he had aboundance, and invented wher he wanted. He was also of gud religion for a poet, bot he was easely abused, and sa facill that he wes led with any company that he hanted for the tym, quhilk maid him factious in his auld dayes; for he spak and wret as they that wer about him for the tym infourmed him. For he was

becom sleperie and cairles, and folowed in many thingis the vulgair oppinion; for he was naturally populaire, and extrem vengeable against any man that had offendit him, quhilk was his gretest falt.

There have been plenty of major writers guilty of greater moral crimes than Buchanan who should be remembered for his poetry. His finest work is the Epithalamium on Queen Mary's marriage to the Dauphin which has a very famous section where the poet describes Scotland and the Scots whom Mary brought as dowry. To Hugh MacDiarmid, "This is one of the great passages in Scottish poetry", and he included a prose translation in his *The Golden Treasury of Scottish Poetry*, but, as far as I know, this Latin work awaits a verse translation that does it justice.

3

St Andrews:
Knox and Many a Beaton

NEGLECT, or lack of dignified patronage, may disturb the creative minds of poets but such sufferings may seem a gentle torture when we stand in front of St Salvator's College and remember that in 1528 Archbishop James Beaton had the young and well-educated Lutherian reformer Patrick Hamilton (1504-28) hideously, and incompetently, burnt hereabouts. His initials are set into the cobbles in front of the tower. The Archbishop was advised by John Lindsay that if he wished to burn any more of his opponents he should do so in deep cellars since "the reek of Maister Patrik Hammyltoun has "infected as many as it blew on." The martyrdom of Hamilton was a spark that further ignited the flame of the Scottish Reformation, but the suppressions continued as did the burnings.

Amongst those who watched Patrick Hamilton slowly die was Alexander Campbell, the Dominican friar who had disputed with Hamilton on his heresies before the Great Council in St Andrews. As so often, Lyndsay of Pitscottie gives a superbly dramatic description of how the dying man summoned Campbell to appear, within the space of forty days, "befor the tribunall saitt of God and Christ Jesus his sone" and of how a great blast of wind from the sea carried the flame and reek from the roaring fire to where Campbell stood and, with superb directness, Pitscottie ends, "it dang him to the erd [earth] and brunt all the foir pairt of his coull and pat him in sic ane fray that he come never to his right spreit againe bot wanderit about the space of XL dayis and then depairttit."

David Beaton, nephew of Archbishop James Beaton, became a Cardinal in December 1538 and Archbishop of St Andrews in September 1539. King James V had given great powers to a fanatical opponent of the Reformers but, following the Scottish defeat at Solway Moss, the King was to die in 1542 and Beaton was to be murdered in 1546. Also, Copernicus had published his great work on the solar system in 1543 and the intellectual thrust was with the Reformers. As John Donne was to write famously, "And new philosopy calls all in doubt:/The element of fire is quite put out". Less well known is Drummond of Hawthornden's "A Cypresse Grove" where he echoes Donne, lists the new uncertainties and states the new insecurities, "Thus Sciences by the diverse Motiones of this Globe of the Braine of Man, are become Opiniones, nay errors, and leave the Imagination in a thousand Labbyrinthes. What is all wee knowe compared with what wee knowe not?" But I jump ahead almost seventy-five years as the first version of Drummond's essay was first printed in 1619.

Set into the roadway outside St Andrews Castle are the initials of the Reformer George Wishart. Wishart's trial, which took place in the magnificent Cathedral of St Andrews in 1546 before assembled nobles and clerics, revealed the defendant's brilliant mind and eloquence, but Wishart was being tried to be condemned and he died at the stake outside the Castle watched from the Castle wall by Beaton and other dignitaries. The murder of the Cardinal in St Andrews Castle by a group of Fife lairds followed on Saturday 29th May 1546. On hearing of Beaton's murder, John Knox rushed to St Andrews to join the Reformers who had taken the Castle, but held it for only fourteen months before it was taken by a French force. Knox was amongst those who "filled the galleys fou". The rest, as they say, is history, and the stones of St Andrews seem to speak of it.

So also did Knox in his very prejudiced but, in parts, still very readable, *History of the Reformation*, which includes a dramatic description of the murder of Cardinal Beaton in St Andrews in May 1546. As Knox says, "These things we write merrily". According to Knox, Beaton had a "treasonable purpose" which was,

> not understood but by his secret council; and it was this: That Norman Leslie "Sherriff of Fife, and apparent heir to his father, the Earl of Rothes, the said John Leslie, father-brother to Norman, the Lairds of Grange elder and younger [Sir James Kirkcaldy and William Kirkcaldy], Sir James Learmonth of Dairsie and Provost of St Andrews, and the faithful laird of Raith [Sir John Melville of Raith] should either have been slain, or else tane, and after to have been used at his pleasure. This enterprise was disclosed after his slaughter, partly by letters and memorials found in his chamber, but plainly affirmed by such as were of the council. Many purposes were devised how that wicked man might have been taken away, But all failed, till Friday, the 28 of May, Anno 1546, when the foresaid Norman came at night to Saint Andrews; William Kirkcaldy of Grange, younger, was in the town before, awaiting upon the purpose; last came John Leslie foresaid, who was most suspected. What conclusion they took that night, it was not known but by the issue that followed.

That is well written and it could be about a discreet gathering of desperate bank robbers in a town of the American west in the days of Marshall Dillon. Knox continues,

> But early upon the Saturday, in the morning, the 29 of May, were they in sundry companies in the Abbey kirk-yard, not far distant from the Castle. First, the yetts [gates] being open, and the draw-brig down, for receiving of lime and stones, and other things necessary for building (for Babylon was almost finished)—first, we say, essayed William Kirkcaldy of Grange, younger, and with him six persons, and getting entrance, held purpose with the porter.
> . . . While the said William and the porter talked, and his servants made them to look the work and the workmen, approached Norman Leslie with his company; and because they were no great number, they easily got entrance. They addressed them to the midst of the close, and immediately came John Leslie, somewhat rudely, and four persons with them. The porter, fearing, would have drawn the brig; but the said John, being entered thereon, stayed, and leapt in. And while the porter made him for defence, his head was broken, the keys taken from them, and he cast in the fosse [moat]; and so the place was seized.

The workmen, more than one hundred says Knox, ran from the walls and unharmed they were put out through the small gate. Then,

> William Kirkcaldy took the guard of the privy postern, fearing that the fox should have escaped. Then go the rest to the gentlemen's chambers, and without violence done to any man, they put more than fifty persons to the yett: The number that enterprised and did this, was but sixteen persons. The Cardinal, awakened with the shouts, asked from his window, What meant that noise? It was answered, That Norman Leslie had taken his Castle. Which understood, he ran to the postern; but perceiving the passage to be kept without, he returned quickly to his chamber, took

his two-handed sword, and gart [made] his chamber child cast kists [chests], and other implements to the door. In this meantime came John Leslie unto it, and bids open. The Cardinal asking, "Who calls?, he answers, "My name is Leslie." He re-demands, "Is that Norman?" The other says, "Nay; my name is John." "I will have Norman", says the Cardinal, "for he is my friend." "Content yourself with such as are here; for other shall ye get none." There were with the said John, James Melville [of Carnbee] a man familiarly acquainted with Master George Wishart; and Peter Carmichael [of Balmedie, or Balmaddie], a stout gentleman.

. . . the Cardinal or his chamber-child, (it is uncertain), opened the door, and the Cardinal sat doun in a chair and cried, "I am a priest; I am a priest, ye will not slay me." The said John Leslie (according to his former vows) strook him first, anes or twice, and so did the said Peter. But James Melville (a man of nature most gentle and most modest) perceiving thame both in choler, withdrew them, and said, "This work and judgment of God (although it be secret) ought to be done with greater gravity"; and presenting unto him the point of the sword, said, "Repent thee of thy former wicked life, but especially of the schedding of the blood of that notable instrument of God, Maister George Wishart, which albeit the flame of fire consumed before men, yet cries it a vengeance upon thee, and we from God are sent to revenge it: For here, before my God, I protest, that neither the hetterent [hatred] of thy person, the luif of thy riches, nor the fear of any trouble thou could have done to me in particular, moved nor moves me to strike thee; but only because thou hast been, and remains ane obstinat enemy against Christ Jesus and his Holy Evangel." And so he struck him twice or thrice through with a stog [thrusting] sword; and so he fell, never word heard out of his mouth, but "I am a priest, I am a priest: fye, fye: all is gone."

Knox relates that a crowd gathered and insistently cried to see the Lord Cardinal,

And so was he brought to the east blockhouse head, and shown dead over the wall to the faithless multitude, which would not believe before it saw. How miserably lay David Beaton, careful Cardinal. And so they departed without *Requiem æternam*, and *Requiescat in pace*, song for his soule. Now, because the weather was hot (for it was in May, as ye have heard), and his funeral could not suddenly be prepared, it was thought best, to keep him from stinking, to give him great salt enough, a cope of lead, and a nuke in the bottom of the Sea-touer (a place where many of God's children had been empreasoned before) to await what exequies his brethren the Bishops would prepare for him.

These things we write merrily. But we would that the Reader should observe God's just judgments, and how they can deprehend the wordly wise in their own wisdom, make their table to be a snare to trap their own feet, and their own presupposed strength to be their own destruction. These are the words of our God, whereby he would admonish the tyrants of this earth, that in the end he will be revenged of their cruelty, what strength so ever follow they make in the contrary. But such is the blindness of man (as David speaks), "That the posterity does ever follow the footsteps of their wicked fathers and principally in their impiety"; for how little differs the cruelty of that bastard, that yet is called Bishop of Saint Andrews from the cruelty of the former, we will after hear.

The bastard Bishop of Saint Andrews is the intelligent and capable John Hamilton, half-brother of the indecisive James Hamilton, 2nd Earl of Arran, the Governor of Scotland who became Duke of Chatelherault. Archbishop Hamilton was to be hanged at the Mercat

Cross in Stirling in April 1571. Cardinal Beaton's cousin Janet was the mother of Chatelherault, being the second wife of James Hamilton, 1st Earl of Arran, who was descended, on the female line, from King James II.

After the murder of Beaton, Norman Leslie, a capable and experienced soldier, may have escaped to the castle of the Leslies at Ballinbreich near Lindores and Newburgh. After the fall of St Andrews Castle to the French, he was one of those who escaped into exile and avoided the hard labour of a French galley which might have been more bearable than the debilitating sense of guilt that was to afflict him. The magnificent Leslie House, in today's new town of Glenrothes, was built by the first Duke of Rothes in the time of Charles II. The Carnbee estate of the Melvilles was north of Pittenweem, on the side of Kellie Law in an area of upland acres, small villages and great country houses; an isolated, upland area from which the great landowners retreated in winter to their town houses in Pittenweem and Anstruther. William Kirkcaldy's Grange estate was near Kinghorn and later his family owned the grander Halyards Castle near Auchtertool.

Following his arrival in St Andrews John Knox taught in private, perhaps in the chapel within the Castle and more publicly in the parish church. It was not until a Sunday in May, or perhaps early June, 1547, that Knox revealed his power as a preacher. In his *History* he abridged his sermon and this may lessen its power but that a great preacher had arrived was apparent to all who heard him that day. As was said, "he struck at the root, while other preachers only sned [pruned] the branches." Amongst those who heard Knox that day would be the murderers of Beaton, but John Mair (or Major), an old and careful provost of St Salvator's, would have been there, as may Sir David Lyndsay, poet and courtier who did not die until 1555. The passionate Knox took as his text part of the 24th and 25th verses of the seventh chapter of the Book of Daniel. Not exactly a subtle choice but a classic for those who would proclaim a new order and conviction politics. "And ane other king shall rise after thame, and he shall be unlyk unto the first, and he shall subdue three kinges, and shall speak great wordes against the maist Heich, and think that he may change tymes and lawes, and thei shal be gevin unto his handis, until a tyme, and tymes, and the deviding of tymes."

The nineteen months in the galleys and the long years of exile followed for Knox, and it was not till June 1559 that he preached again in Fife. He famously preached "revolution" in Perth on 11th May 1559. He was in Anstruther on 2nd June 1559 and when, a few days later, he preached in Crail, he announced that he intended to preach in the Parish Kirk of St Andrews on Sunday, only two days later. This was dangerous, with Archbishop Hamilton able to call out spearmen and Mary of Guise at Falkland with French soldiers. He preached to the text of Jesus throwing the buyers and sellers out of the temple. On 29th June Knox preached in St Giles, Edinburgh, and by July not only had the Reformers taken over St Andrews and Dundee but in Edinburgh Knox was installed as its first Protestant minister.

In some ways Knox's most interesting years in Fife were as an old and ill man. It was in July 1571 that the old Knox came to St Andrews and he remained there until 17th August 1572. He was recovering from a stroke and in Edinburgh his old ally and friend Kirkcaldy of Grange had changed sides and was holding the Castle for Mary, Queen of Scots. The betrayal of a cause by a friend must have hurt Knox more than the arrival of a new enemy or of compromisers such as Mar and Morton. Edinburgh Castle became a powerful symbol in the old man's imagination. He wrote to the laird of Drumlanrig, "That Babylon, the Castle of Edinburgh, sall ones bring Scotland in that miserie that we and our posteritie sal murne for a tyme. Bot yit, schir, be nocht ye nor the faithful afraid, for to destructione sall it come, and they that presently sufferis sall rejoice in his life and eternallie" And Knox signed his letter, "Yours, lying in Sanct Androis half deid, the 26 of May 1572."

The ill man had the will to preach every Sunday and as Richard Bannatyne, his rigidly righteous and loyal secretary, said, "He always applied his text to the time and state of the people: whereby the wicked and troublers of God's Kirk might be pointed out in their colours." Again Knox was taking his texts from Daniel. The religious victory of the Reformers was not absolute in the terms of an extremist such as Knox. Thankfully it never could be.

The religious divisions in Edinburgh were also there in St Andrews. It was a struggle for power. Knox encountered the opposition of John Rutherford, the provost of St Salvator's, the parish minister Robert Hamilton, and other Hamiltons, which was not surprising since Knox had described all Hamiltons as murderers. The public statements were extreme with Knox described as being as great a murderer as any Hamilton. The inter-college rivalry added to the pressures on Knox, with the students of St Leonard's sitting at his feet whilst those of St Salvator's attacked him. The academics naturally still bucked against the power of parish ministers. On the plus side for the old preaching warrior, the printer Lekprevick showed his support by taking his press out of Edinburgh and the ferries of both Forth and Tay were busy with ministers wishing to see Knox.

We are fortunate that James Melville, a youth of fifteen, had left a manse near Montrose to attend St Leonard's and was there during Knox's months in St Andrews. In his diaries he gives quite remarkable descriptions of the old John Knox,

> Bot of all the benefites I haid that yeir [1571] was the coming of that maist notable profet and apostle of our nation, Mr Jhone Knox, to St Androis; wha, be the faction of the Quein occupeing the castell and town of Edinbruche, was compellit to remove thairfra with a number of the best and chusit to com to St Androis. I hard him teatche ther the prophecie of Daniel that simmer, and the wintar following. I haid my pen and my little book, and tuk away sic things as I could comprehend. In the opening upe of his text he was moderat the space of an halff houre; bot when he enterit to application, he maid me sa to grew [shudder] and tremble, that I could nocht hald my pen to wryt. I hard him oftymes utter these thretenings in the hicht of their pryde, quhilk the eis of monie saw cleirlie brought to pass within the yeirs upon the Captean of that Castle, the Hamiltones, and the Quein hir selff.

> . . . At Mr Knox coming to St Androis, Robert Lekprevik, printar, transported his lettres and press from Edinbruch to St Androis, whar first I saw that excellent art of printing; and haid then in hand Mr Patrik Constant's Catechisme of Calvin, converted in Latin heroic vers, quhilk with the author was mikle estimed of.

> . . . The town of Edinbruche recovered againe, [1572] and the guid and honest men thereof retourned to thair housses. Mr Knox with his familie past hame to Edinbruche. Being in St Androis he wes verie weak. I saw him everie day of his doctrine go hulie and fear, with a furring of marticks [marten fur] about his neck, a staff in the an hand, and guid and godlie Richart Ballanden, his servand, halding uupe the uther oxtar [armpit], from the Abbay to the paroche kirk; and be the said Richart and another servant, lifted upe to the pulpit, whar he behovit to lean at his first entrie; bot or he haid done with his sermont, he was sa active and vigorus that he was lyk to ding that pulpit in blads, and fly out of it!

Almost 250 years later the superb phrase that Melville used to describe Knox, as being so vigorous as to be likely to beat the pulpit into pieces, was gathered, magpie-like, by William Tennant for use in his poem "Papistry Storm'd". Tennant (1784-1848) is best known for his mock epic poem "Anster Fair" but his "Papistry Storm'd" is a true *tour de force*. The poet takes the Reformers' attacks on the structures of St Andrews Cathedral and turns their most serious endeavours into a riotous celebration that belongs within the comic Scots tradition that was formed by poems such as "Peblis to the Play" and "Chrystis Kirk on the Green". Tennant was born in Anstruther and became Professor of Oriental Languages at St Andrews. His other works, deservedly neglected, include a verse drama "Cardinal Beaton" and a long poem "The Thane of Fife". The mock-heroics of "Papistry Storm'd" begins,

> I sing the steir, strabush, and strife,
> Whan, bickerin' frae the towns o Fife,
> Great bangs of bodies, thick and rife,
>   Gaed to Sanct Androis town,
> And, wi John Calvin i' their heads,
> And hammers i' their hands and spades,
> Enrag'd at idols, mass, and beads,
>   Dang the Cathedral down:

It is the younger Knox who first preached in St Andrews in 1547 that Tennant comically celebrates,

> He prechit east, he preachit wast;
> His voice was as the whirlwind's blast,
>   That aftentimes, in days o' simmer,
> Comes swirlin' sudden frae the sea,
> And swoops the hay-cocks aff the lea,
>   And tirls the kirks, and strips the timmer;
> The vera steeples round about
> Rebellow'd to his nobill shout,
> And rang wi' texts baith in and out;
> The dows and daws that there aboundit,
> As if affrichtit and confoundit,
> Out-whirr'd and whitter't at the sound o't;
> The bells and bartisans reboundit,
> Strang pupits flew about in blads,
> Breakin' the hearers' pows wi dads;
> Men, women, kirtled girls, and lads,
> Were fir'd and furiated in squads;
> Sae wud and wicket was their wraith . . .

dows and daws: pigeons and jackdaws   bartisans: parapets
Strang pupits: strong pulpits   blads: fragments   dads: bits
wud: mad

Nepotism was commonplace in these times—at least for those in power—and following David Beaton's murder his nephew, another James Beaton, became Archbishop of Glasgow, but the Beaton family were of significance in Fife far beyond the three famous clerics who were powerful secular administrators. The various lines of the family were important landowners around Markinch, Anstruther and Kilconquhar, and also in Creich with a castle near the banks of the Tay half way between Newburgh and Newport. They also married into most of the other land-owning families of Fife including Anstruther, Sandilands of St Monans, Lyndsay of the Byres, Leslie (a daughter of the Earl of Rothes) and an Earl of Crawford. The spelling of their name has varied perhaps even more than is usual. It has been suggested that it could be derived from Bethune a town in Picardie in Northern France although others believe the name was Betun which members of the family altered to Bethune to associate themselves to a more ancient house, but we also have the Scottish Beton, Betoun and, of course, Beaton which I have used here.

We have to distinguish between the Balfours of Balbirnie and the longer-established Balfours of Balgonie. Balfour House stood to the south-east of Balgonie in a beautiful position between the Rivers Leven and Ore which unite near Windygates. Balfours have been at Balgonie and Markinch since the time of King Duncan. A charter of Duncan, Earl of Fife, is confirmed by one of Robert II dated 1378 which shows Beaton holding the lands of Balfour, Newton and Kettel. A David de Balfour died fighting with Wallace. A Sir John Balfour of that ilk died in 1375 leaving only a daughter and she it was who married into the Beaton family. About 1360 she married Sir Robert Betoun, probably younger son of Alexander de Betoun of not Fife but Angus. From this couple were descended the Balfours of Balgonie and also many a Beaton.

In the 1460s there was a John Beaton and he seems to have been married twice; first to Marjory Boswell of Balmuto, in the old parish of Auchtertool, and second to Elizabeth Melville of Raith, Kirkcaldy. James Boswell, the biographer of Samuel Johnson, is related to the Boswells of Balmuto. John Beaton and Marjory (or Mary) Boswell are certainly the parents of James Beaton, Archbishop of Glasgow in 1508 and Archbishop of St Andrews in 1522, and the grandparents of David Beaton, the Cardinal who was murdered in 1546.

Two of John Beaton's sons are John, father of the Cardinal and David who acquired Creich estate in 1502. There is some documentary evidence that a John Beaton of Balfour, and his brother David Beaton of Creich, sons of John Beaton of Balfour, were buried in Markinch in the early decades of the sixteenth century. John Beaton, the Cardinal's father, died in 1532. Until recently a pub in Markinch was named the Bethune Arms.

The Cardinal's father, John Beaton, possibly of Balfarg as well as Balfour, married Elizabeth or Isobel Monypenny of Kinkell and Pitmilly. I have previously referred to the dykes at Pitmilly near Boarhills, and today's Kinkell Farm sits off the A917 halfway between St Andrews and Boarhills. On the coast is Kinkell Ness with the braes above. One of the Cardinal's older brothers, John or James Beaton of Balfarg, may have married Helen Melville of Drummaird and their children included James Beaton, Archbishop of Glasgow in 1551, loyal ambassador for Queen Mary, who fled at the Reformation and, aged 86, was buried in Rome. Balfarg lands were to become part of the Balfours of Balbirnie estate and today the name lives on within Glenrothes.

Locally it has been taken as read that Cardinal David Beaton was born in the grand Balfour House that stood between the Leven and the Ore and which was demolished in the early 1930s. Other less local writers, who may also be inclined to jump to unfounded conclusions, have preferred to believe that he was born in the nearby Balgonie castle-tower which was owned not by Balfours but by the Lundin family who were at Balgonie until early in the seventeenth century.

The Cardinal's uncle, Sir David Beaton, acquired the lands of Creich about 1500. He was familiar with King James V as a boy and "grew into great favour" becoming Comptroller of the Exchequer and, on the death of Sir Robert Lundin, Lord High Treasurer. True to that time, David Beaton was succeeded as Treasurer by his brother James Beaton who became an Archbishop. The heir to Creich, Sir John Beaton, expanded the estate and he probably built Creich Castle and became Captain of Falkland Palace. Sir David's daughter, Janet Beaton, seems to have had three husbands. So also did his granddaughter, another Janet Beaton, the third of them being Sir Walter Scott of Branxholm and Buccleuch whose third wife she was. Janet Beaton, or Lady Scott of Buccleuch, became more lastingly famous through the prominence given to her in an even more illustrious Sir Walter Scott's *The Lay of the Last Minstrel,*

> In sorrow o'er Lord Walter's bier
>   The warlike foresters had bent;
> And many a flower, and many a tear,
>   Old Teviot's maids and matrons lent:
> But o'er her warrior's bloody bier
> The Ladye dropp'd nor flower nor tear!
> Vengeance, deep-brooding o'er the slain,
> Had locked the source of softer woe;
> And burning pride, and high disdain,
>   Forbade the rising tear to flow;
> * * *
> Of noble race the Ladye came,
> Her father was a clerk of fame,
>   Of Bethune's line of Picardie:
> He learned the art that none may name,
>   In Padua, far beyond the sea.
> Men said, he changed his mortal frame
>   By feat of magic mystery;
> But when, in studious mood, he paced
>   St Andrew's cloistered hall,
> His form no darkening shadow traced
>   Upon the sunny wall!
>
> And of his skill, as bards avow,
>   He taught that Ladye fair,
> Till to her bidding she could bow
>   The viewless forms of air.
> And now she sits in secret bower,
> In old Lord David's western tower,
> And listens to a heavy sound,
> That, moans the mossy turrets round.

The real life Lady was said to be as physically brave as any man and when her husband, Sir Walter Scott of Branxholm, who was involved in a feud between the Scotts and the Kerrs, was killed on the streets of Edinburgh in 1552, she led out the Scotts to revenge his death. Some who were astounded by her abilities attributed them to the magic powers which the poet refers to in his Lay. The real-life Branxholm Tower, Branksome in the poem, stood three miles south-west of Hawick.

Sir John Beaton's heir was Sir Robert Beaton who was a page in the household of King James V. It is often said that he was one of the pages who accompanied Mary, Queen of Scots, to France but he was too old to hold that position. He did, however, marry one of the maids-of-honour to Queen Mary of Guise and although her name has been much debated she appears as Johanne de Lareyneville on a charter of Queen Mary that confirms "the lands of Creich with the tower, fortilice, and manor thereof in the county of Fife . . .." After the Queen's return from France in 1561, Sir Robert Beaton of Creich was made Master of the Household, Heritable Steward of Fife, and Keeper of Falkland Palace.

The heir to Robert of Creich, David Beaton, married Beatrice Leslie, daughter of the Earl of Rothes, but more famous is Beaton and Lareyneville's daughter Mary who is one of the four Maries, or maids-of-honour, of Mary, Queen of Scots, who are celebrated in the ballad of Marie Hamilton. Historically the Maries do not include a Hamilton, being: Mary Fleming, whose mother had royal blood, and who married Maitland of Lethington; Mary Seton, daughter of George, 4th Lord Seton, who did not marry; and Mary Livingstone, daughter of the Queen's guardian, Alexander, 5th Lord Livingstone, who married John Sempill. Mary Beaton was to marry Alexander Ogilvie of Boyne and the marriage contract had the distinction of being signed by Queen Mary, Darnley, Huntly, Argyll, Bothwell, Murray and Atholl. Locally it was well known that there was a portrait of the beautiful Mary Beaton in Balfour House. It was also said that in the same room in Balfour House hung portraits of Cardinal David Beaton and of his uncle Archbishop James Beaton. I have wondered what happened to them but my efforts to find information on them have been unfruitful. It would be a regrettable if they have been lost, or never existed—which would undermine local history and pride!

In his *History of the Reformation* John Knox merrily attacks his Queen and the goings-on at her artistic and musical Court. He writes of the year 1563,

> At the very time of the General Assembly, there comes to public knowledge a heinous crime committed in the Court, yea, not far from the Queen's own lap; for a French woman, that served in the Queen's chamber had played the whore with the Queen's own apothecary. The woman conceived and bore a child, whom with common consent the father and the mother murdered. Yet were the cries of the new born bairn heard; search was made, the child and mother were both deprehended: and so were both the man and the woman damned to be hanged upon the public street of Edinburgh.

This is propaganda against the Catholic Queen Mary; Knox also refers to another affair in which "shame hastened marriage betwixt John Sempill, called the Dancer, and Marie Livingstone, surnamed the Lusty. What bruit the Maries and the rest of the dancers of the Court had, the ballads of that age did witness, which we may with modesty omit." This Mary Livingstone is the Marie who accompanied the Queen to France and she was to marry John Sempill in Fife—in Auchtermuchty. Sempill may have been a natural son of Lord Sempill, but Knox libelled them in the phrase, "shame hastened marriage". In the ballad the apothecary has become the Queen's husband Darnley although by Knox's dating of his story Darnley was nowhere near Edinburgh at the crucial time. Not that the ballad is about history or, if it is, it belongs as much in an incident at the Russian Court of Peter the Great at the end of the seventeenth century as in Mary's Holyrood. Also the names of the four Maries vary in versions of the ballad,

Word's gane to the kitchen,
  And word's gane to the ha,
That Marie Hamilton gangs wi bairn
  To the heichest Stewart of a'.

He's courted her in the kitchen,
  He's courted her in the ha,
He's courted her in the laigh cellar,
  And that was warst of a'.

She's tyed it in her apron
  And she's thrown it in the sea—
Says, "Sink ye, swim ye, bonny wee babe!
  That I heard greet sae sare.

. . .

"O Marie, put on your robes o black
  Or else your robes o broun
For ye maun gang wi me the nicht,
  To see fair Edinbro toun."

"I winna put on my robes o black
  Nor yet my robes o broun;
But I'll put on my robes o white,
  To shine through Edinbro toun."

When she gaed up the Cannogate,
  She laughd loud laughters three;
But whan she cam doun the Cannogate
  The tear blinded her ee.

When she gaed up the Parliament stair,
  The heel cam aff her shee;
And lang or she cam doun again
  She was condemnd to dee.

And so through the tale to the final two verses of this version,

"Last nicht I washed the queen's feet,
  And gently laid her doun;
And a' the thanks I've gotten the nicht
  To be hangd in Edinbro toun!

"Last nicht there was fowre Maries
  The nicht there'll be but three—
There was Marie Seton, and Marie Beaton,
  And Marie Carmichael, and me."

$$4$$

Kinaldy and Dunino
& by the Coast to Fife Ness & Crail

THE BROWNHILLS Brae climbs out of St Andrews to lead to the coastal road (A917) which goes past Brownhills to Boarhills, Kingsbarns, across to Crail and along the coast to Largo; a very fine coastal road and the beaches between St Andrews and Crail are perhaps the most isolated in Fife. Again we may turn to look down to St Andrews and its bay and over Angus to the distant Grampian mountains. The Brownhills road also goes to the B9131 and across country, past Stravithie and Dunino, to Anstruther.

When the teenage Robert Fergusson left St Andrews to visit Professor Wilkie's farm in the parish of Cameron it could be that he took a road equivalent to the A915 which goes to Upper Largo via Largoward. This is an admirable road from which to see the lands of the Riggin o Fife. Also, from points on that road we could be on another ridge, or backbone, that gives splendid views not only of the varied green acres of this north-east of the county but also of the Forth and over to Berwick Law and the Bass Rock. There is a high open stretch of road from which St Monans Kirk looks like a sturdy miniature of geometric perfection on the edge of the world. The rooflines of Elie and Earlsferry continue this distant-seeming silhouetted coastscape.

The inland view towards where Ceres lies is more enclosed but westwards there are fine sightings of Largo Law. Northwards, off the A915, lies Peat Inn where David and Patricia Wilson have established a national reputation for exceptional cooking.

A minor road that links the A915 to the B9131 takes us past Kinaldy to Dunino. Alternatively the St Andrews to Anstruther bus (no.61) can be taken directly along the B9131 to Dunino. Once, about half way between St Andrews and Dunino, there was a Stravithie Station on the St Andrews to Crail railway line that continued to Thornton Junction. The bridge can still be recognised and, perhaps, also the station house. The bus stops at Dunino Primary School the existence of which may give a false idea of the size of this very small village. Back down the hill towards Stravithie, and facing the avenue that goes to Stravithie House, a sign indicates a Public Footpath to Dunino Church and Den.

To some visitors the name seems to belong more in Italy, or Spain, than in Fife. It has been variously: Dunnigheanach, Duninow, Dununnow on the communion cups bought in 1736, although the Kirk Session used the form Deninno (or Denino) which was widely used throughout the eighteenth century as milestones reveal, and currently Dunino which is only the latest "corruption" of a name lost in pre-mapmaking times.

Even in winter, standing by the Primary School, it is difficult to see Dunino Kirk through the trees that line the burn, but the elusiveness of that jaggy bellcote and these well-cut windows adds to its rural attractiveness. Bishop David Bernham consecrated a Church at Dunino about 1240 as a rectory of St Salvator's College, St Andrews, but long before that date a Culdee church would have been set up at the site chosen by the Druids. The present building dates from 1826-27 and was designed by J. Gillespie Graham. Rev Alexander Macdonald was uncomfortable with a west-facing church and the building was redesigned in 1928 when a chancel and porch were added. The bare but superbly cut and pointed stone and the pine roof must give pleasure to all who go into the building for the first time, as I did in 1998. Also, the natural surface of the pine pews is well set off by the brass fittings of the umbrella stands, and the plain glass of the side windows not only acts as a foil to the stained glass in the chancel but allows us to incorporate the surrounding trees into our view of this fine interior. There is a pink stone font by Sir Robert Lorimer which has good strong lines that balance the more intricate carvings of birds and bells. When I was at Dunino Church in 1998 I was intrigued by what looked like a very recent extension to the porch alongside the west window. This is indeed an addition of late 1997 and early 1998.

In the Spring of 1998, the public footpath to the church was dry and firm and the crisp sound of beech nuts being crunched underfoot added to my enjoyment of this tree-lined path. Soon the sound of a fast-running burn added further interest, as did the old iron bridge. In another few yards this burn meets with another—Kinaldy and Dunino I guess. Further down, beyond Dunino, these two waters join the Kenly Water on its way to the sea at Boarhills. Another helpful sign directs away from a private house and uphill along the edge of the wooded gorge of the burn. Two minutes walking through that glen, lined by snowdrops when I was there, and the Gothic bellcote of Dunino Church can be seen, fronted by a large yew, and backed by the frondy tracery of a single, taller tree. A short climb and the headstones of the kirkyard come into view as, to the left, does the large manse. The final stretch of this idyllic approach to the church has the contrast of one open aspect of fields that are adorned only by a wall and a solitary tree. Over the gorge and through the enclosing wood, the few houses of Dunino village can just be seen. In summer this will be an enclosing wood.

The main path continues round to go alongside the kirkyard but, to the right, a lesser path goes down to the Bel Crag. This is a rock of inspiring proportions. It rises in a great craggy, yet bulbous, mass above the burn and, on its flat circular top, is a dark, deep-looking pool some four feet wide; a pool to step back from. Long ago a stairway has been cut many through the towering bedrock to enable direct access to the gorge with its enclosing cliffs and fast-running burn; a slippery and dangerous stairway for those not sure of foot and eye; a gorge that can encourage us to whisper and look anxiously into these dim woods. Fortunately a path goes alongside the burn and up into the sunshine and to a side gate to the kirkyard.

Not far from this Den, a stone circle (henge) stood in a field close to Beley Farm. In 1922 a burial cist, with Food Vessel dating from about 1800 BC, was found in this field— it is now in the National Museum of Scotland. We can perhaps accept that the farm's name has a long history that goes back to times of sun worshiping; of Bel worship and Beltane ceremonies on 1st May. As with so many old and rural Christian churches, this is a place where there were religious ceremonies before the arrival of the Christian missionaries who tended to place their small churches near the old religious places but, where possible, on the other side of the burn. This is so, also, for Glasgow Cathedral which stands close to where the Molendinar burn ran, and St Kentigern founded his small church, but across the burn from the Necropolis Hill where the Druids may have performed their ceremonies.

The kirk of the parish of Cambuslang where I was born stands above another such gorge through which flows the Kirkburn. Dechmont Hill looks down on Cambuslang Parish Church and, outside the village, the burn flows through a smaller, darker gorge heavily overhung with trees. I knew that place as a boy, and tradition told us that at it there had been strange ceremonies. Later I learned that this was regarded as a sacred grove of the Druids, a place where as the Bible says of the children of Israel, they "made a grove, and worshipped all the host of heaven, and served Baal. And they caused their sons and their daughters to pass through the fire, and used divinations and enchantments." Without doubt Beltane fires were lit on Cambuslang's Dechmont Hill, and the term "till Beltane night" appears in the Parish Church records into the seventeenth century. When I returned to the gorge of the Kirkburn as a grown man, on a sunny but showery day, I was reminded of Titian's small dark painting in the Louvre of Saint Jerome crouching before a symbol of his Christ God in which the landscape is not that of the Saint's usual rocky desert, but of a dark wood. The gorge, or Den, at Dunino has that same sense of mystery. In 1998 I was told that dogs can become disturbed when walked through Dunino Den. My rational mind posed the question, "Are they responding to a nervousness in their owners, rather than to memories of past happenings supposedly retained by the stones and the earth?" My informant joined me in laughter. I cannot claim to have any sense of the mystery of a reputed Druid Grove in Dunino but then I did not know it as a boy.

The minister of Dunino who wrote both the *Statistical Account* and the *New Statistical Account* for the parish was Rev James Roger and he gives details, in the later volume, of a "tabulated stone" on which, tradition had it, the Druids "collected dew on 1st May, Beltane, and having sprinkled the people, blessed them from the God of Fire." A shallow footprint carved on the rock has encouraged the idea that the Druids also swore in each new chief on the stone.

From Rev James Roger's headstone in Dunino kirkyard I learned that he was minister of the parish for forty-four years and died in 1849, age 83. The stone was erected by his son Charles who added an "s" to their name, and who, the inscription informs, was "Revd Charles Rogers, DD, LLD, born at Dunino manse 18th April 1825. Died Edinburgh 17th September 1890 and buried in the Grange Cemetery there. Author of many antiquarian, biographical and historical works." Charles Rogers's edition of the collected poems and songs of Lady Nairne has yet to be properly superseded. He also, unexpectedly as he seems to have had no family links, wrote a history of the Glen family. At a national level he is important for launching the idea of a Wallace Monument on the Abbey Craig, Stirling. It was he who, in 1845, investigated the Bel Craig and, removing the soil from the top, found the pot-holes and the shallow foot print.

In their most useful and interesting *Dunino: Place of Worship*, which was published in June 1993, D. and L. MacGilp write some cautionary words,

We know nothing certain about our Den and it has certainly been suggested that the excavations there were part of a hoax built on local legend. Still, in its favour, are the undisputed importance of the earlier henge site, the long attachment of the name Bel, the proximity of the place called "Druid's grave", Pittendreich, the Roman visit in strength and the importance attached by early Christians. The early Christian missionaries were attracted to the sacred groves of earlier worship as part of their process of gradual conversion and because of the natural affinity with nature and open air worship of the early church. A Culdee Celtic monk scribbled this poem in the margin of the book he was copying:

> A hedge of tree surrounds me,
> A blackbird's lay sings to me;
> Above my lined booklet
> The trilling birds chant to me.

> In a grey mantle from the top of bushes
> The cuckoo sings:
> Verily—may the Lord shield me—
> Well do I write under the greenwood.

What we can be sure of on high moorlands is that the imaginations and tall stories, traditional or otherwise, of ordinary folk can encourage not only archaeological investigations such as that of Charles Rogers who discovered the Bel Crag, but also superstitious imaginings. So we had the story of Alison Peirson leaving Boarhills to wander on the moor when the moon was right to harvest the ingredients for her concoctions, and meeting the man "cled in green claithes", as the Scots Deil (or Devil) has been described. There she was also spirited into fairyland where the magical seven years seemed like three days to her. Fortunately she "cam hame again". Such women, or others with strange ways, if unfortunate, could be identified as witches. When responding to the sounds and light of lonely places, the brain can encourage the eyes of those whose heads are full of often-told tales, to see a village that is not there. The odds are that given enough such sightings, some will occur at the site of a long-forgotten hamlet or of a house where some killing took place.

The "fairies", like the deil, were real enough to those who lived confined lives, and indeed to highly sophisticated Archbishops—or their detractors; including those who whispered of Archbishop Sharp having ceremonial meetings with the lord of darkness! The new scientific views of Copernicans must have influenced Shakespeare but we cannot know how many of the old beliefs were accepted by the dramatist in the scene in which the ghost of Hamlet's father faded, "on the crowing of the cock",

> Some say that ever 'gainst that season comes
> Wherein our Saviour's birth is celebrated,
> The bird of dawning singeth all night long;
> And then, they say, no spirit can walk abroad,
> The nights are wholesome; then no planets strike,
> No fairy takes, nor whitch hath power to charm,
> So hallow'd and so gracious is the time.

Horatio's response could be said as being sceptical but he certainly points to a sunny dawn which must have been welcomed by many, Christian or otherwise, who lived and worked the lands of Dunino, Kinaldy and Kingsmuir, as in rural communities everywhere,

> So I have heard and do in part believe it.
> But, look, the morn in russet mantle clad,
> Walks o'er the dew of yon high eastern hill;

Fir some years, the poet William Tennant was Dunino's schoolmaster, and he was also Session Clerk. From memorials in Dunino kirkyard I learned of the Purvis family of Kinaldy but previously I had associated that estate with Aytouns who were there for generations, and they may have had a royal, and illegitimate, Stewart ancestor. Their most literary son is Sir Robert Aytoun (1570-1638) a poet who lived between the Scottish tradition, which King James VI fostered before he left for London in 1603, and that of the English metaphysical poets. Aytoun followed James to London and became secretary to the

46

Queen, with a knighthood in 1612, and burial in Westminster Abbey. The Latin inscription on the tomb certainly cannot claim brevity, although a translation takes more words than the original. Not only does it provide biographical information but also a style of inscription that is, shall I say, a curiosity of its time—not that every comic title has yet left our United Kingdom,

> Sacred to the memory of a very illustrious knight, Sir Robert Aytoun, most adorned by every virtue and species of learning, especially poetry. He was descended from the ancient and eminent family of Aytoun, at the castle of Kinaldie in Scotland. Being appointed Gentleman of the Bedchamber by his Most Gracious Majesty King James, he was sent to the Emperor and Princes of Germany with Royal little work defending the Royal Authority; and having been made Prefect of St Catherine, he became Private Secretary first to Anne and then to Mary, the Most Serene Queens of Great Britain. He was also a Privy Councillor, Master of the Requests and Master of the Ceremonies. His soul, being restored to its Creator, while his mortal remains are here deposited, awaits the second coming of the Redeemer. Leaving King Charles he returns to his Royal sire; and bidding adieu to Queen Mary here visits Queen Anne; and exchanges the honour of the Palace for the exalted glory of Heaven. He died unmarried in the Palace of Whitehall, not without the greatest grief and lamentation of all good men, in 1638, aged sixty-eight years. As a testimony of his beloved and grateful mind, John Aytoun has erected this mournful monument to the best of uncles. Here lies entombed the unrivalled example of worth—the glory of the Muses—of the Court and Country—of Home and Abroad.

An early editor of Aytoun's poems was Rev Charles Rogers, son of Dunino manse, whose edition was published in 1844 with a brief biographical note on Aytoun. He has early work in Scots which belongs to the King's Castilian movement; polished but unsparkling poems in English; and Latin poems in *Delitiae Poetarum Scotorum* edited by Arthur Johnson and Sir John Scot of Scotstarvit. In the eighteenth century a version of "Auld Lang Syne" appears under Aytoun's name in James Watson's *Choice Collection of Comic and Serious Scots*. We'll never know for certain if Aytoun wrote the following lines but we can see that he lacked the genius of Robert Burns:

> Should old acquaintance be forgot,
>   And never thought upon,
> The flames of love extinguished,
>   And freely past and gone?
> Is thy kind heart now grown so cold
>   In that loving breast of thine,
> That thou canst never once reflect
>   On old-lang-syne?

From Dunino to Anstruther is five miles and the first of these is over the flat, and now fertile, toplands that give a view of only themselves but soon the road drops down and the individualistic spires of the kirks of the East Neuk can be identified, St Monans, Pittenweem, Anstruther, and soon, inland and further east, the elevated weathercock of Kilrenny.

To King James VI Fife was "a beggar's mantle fringed with gold". The seaports and fertile fringe were the gold and the muirs the waste lands that produced no income. Today's fertile Howe of Fife was in James's time very boggy, with a loch, and generally suited only for hunting. Kingsmuir south of Dunino was part of that waste land and it took in the Boar's Chase that stretched in the west to Kemback north of Pitscottie to, presumably, Boarhills on the coast although there were more cows there than swine which were feared by the fishing communities. If a fisherman allowed his eye to fall on that evil beast he had to allow a tide to ebb and flow before putting to sea. Not one pig was willingly allowed in St Monans for over a century. And to hear this word of the devil was equally feared. Some protection was possible by touching "cauld iron". A much-repeated story is that of the new minister of St Monans who chose to preach around the parable of the prodigal son and announced that he would read from Luke chapter XV at the 11th verse. Even this ignorant stranger sensed a wave of unease moving through the congregation. He was aware of the apprehension growing as he read through verse fifteen towards the final dreaded word, "and he sent him into his fields to feed swine". "Touch airn" was the whisper. Startled the minister repeated the last phrase. "Touch airn" was the louder cry. The tension grew as he read verse 16 but he never reached the final evil word. The congregation panicked, those in the galleries dropped down on those below, and all rushed out into the clean sea air. For many a day few dared to cross into the kirk.

In medieval times, inland on the muirs, there had rooted and charged the mighty boar. A great stretch of land, from the River Eden to the Kenly Burn and taking in Dunino, was known as the "Boar's Raik". About 1120, King Alexander I is said to have given these lands to the religious community of Kinrimund—"head of the King's hill", later Kilrymont (church on the King's hill) and later St Andrews—to commemorate a great hunt. This great event is also commemorated by the tusked boar in the arms of the burgh of St Andrews. The suffering Covenanters were to hold illegal conventicles on these moors and yet more blood stained them when Archbishop Sharp was murdered at Magus Muir. Drumcarrow Craig looks down equally on Magus and the peaceful farm at Cameron where professor and poet strolled talking of poetry, a good potato crop and, who knows, perhaps a hare that "chanc'd to see/ A partan creepin on a lee."

As the name Kingsmuir suggests, these moors were lands held by kings. King David I is said to have favoured Crail Castle (now demolished) as a residence, and grain for the royal palaces at Falkland and Crail was gathered into barns at Kingsbarns. From the road end leading to Boarhills the A917 makes the twists and turns that, proverbially, offer shelter from the winds whether they come from north, south, east or west. We are at Pitmilly and lands that, for many centuries, belonged to the Monypenny family.

The Monypennys also had Pittarthie Castle built, about 1580, but sold it to the Bruces about 1636. Moving on two centuries, David Monypenny, who took the title Lord Pitmilly, was a friend of Sir Walter Scott at Edinburgh High School. Monypenny became a more successful lawyer than the novelist who helped to shape how the outside world saw Scotland; a view of Scotland that has still to be quite balanced by a more realistic view of a nation that views Balmorality as an irrelevance and knows nothing of the life style of the *ancien regime* of landed gentry that Scott favoured at Abbotsford. Lord Cockburn, who at one time lived next door to Monypenny in Charlotte Square, Edinburgh, wrote, "looking out of a window in the High Street at the foot procession of the Lord High Commissioner to the General Assembly saw Monypenny walking before his Grace the Earl of Leven dressed like a macaw as the Commissioner's purse-bearer. Little did he, or anybody then, dream that the day was to come when he was to have a seat on the supreme benches and become famous in his profession." He was promoted to the bench in 1813 and amongst the trials he took part in was that of the infamous Burke and Hare. His memorial was placed in a corner of Kingsbarns kirkyard.

The learned judge's father, Sir Alexander Monypenny, has been credited with a poem on Crail and some of those who lived there. According to Charles Rogers, Colonel Sir Alexander Monypenny was poet-laureate of a social club named "The Beggar's Benison". The old ballad "Of Sir John Malcolm" was given by Chambers as the inspiration for Robert Burns's song, "Ken ye ought o' Captain Grose?" which is sung to the tune "Sir John Malcolm". Professor James Kinsley, who edited the three-volume Oxford edition *The Poems and Songs of Robert Burns* which was published in 1968, says that Burns's model "is a dreg-song from the Forth, probably on the seventeenth-century Sir John Malcolm of Grange, Burntisland". There is a version printed in David Herd's *Ancient and Modern Scottish Songs, Heroic Ballads, etc*, the enlarged edition of which was published in 1776. So, it would seem that Monypenny, like Burns and many singers of ballads, was giving his fellow club members his version of an old song that belongs within the tradition of the oyster dredging songs of the Forth. The old version has these lines,

> Keep ye well frae Sir John Malcolm, Igo and ago,
> If he's a wise man, I mistak him, Iram coram dago.
> Keep ye weel frae Sandie Don, Igo and ago.
> He's ten times dafter than Sir John, Iram coram dago.
> . . .
> Was ye e'er in Crail town? [Igo and ago.}
> Did ye see Clark Dishingtoun? [Iram coram dago,] etc.

In the text given by Charles Rogers, Alexander Monypenny's Crail poem begins,

> Oh were you e'er in Crail toun?
>   Igo and ago;
> An' saw there Clerk Dishingtoun?
>   Iram coram dago.
>
> His wig was like a droukit hen,
>   Igo and ago,
> The tail o't like a grey goose pen,
>   Iram coram dago.
>
> Ken ye ought o' Sir John Malcolm?
>   Igo and ago;
> If' he's a wise man I mistak' him,
>   Iram coram dago.
>
> Ken ye ought o' Sandy Don?
>   Igo and ago,
> He's ten times dafter than Sir John
>   Iram coram dago.

Captain Francis Grose, author of *Antiquities of Scotland*, had the great honour and privilege of prompting Burns into writing "Tam o' Shanter". An introductory note to the Glenridell Manuscript explains, "When Captain Grose was at Friars-Carse in Summer 1790 Collecting materials for his Scottish Antiquities he applied to Mr Burns then living in the neighbourhood to write him an account of the Witches Meeting at Alloway church near

Ayr who complied with his request and wrote for him the following Poem". Gilbert Burns says that the poet asked Grose to include a drawing of Alloway Kirk in the second volume of his *Antiquities* which Grose agreed to do if Burns provided him with something to print with it. Burns gave Grose three prose witch-stories and one of these became the poem, "Tam o' Shanter". Burns's poem "Ken ye ought o' Captain Grose?" is addressed "extempore and anonymous" to Adam de Cardonelle Lawson, antiquary and numismatist, who assisted Grose,

> Ken ye ought o' Captain Grose?
> Igo and ago—
> If he's amang his friends or foes?
> Iram coram dago.—
>
> Is he South, or is he North?
> Igo and ago—
> Or drowned in the river Forth?
> Iram coram dago.—

The dykes around Pitmilly may give protection from winds from all the airts, but the view is an open one over the sea. Soon a sign welcomes us to the East Neuk and ahead is Kingsbarns with Crail three miles further on. It is said that the eight hundred acres of fine corn land owned by the Kings was the most productive in these parts. As Kingsbarns is approached, the spire of the church just tops the green fields but, closer to, the tower is revealed as a succession of interesting levels with round windows, tall windows and belfry angled into parapet and topped by a soaring spire.

The royal barns may have gone from Kingsbarns but there are still Erskines at Cambo and the Gardens are more colourful than most granaries, and seem especially so to those who leave them to venture down onto the eye-stretching beaches that are no place for sufferers from agoraphobia. Here also is Cambo Country Park. The name may be from the de Cambhou family who came here in the time of the long-reigning William the Lion. The Erskine family came to Cambo in the 1660s. Following a fire Sir Thomas Erskine had the current house built in 1879 to stand amongst the many greens of Cambo woods.

A sign indicates that the Secret Bunker is 3 miles away. Until recent years travellers were unlikely to know that deep below these flat lands, off the B940, was the secret bunker that, if there had been a nuclear war, would have been used as government HQ for Scotland. Now, from late March to October, tourists can walk into the operations room and envisage a war being conducted. There's also a café and gift shop. To the west of the bunker, standing on exposed, high ground north of Kingsmuir and south of Dunino, the castle of Pittarthie can *seem* almost benevolent despite its shot holes.

On this road from Cambo to Crail, the May Isle is a more calming sight than any operations room, as is the spire of Crail Parish Church which is first glimpsed over the varied rooftops of the old burgh. Today Crail is seen as picturesque, which it surely is, and as such it has one of the most photographed and painted of Scottish harbours. The early-seventeenth-century Mercat Cross, topped by its unicorn, in the Marketgate has attracted almost as many artists as the harbour, and the solid sixteenth-century Tolbooth has an eye-catching curved roof that tops a layered tower with round windows that are echoed in the face of the clock. This masterpiece of Scottish architecture is topped by a weathervane that carries the fine and famous Crail capon, or smoked haddock.

In centuries past Crail was a royal centre with the castle favoured by Kings. In medieval Europe, the market in Crail's Mercatgait was one of the largest. Crail was also a most important harbour, superior to Anstruther, Pittenweem, Elie and Earlsferry. The Mercatgait has now been Anglicised to Marketgate, although gait is guid Scots for a way or thoroughfare—not a gate. Union with England, and laws passed in Westminster, did the villages of the East Neuk no favours. Today Crail is neither royal nor an exporting and importing port; the fishing has gone also. Its main trade is with tourists, and the old Royal Burgh (created in 1310) can disappoint few visitors no matter how high their expectations. A recently-come resident in Crail is Gavin Bowd, young poet and scholar, who was born in Galashiels but attended St Andrews University where he now teaches in the French Department of St Andrews University.

The tower of Crail Parish Church is a worthy associate of the Tolbooth tower in the Marketgate. The church has at least part of a wall that is Norman, and its dedication of 1243 was to the Celtic Saint Maelrubhha but it became Romanised as St Mary, not a dedication that would please John Knox who preached here in June 1559. Approached from Marketgate, the trimmed masses of ivy that covers the walls between the high windows are a pleasing surprise. The interior is another surprise—so open, so white, and with chestnut pews and a sky-blue, panelled ceiling. Also, the arches of the nave and the magnificent pillars have been stripped of plaster to reveal very beautiful and smooth stones that invite our fingers to appreciate the work of the masons who cut and laid them. The interior of the tower has a delicacy that cannot be anticipated from its exterior, and its narrow stained-glass windows not only throw colours onto the walls of the tower but act as a contrast to the tall clear windows of the nave through which shines the clear light of this sea-washed burgh. This very successful restoration work, and the stained glass in the tower, was undertaken by Judith Campbell.

To leave the peaceful interior of the church to inspect the old memorials of the kirkyard requires a major change of attitude. These are, certainly, very interesting as is to be expected with dates on them of, for example, 1645, 1649, 1663, and 1689. The spectacularly large, and vigorously vernacular, memorial of James Lumsden of Airdrie, on the Riggin o Fife, has much lettering that is now unreadable but the date is 1598. A very emotive memorial is that of William Bruce of Symbister which may be of 1630. When new this would be unusual; now, in its ruined condition, it is highly dramatic. The very tall and heavy effigy of this warrior knight has deteriorated into what could be a modern, but unfinished, sculpture of a headless knight in armour. In the context of this graveyard, this heavy, worn and broken figure becomes a graveyard symbol that is more potent than the conventional skulls and bones, or formally sculpted broken columns, of other memorials.

Emerging from the beautiful interior of the church into a sunny Crail, a route to the harbour can be via Castle Terrace where seats are set against the old wall. This can be a sun trap and the view is superb. To the east is a rocky point and the Roome Rocks; but the best aspect of this view lies westwards; to the sun-danced sea and the May Isle, Bass Rock and Berwick Law. Beside the sundial at the end of the Terrace stands a viewfinder that enables Tantallon Castle to be identified, just west of the Bass Rock and east of North Berwick; and, to the east and thirty miles across the sea, St Abbs Head can be brought into focus. As a crow might fly, from there to Berwick-on-Tweed is not so very far. Below the Terrace lies the much-photographed harbour although the classic view is from the west side of the town. Again the Firth of Forth is revealed as one of the scenic splendours of Scotland.

East of Crail is Fife Ness; a name that almost tastes of sea salt. At the Ness, Wormiston was once the property of the Spens family but here also were Lyndsays. At nearby Balcomie the lands of that estate came into the possession of James Learmonth in 1526 and he may not have waited many years to build the castle. That first building has mostly gone and what remains has been merged into a later farmhouse and buildings. One of the panels on the entrance arch carries the date 1602. According to John Knox, Sir James Learmonth of Dairsie, and also Clatto, who was Provost of St Andrews, was one of those on the hit list of Cardinal Beaton. When James V's second French wife, Mary of Guise-Lorraine, landed at Fife Ness and awaited a horse at Balcomie, she was welcomed by Sir James Learmonth. If the Queen had turned as she landed at this bracing and invigorating place to look out over the edge of the East Neuk she would have seen, over the dangerous rocks that her boat had just negotiated, to the north and east an open sea. Today if the tide is out we may just see the outline of the natural harbour where she landed.

Although many have disagreed with him, Sir Walter Scott, a Borderman, suggested that the earliest Learmonth of Dairsie was a son of Learmonth of Ercildoun, in Berwickshire, who married Janet de Dairsie. The most famous Learmonth of Ercildoun is the poet and seer known as Thomas the Rhymer out of whose work came the ballad "True Thomas" in which Thomas spends seven years in elfland with his "ladye bright", the Queen of Faerie,

> True Thomas lay on Huntlie bank;
>   A ferlie he spied wi' his ee;
> And there he saw a ladye bright,
>   Come riding down by the Eildon Tree.

Today near Crail lives Professor A. Norman Jeffares, poet and biographer, editor and scholarly critic of W.B. Yeats. By Fife Ness we may imagine, with Yeats, a child dancing in the wind and ask of her, "Dance there upon the shore;/What need have you to care/For wind or water's roar?" Almost one hundred years after Yeats wrote these words, surely we should be more confident than we are when asking the young and innocent, "What need have you to dread/The monstrous crying of wind?"

On the edge of what became the parish of Crail, there was a barony of Barns and on a promontory to the west of Crail stood the house of the Cunninghames of Barns where, in the early 1620s, the poet William Drummond of Hawthornden came courting. In his poem, "To the Principal and Professors of the University of St Andrews, on their Superb Treat to Dr Samuel Johnson", Robert Fergusson writes of Drummond,

> Drummond, lang syne, o Hawthornden,
> The wyliest an' best o' men,
> Has gi'en you dishes ane or mae,
> That wad ha' gard his grinders play,
> Not to *roast beef*, old England's life,
> But to the auld *east nook of Fife*,
> Whare Creilian crafts cou'd weel ha'e gi'en
> Scate-rumples to ha'e clear'd his een;
> Than neist whan Samy's heart was faintin,
> He'd lang for scate to mak him wanton,.

> *roast beef . . east nook of Fife:* references to tunes
> Creilian crafts: fishing vessels from Crail

The phrase "wyliest an' best o' men" may be words that came to Fergusson to meet the needs of the metrics of his poem, and to provide a Fife connection, but they could be sincerely meant. Perhaps it was a phrase used in Fergusson's company by Professor William Wilkie who would know of Drummond's connections to the Cunninghames of Barns, the lairds of Thirdpart, near Crail. The mansion at Thirdpart has gone so completely it might have a fiction of the poet's imagination but in the 1840s the minister of Crail wrote in his contribution to the *New Statistical Account* of an "old house with vaulted cellars and rooms above occupied by farm servants" as "the chief remain of the extensive mansion of the Cunninghames of Barns."

The work by William Drummond that Robert Fergusson alludes to is "Polemo-Middinia", or "The Battle of the Midden", written about 1620. This work is rather like the radio Goon Show in that it either induces gleeful laughter or scornful rejection as over-done, childish posturing nonsense. The verse—or doggerel to the scornful or the embarrassed—describes, in fantastic macaronic Scots-Latin, a quarrel over a road to a midden between the Lady of Barns and her neighbour the Lady of Scotstarvit whose husband, Sir John Scot, also owned land at Thirdpart. Scot also owned Easter and Wester Pitcorthie, which lie north and east of Crail and Kilrenny, although Scotstarvit Tower stands near Ceres and Cupar. In the poem Scotstarvit is Vitarva and Barns is Nebarna. Between West and East Pitcorthie there is a standing stone and it is, perhaps, possible that it stood there in the time of Drummond and the feuding ladies of Thirdpart and Barns. Today there is still a road running between these properties.

A few lines from the start of "Polemo-Middinia" give a hint of the style and tone of this most phonetic 170-line poem,

> Nymphae quae colitis highissima monta *Fifaea*,
> Seu vos *Pittenwema* tenent seu *Crelia* crofta,
> Sive *Anstraea* domus, ubi nat haddocus in undis,
> Codlineusque ingens, et fleucca et sketta pererrant
> Per costam, et scopulis lobster mony-footus in udis
> Creepat, et in mediis ludit whitenius undis;
> Et vos skipperii, soliti qui per mare breddum
> Valde procul lanchare foris, iterumque redire
> Linquite scellatas bottas shippasque picatas,
> Whistlantesque simul fechtum memorate bloodaeam,
> Fechtum terribilem, quam marvellaverit omnis
> Banda Deum, et Nymppharum Cockelshelleatarum,
> *Maia* ubi sheepifeda atque ubi solgoosifera *Bassa*
> Suellant in pelago, cum Sol boottatus *Edenum*
> Postabat radiis madidis et shouribus atris.

The Isle of May and Bass Rock can be seen from Pittenweem, Anstruther and Crail and the river Eden flows into the sea at St Andrews Bay.

There have been pompous literary historians who, concerned to maintain the high tone of this "wyliest an' best o' men", deny to Drummond the authorship of his comic masterpiece. There is also disagreement amongst local historians as to whether he wrote it at Thirdpart, near Crail, where Alexander Cunninghame of Barns lived, or at Scotstarvit Tower, near Ceres and Cupar, where Lady Scot, his sister, lived.

The tragedy of Drummond's younger years occurred at Crail, as Euphemia Cunninghame, the lady he came to court and intended to marry, died and so provided some romantically inclined literary biographers with a love story and a tragedy that enabled, such biographers suggest, the poet to produce poems that are a "little history of love"—to become the "Scottish Petrarch". Drummond's sonnets read on the page as if written in over-wrought English but we should remember that the poet had learned his English from books and spoke Scots. When read aloud with that in mind they become less literary and more acceptable, at least to my ear,

> All other Beauties how so e're they shine
> In Haires more bright than is the golden Ore,
> Or Cheekes more faire than fairest *Eglantine*,
> Or Hands like Hers who comes the Sunne before:
> Match'd with that Heavenly Hue, and Shape divine,
> With those deare Starres which my weake Thoughts adore,
> Looke but like Shaddowes, or if they bee more,
> It is in that they are like to thine.
> Who sees these Eyes, their Force and doth not prove,
> Who gazeth on the Dimple of that Chinne,
> And findes not *Venus* Sonne entrench'd therein,
> Or hath not Sense, or knowes not what is Love.
> > To see thee had *Narcissus* had the Grace,
> > Hee sure had died with wondring on thy Face.

Eglantine: the wild rose   Venus Sonne: Cupid

As a student in France, Drummond travelled in Europe but apart from his visits to the East Neuk of Fife he does not seem to have ventured far out of the Lothians. Indeed he became something of a recluse at his beautiful Hawthornden Castle which stands high above the river Esk near Roslin and Lasswade in Midlothian. He signed the Covenant of 1638 but was conservative and royalist by nature and played safe by sitting tight in his extensive library at Hawthornden, that "sweet solitary place". Today the castle is owned by a member of the Heinz beans family who has created a much-favoured retreat for writers.

The Lady of Scotstarvit, Anne Drummond, was the poet's sister and the first wife of Sir John Scot of Scotstarvit (1585-1670). As heir to Knightspottie in Perthshire Sir John Scot, knighted by 1617, acquired lands in Fife including, in 1611, those of Tarvit from Alexander Inglis which he renamed as the barony of Scottis-Tarvit. Sir John's second wife was Elizabeth Melville, granddaughter of Sir James Melville of Halhill, near Collessie, and his is another name of literary note. His third wife was Eupham Monypenny of Pitmilly.

The tower-houses of Scotland began to replace the motte castle in the fourteenth century and remained popular with the feudal lords for three centuries. In recent years many towers have been restored, some to be used as modern homes. In Fife Scotstarvit is not lived in but its tower and newelstair jamb are very well preserved and open to the public who, currently, can get the key at Hill of Tarvit house. A panel in the tower has the initials (S.I.S.) of Sir John Scott and his first wife (D.A.D.) Dame Anne Drummond and the date 1627 which is when Sir John altered a late-fifteenth or early sixteenth-century building. The nearby Hill of Tarvit is owned by the National Trust for Scotland and the house and fine gardens can be visited.

Like his father, John Scot was a student at St Andrews being there in the first years of the seventeenth century, graduating in 1605. He was to found a Chair in Humanity in St Leonard's College, donated books to the library and persuaded others, including Drummond, to do likewise. Scot had an interesting career as a counsellor to King James VI and Charles I, and Lord of Exchequer and a Lord of Session. For some forty years he was Director to the Chancery but lost that office during the Cromwellian years. He petitioned Cromwell to restore the Chancery post to him and this willingness to collaborate with the Protector was held against him by Charles II on his Restoration. The Chancery post was given to Sir William Kerr, son of Lord Lothian, who Sir John said, "danced him out of office, being a dextrous dancer." Beyond an old literary expression, Kerr was indeed famous for his ability as a swordsman and dancer. In his *Staggering State of the Scots Statesmen*, Scot gives his views on the greedy Scottish nobility and the misfortune that can follow the acquisition of too much wealth and power.

What no-one can take away from Scot of Scotstarvit are his work as a man of letters and patron of the cartographer Timothy Pont. He it was who supplied Pont's maps to Johan Blaeu for his important atlas and Sir John even went to Amsterdam to assist with the publication of the maps of the Scottish counties. Also, he initiated *Delitiae Poetarum Scotorum*, which was modelled on anthologies of the Latin verse of various countries published in the early years of the seventeenth century by Janus Gruter, a Dutchman whose mother was English. The Scottish collection was published by Johan Blaeu at Amsterdam in 1637 in two small volumes which printed work by thirty-seven names. I was pleased to find both volumes in the Scottish Department of Edinburgh's Central Library. Scot may have been assisted by his brother-in-law, Drummond of Hawthornden who had, in 1627, given to Edinburgh University many books and manuscripts that were used in the compilation of *Delitiae*.

It has often been said that Scot's collaborator was Arthur Johnston (1587-1641) a poet of considerable stature in Latin who was also court physician to King Charles and in 1637 became Lord Rector of King's College, Aberdeen. He died in Oxford in 1641. In 1784 Dr Samuel Johnson wrote to James Boswell, "if you procure heads of Hector Boece, the historian, and Arthur Johnston, the poet, I will put them in my room." William Drummond wrote a letter on the nature of poetry to Johnston, whom he described as his "much honoured friend M. Arthur Johnston physician to the King."

A major omission from *Delitiae* is work by George Buchanan (1506-82) whom many regard as the greatest of Scottish writers in Latin and whose Latin versions of the Psalms are superior to those by Johnston. We do not know the attitude of Arthur Johnson, but the laird of Scotstarvit certainly did not lack generosity when he acted as patron to Pont and paid for the printing of the Scottish Latin poets. Religious bias must have been at work here. There are poems by Andrew Melville but none that attack Episcopacy. Here, also, are poems by James Crichton, "the Admirable", who had been taught at St Andrews by Buchanan. Sir John Scot included some of his own poems in *Delitiae* and one of these, which begins "Quod vitae sectabor iter", was translated by Drummond as,

> What course of life should wretched Mortalles take?
> In books hard questions large contention make;
> Care dwelles in houses, labour in the field.
> Tumultuous seas affrighting dangeres yield.
> In foreign landes thou never canst be blest,
> If rich, thou art in feare, if poore, distrest.

In wedlock frequent discontentmentes swell,
Unmarried persones as in desertes dwell.
How many troubles are with children borne?
Yet he that wants them countes himself forlorne.
Young men are wanton and of wisdome void,
Grey hairs are cold, unfit to be imployd.
Who would not one of these two offeres choose:
Not to be borne; or breath with speed to loose?

The Cunninghame family of Barns make an appearance in William Tennant's long satirical poem "Anster Fair", as do the Melville family at Carnbee which sits east of Kellie Law. They, and others, if they had been alive, would not be best pleased by the descriptions of them by Maggie Lauder, a lady of "disrepute'"

"Then come, let me my suitors' merits weigh,
    And in the worthiest lad my spouse select:-
. . .'
Then for the lairds—there's Melvil of Carnbee,
    A handsome gallant, and a beau of spirit;
Who can go down the dance so well as he?
    And who can fiddle with such manly merit?
Ay, but he is too much the debauchee—
    His cheeks seem sponges oozing port and claret;
In marrying him I should bestow myself ill—
And so, I'll not have you, thou fuddler, Harry Melvil!

There's Cunningham of Barns, that still assails
    With verse and billet-doux my gentle heart—
A bookish squire, and good at telling tales,
    That rhymes and whines of Cupid, flame, and dart;
But, oh! his mouth a sorry smell exhales,
    And on his nose sprouts horribly the wart;
What though there be a fund of lore and fun in Him?
He has a rotten breath—I cannot think of Cunningham!

Why then, there's Allardyce, that plies his suit
    And battery of courtship more and more;
Spruce Lochmalonie, that with booted foot
    Each morning wears the threshold of my door;
Auchmoutie too and Bruce, that persecute
    My tender heart with am'rous buffets sore:-
Whom to my hand and bed should I promote! —

From Crail the coastal road goes west to give a view of Kilrenny steeple as a landmark that leads to yet more views of other East Neuk spires—Anstruther, Pittenweem and St Monans.

5

Kilrenny & Cellardyke, Anstruther, Pittenweem and St Monans

THE TIDAL harbour of Cellardyke is a simple rather square structure but, especially when the tide is out, its rugged high walls give an imposingly fierce aspect to this safe haven. Judging the way into its narrow entry must always have required good seamanship. The harbour was once known as Skynfast Heyvne (Skinfasthaven) and the area where the harbour was built as Nether (or Lower) Kilrenny. Today The Haven restaurant by the harbour keeps alive the name. As always I am suspicious of obvious explanations for place names and often any relationship to modern English is incidental to a corruption out of another language. Here I am pleased to learn from Harry D. Watson's excellent *Kilrenny and Cellardyke: 800 Years of History*, 1986, that the local pronunciation of the Scots word siller (English silver) was Anglicised into cellar, which rather undermines suggestions that the name comes from cellars where the Kilrenny fishermen kept their gear to save them the labour of carrying it up to their village.

The Beatons were powerful here and the even more powerful Cardinal Beaton was concerned to give advantages to his kinsfolk. When the idea of the new harbour of Skinfasthaven was proposed it was seen as not only developing trade in the area but also providing extra income for the vicar of Kilrenny This previously isolated place would attract new parishioners. Also, but not least, John Beaton, laird of Kilrenny, former captain of St Andrews Castle and nephew of Cardinal Beaton, would be granted a charter allowing him to receive an income from the new harbour and the fish landed at not only Skinfasthaven but also at Easter Anstruther by boats sailing out of Kilrenny. The laird of Anstruther, who had the income from Anstruther Wester, was a brother of Agnes Anstruther, the wife of John Beaton of Kilrenny. The arrangement seems to have been financially cosy for both families.

The modern tidal swimming pool at Cellardyke (now abandoned) was the Cardinal's Steps Pool. When the Cardinal landed at Skinfasthaven from Edinburgh to rest before riding with his entourage over the moors to St Andrews he would step ashore at the mouth of the burn between the Wolves and the Cutty Skelly rocks. And, if he wished to take his Chancellor of Scotland's barge from Kilrenny to St Andrews, he could leave from these same steps.

Near the swimming pool a long flight of steps leads up to the 1914-1918 War Memorial of the Parish of Kilrenny which carries a most disturbing number of names for such a small place. Across the fields the steeple of Kilrenny Church is reminiscent of that at St Monans although less so close up. Today the church is offset by a number of new houses that await weathering to merge them into the landscape. The old church in Kilrenny was demolished in 1806 and a new kirk built onto the fifteenth-century tower. To fishermen who used it as a mark it was St Irnie and the fat cockerel on the weathervane stands on a pole that raises it higher than usual above the steeple. In its kirkyard are several large burial chambers, some gated some not, but all rather desolate and especially so in the half light of early evening. The arms of the Beatons are crumbling within the walls of their burial enclosure; the forbidding gates of the mausoleum of Scott of Balcomie seem more imposing than the uplifting arch and dome. The more complex walls, columns and monuments of the Lumsdaines of Innergellie are given further significance by being so close to the fifteenth-century tower. Here, also, are memorials of more modern Lumsdaines. The memorials of some members of the Anstruther family are also more recent. Sir James Lumsdaine, like the Leslies, fought for King Gustavus Adolphus of Sweden in the Thirty Years War. Innergellie House was built north-east of Anstruther for the Lumsdaines in 1740. Sir John Scot of Balcomie was of Scotstarvit and Barns when he bought Balcomie in the 1760s. There are those who believe that the body of the murdered Cardinal Beaton was brought from St Andrews to be buried in the Beaton family vault in Kilrenny kirkyard. The more national view, which may be no more accurate, is that Beaton's ashes lie in the ground behind the remnant of the Blackfriars Chapel in South Street, St Andrews. Behind the remains of the chapel are the buildings and lawn of Madras College which was planned, by William Burn in 1832, to reveal the ruined chapel rather than overpower or conflict with it.

The village of Cellardyke is squeezed into the limited space between the sea and the hillside but the narrowness of the streets from Cellardyke Town Hall to the harbour could have been designed to give shelter from even a January blizzard carried on an east wind. At places the street is made to seem even tighter by forestairs that protrude from the old houses and near the harbour are two houses built with beautifully rugged stones, with reddish brown tints, that remind me of sections of the harbour walls. The house nearer to the harbour stands on exposed bedrock that cuts into where the pavement should be and these stones could be part of a well-chiselled piece of sculpture.

On a wall near the harbour a plaque informs that "Peter Smith known as Poetry Peter was born in this house in 1874. Fisherman Poet of Cellardyke." Today the best-known poet in Cellardyke must be John Burnside, although he is not native to the village having been born in Dunfermline in 1955. He also writes fiction.

The first full-time minister of the Parish of Kilrenny, which then included Anstruther Easter, was Rev James Melville. It was in Anstruther that Melville acquired material for some of the most interesting sections of his *Diary* which is amongst the best in Scottish literature; this despite Melville's attention to religious controversies which are of little interest to most of us today. The fully-committed reformer, scholar and minister somehow managed to retain something of the awareness of a child and a lack of inhibition that allowed him to reveal sophisticated truths and perceptions through a very lively prose. As with many very good writers, Melville wished to tell it as it was.

The manse built by Melville in Anstruther still stands off Back Dykes. The parishioners promised to build a house for their minister on a piece of land given to Melville by the laird of Anstruther but they made slow progress and Melville took the work in hand himself, paying the workmen weekly, with never a break from the beginning to the completion, and never a sore finger during the whole labour. At least that is what Melville wrote in his diary. The work began in June of 1590 and was completed by March the following year. So it was Melville's property, and he may have passed it to his grandson before Sir William Anstruther bought it in 1637. In 1753 a west wing was added to Melville's original three-storey L-plan building to make it T-shaped. The Church of Scotland bought the manse back and so enabled its many admirers to claim it as Scotland's oldest inhabited manse. The house was excellently restored in the 1970s and, with its high, tight hedges and grassed garden, it must have a gentler aspect than in Melville's day but it remains a manse he could be proud of and we can enthusiastically admire.

Born in the manse of Mayton near Montrose, James Melville was admitted BA of St Leonard's College, St Andrews in 1572. He accompanied his uncle Andrew Melville to Glasgow when the great Reformer became Principal of the University there. No doubt his uncle was influential in having James elected as a regent at Glasgow. When Andrew returned to St Andrews in 1580 to become Principal of what was then New College but became St Mary's his nephew came with him to be Professor of Oriental Languages. Of course these extreme Presbyterians opposed the Episcopalians, including Bishop Patrick Adamson of St Andrews, and when, in 1584, Principal Melville had to flee to Berwick the young James took charge of the College. Soon, however, he too was in flight to England.

He was no less outspoken on his return to St Andrews and was pressurised by King James to restrict his activities to university teaching; not that the Melvilles avoided trouble from the people of St Andrews as this account of a protest movement of 1592 shows,

In that simmer [1592] the devill steired upe a maist dangerus uproar and tumult of the peiple of St Androis against my uncle, Mr Andro. . . . The wicked, malitius misrewlars of that town . . . hated Mr Andro, because he could nocht bear with thair ungodlie and unjust delling, and at thair drinking, incensit the rascals be fals information against Mr Andro and his Collage, making tham to think that he and his Collage sought the wrak and trouble of the town; sa that the barme [yeast] of thair drink began to rift [belch] out crewall thretnings against the Collage and Mr Andro. They being thus prepeared, the devill devyses tham an appeirance of just occasion to fall to wark.

Ther war a certean of Students in Theologie, wha weireing to go out of the Collage to thair exerceise of bodie and gham [game], big [built] a pear of buttes in the Collage garding, joyning to a wynd and passage of the town. Wharat a certean of tham shootting a efter noone, amangs the rest was Mr Johne Caldcleuche, then an of the Maisters of Theologie, bot skarse yit a schollar in archerie, wha missing the butt and a number of thak housses beyonde, schouttes his arrow down the hie passage of the wynd, quhilk lightes upon a auld honest man, a matman [maltster] of the town, and hurts him in the crag [neck].

This coming to the eares of the forsaid malitius and seditius, they concitat the multitud and popular crafts and rascall, be thair words and sound of the comoun bell; wha setting upon the Collage, braks upe the yett thairof, and with grait violence unbesets [attacks] the Principall's chalmer, dinging at the forstare [outside stair] thairof with grait gestes [joists], crying for fyre, etc. Bot the Lord assisting his servant with wesdome and courage, maid him to keipe his chalmer stoutlie, and dell with sum of tham fearlie, whom he knew to be abbusit, and with uthers scharplie, whom he knew to be malitius abbusars of the peiple. . . . Efter lang vexation and mikle adoe, the peiple's insurrection was sattelit.

For a time James Melville seemed to be in the favour of the King but both Melvilles were quite beyond compromise with regard to Episcopacy and, when they went to London in 1606, the King soon put Andrew Melville in the Tower and pressure was put on his nephew to bend, which he could not do. He was virtually a prisoner until allowed to return to Scotland shortly before his death in 1614.

At the time of the feared Spanish Armada, in 1588, Melville was ministering at Anstruther and Kilrenny, and wrote,

For a lang tyme the newes of a Spanish navie and armie had been blasit abrode; and about the Lambes tyde of the 1588, this Island haid fund a feirfull effect thereof, to the utter subversion bathe of Kirk and polecie, giff God haid nocht woudderfullie watched ower the sam, and mightelie fauchten and defeat that armie be his souldiours, the Elements, quhilk he maid all four maist ferclie to afflict tham till almost utter consumption. Terrible was the feir, persing war the pretchings, ernest, zealus, and fervent war the prayers, sounding war the siches and sobbes, and abounding was the teares at that Fast and Generall Assemblie keipit at Edinbruche, when the news war credible tauld, sum tymes of thair landing at Dumbar, sum tymes at St Andros, and in Tay, and now and then at Aberdein and Cromertie firth. And in verie deid, as we knew certeanlie soone efter, the Lord of Armies, wha ryddes upon the winges of the wounds, the Keipar of his awin Israell, was in the mean tyme convoying that monstrus navie about our coustes, and directing thair hulkes and galiates to the islands, rokkes, and sandes, wharupon he haid destinat thair wrak and destruction.

Soon after, Melville and the people of his parish and the town of Anstruther had a more personal experience involving the Spanish. Melville tells the story very well,

. . . earlie in the morning, be brak of day, ane of our Bailyies cam to my bedsyde, saying, (but nocht with fray,) "I haiff to tell yow newes, sir. Ther is arryvit within our herbrie this morning a schipe full of Spainyarts, bot nocht to giff mercie bot to ask." And sa schawes me that the Commanders haid landit, and he haid commandit tham to thair schipe againe till the Magistrates of the Town haid advyfit, and the Spainyards haid humblie obeyit: Therfor desyrit me to ryse and heir thair petition with tham. Upe I got with diligence, and assembling the honest men of the town, cam to the Tolbuthe; and efter consultation taken to heir tham, and what answer to mak, ther presentes us a verie reverend man of big stature, and grave and stout countenance, gray heared, and verie humble lyk, wha, efter mikle and verie law courtessie, bowing down with his face neir the ground, and twitching my scho with his hand, began his harang in the Spanise toung, wharof I understud the substance, and being about to answer in Latine, he haiffing onlie a young man with him to be his interpreter, began and tauld ower againe to us in guid Einglis.

A storm had swept the Spanish navy past England and Scotland and the General and his captains with twenty hulks had been shipwrecked off the Fair Isle. The General had been able to sail south and the poor suffering captains and their soldiers were now seeking shelter and help in Anstruther. Melville advised the laird of Anstruther and the next morning Anstruther,

. . . with a guid nomber of the gentilmen of the countrey round about, gaiff the said Generall and the Capteanes presence, and efter the sam speitches in effect as befor, receavit tham in his hous, and interteined tham humeanlie, and sufferit the souldiours to com a land, and ly all togidder, to the number of threttin score, for the maist part young berdles men, sillie, trauchled, and houngred, to the quhilk a day or twa, keall, pattage, and fishe was giffen; for my advys was conforme to the Prophet Elizeus his to the King of Israel in Samaria, "Giff tham bred and water," &c. The names of the Commanders war Jan Gomes de Medina, Generall of twentie houlkes, Capitan Patricio, Capitan de Legoretto, Capitan de Luffera, Capitan Mauritio and Seingour Serrano. . . .
In the mean tyme they knew nocht of the wrak of the rest, but supposed that the rest of the armie was saifflie returned, till a day I gat in St Andros in print the wrak of the Galiates in particular, with the names of the principall men, and whow they war usit in Yrland and our Hilands, in Walles, and uther partes of Eingland; the quhilk, when I recordit to Jan Gomes, be particular and speciall names, O then he cryed out for greiff, bursted and grat. This Jan Gomes schew grait kyndnes to a schipe of our town, quhilk he

fund arrested at Calles at his ham coming, red to court for hir, and maid grait rus of Scotland to his King, tuk the honest men to his hous, and inquyrit for the Lard of Anstruther, for the Minister, and his host, and send hame manie commendationes. Bot we thanked God with our hartes, that we haid sein tham amangs us in that forme.

In 1589 the fifth Earl of Bothwell, Francis Stewart, who succeeded James Hepburn, the fourth Earl and husband of Queen Mary, was allowing his soldiers to harass the towns and villages along the coast for food and pieces of armour. But, Melville wrote,

Carell [Crail], Anster [Anstruther] and Pittenweim, with assistance of sum gentilmen of the countrey about, resolved to resist and feght tham. The quilk when I perceaved, I maid hast to Court, and informed the King of the abbus and commotion that was lyk to be, and purchased Letters to discharge the Capteanes from proceiding anie farther, and if they wald nocht, to warrand the subjects to resist. The Erle being Admirrall, discharges the bottes at Leithe from giffing me passage; bot taking jorney to Queins ferrie, I cam with sic diligence as I could, bot or I cam, the Coronell, with his men of wear, war fean to tak the steiple of St Monians on thair head, utherwayes haid gotten sic wages peyed tham as wald haiff interteined tham all thair dayes.

The poet William Tennant was born in 1787 in a house on Anstruther High Street that now carries a plaque. In 1998 part of the building was a shop called "Pets Pantry". As the plaque says, Tennant became Professor of Oriental Languages in St Mary's College, St Andrews. Tennant is buried at St Adrian's Church on Burial Brae where his well-preserved memoriam, in the shape of an obelisk, carries a formal inscription in Latin which was written by Professor Scott of Aberdeen University. The larger gate into the kirkyard was locked each time I tried it but a smaller one, nearer the top of this most precisely named brae, seems to be open most days. As I have said, Tennant is best known for the long poem *Anster Fair*, although sometimes I think that it is mostly referred to by literary critics because Tennant's use of a modified form of Ariosto's *ottava rima* may have influenced Byron's use of it in *Don Juan*. Tennant's *Fair* is written in what looks like English but often it cries out for a Scottish pronunciation. Tennant's wild extension of Rab the Ranter's wooing of Maggie Lauder into a competition between rival suitors certainly goes vigorously when the suitors demonstrate their powers of piping,

> Nor ceas'd the business of the day meanwhile;
>   For as the monarch chew'd his sav'ry cake,
> The man, whose lungs sustain the trumpet's toil,
>   Made haste again his noisy tube to take,
> And with a cry, which, heard full many a mile,
>   Caus'd the young crows on Airdrie's trees to quake,
> He bade the suitor-pipers to draw nigh,
> That they might, round the knoll, their powers of piping try.
>
> Which when the rabble heard, with sudden sound
>   They broke their circle's huge circumference,
> And, crushing forward to the southern mound,
>   They push'd their many-headed shoal immense
> Diffusing to an equal depth around
>   Their mass of bodies wedg'd compact and dense,
> That, standing nigher, they might better hear
> The pipers squeaking loud to charm Miss MAGGIE's ear.

And soon the pipers, shouldering along
   Through the close mob their squeez'd uneasy way,
Stood at the hillock's foot, an eager throng,
   Each asking license from the king to play;
For with a tempest, turbulent and strong,
   Labour'd their bags impateint of delay,
Heaving their bloated globes outrageously,
As if in pangs to give their contents to the sky.

. . .

Then rose, in burst of hideous symphony,
   Of pibrochs and of tunes one mingled roar;
Discordantly the pipes squeal'd sharp and high,
   The drones alone in solemn concord snore;
Five hundred fingers, twinkling funnily,
   Play twiddling up and down on hole and bore
Now passage to the shrilly wind denying,
And now a little rais'd to let it out a-sighing.

Maggie is reputed to have lived in East Green, Anstruther, sometime before 1650, and her house to be of "ill-repute". My good friend Forbes Macgregor suggested that the site of Maggie's cottage is now a rock garden with benches or, more facetiously, a "sitooterie". The use of walls of old buildings makes this terraced area rather more interesting than Forbes's words might suggest. Also, local men suggested to me that the site of Maggie's house is on the other side of East Green and nearer to the Baptist Church. One of my informants said that the house was demolished in the 1930s, just before the war. From this vacant piece of ground by a sea wall there is an open view to the harbour wall and the rising seas that surge, and throw great white waves into the air. To the east the cliffs of the Isle of May rise from the open-seeming sea. A small movement of the eyes, however, reveals the tip of the Lothian coastline, the Bass Rock and Berwick Law. Completing this scanning of the Firth, the harbour light looks, from this angle, as if it is large enough to be a major lighthouse on May.

For many years I regarded the song "Maggie Lauder" as being by an unknown poet, but gradually authorship for this lively piece has been more firmly ascribed to Francis Sempill (c.1616-82), the son of Robert Sempill (c.1595-c.1665) who wrote the influential poem, "The Life and Death of Habbie Simpson, the Piper of Kilbarchan". Habbie gets a mention in "Maggie Lauder" but his name is especially famous because Allan Ramsay named this six-line stanza "Standart Habbie" and used it to such good effect that it was taken up by Robert Fergusson and the genius of Robert Burns raised the stanza to the level of high art poetry. Not that the form of "Maggie Lauder" is to be looked over-far down on,

Wha wad na be in love
   Wi' bonny Maggie Lauder?
A piper met her gaun to Fife
   And speir'd what was't they ca'd her.
Right scornfully she answer'd him,
   "Begone, you hallanshaker,
Jog on your gate, you bladderskate,
   My name is Maggie Lauder."

"Maggie," quoth he, "and by my bags,
    I'm fidging fain to see thee;
Sit down by me, my bonny bird,
    In troth I winna steer thee;
For I'm a piper to my trade,
    My name is Rob the Ranter;
The lasses loup as they were daft,
    When I blaw up my chanter."

"Piper," quoth Meg, "hae you your bags,
    Or is your drone in order?
If you be Rob, I've heard o' you;
    Live you upo' the Border?
The lasses a', baith far and near,
    Have heard o' Rob the Ranter;
I'll shake my foot wi' right goodwill,
    Gif you'll blaw up your chanter."

Then to his bags he flew wi' speed,
    About the drone he twisted;
Meg up and wallop'd o'er the green,
    For brawly could she frisk it.
"Weel done," quoth he: "Play up," quoth she:
    "Weel bobbed," quoth Rob the Ranter;
"'Tis worth my while to play indeed
    When I hae sic a dancer."

"Weel hae ye play'd your part," quoth Meg,
    "Your cheeks are like the crimson;
There's nane in Scotland plays sae weel
    Since we lost Habbie Simson.
I've liv'd in Fife, baith maid and wife,
    These ten years and a quarter;
Gin you should come to Enster Fair,
    Speir ye for Maggie Lauder."

William Tennant's contemporary, Charles Gray (1782-1851) wrote a much shorter "Sequel to Maggie Lauder" in which a certain douce domesticity seems to dominate,

For a' the talk an' loud reports
That ever gaed against her,
Meg proves a true and carefu' wife
As ever was in Anster;
An' since the marriage knot was tied
Rob swears he couldna want her,
For he loes Maggie as his life,
An' Meg loes Rob the Ranter.

Twenty years after William Tennant was buried in Anstruther, Robert Louis Stevenson was brought there by his father who was supervising the building of a new harbour. The youth dutifully spent time watching the building of the breakwater but he had already

63

committed himself to be a writer. As a poet Stevenson is best known for his verse for children, and he retained something of the ability to remember how a child moves in a special world. It is a world that can haunt the mature man or woman as do Stevenson's lines entitled "To Any Reader",

> As from the house your mother sees
> You playing round the garden trees,
> So you may see, if you look
> Through the windows of this book,
> Another child, far, far away,
> And in another garden, play.
> But do not think you can at all,
> By knocking on the window, call
> That child to hear you. He intent
> Is all on his play-business bent.
> He does not hear; he will not look,
> Nor yet be lured out of this book.
> For, long ago, the truth to say,
> He has grown up and gone away,
> And it is but a child of air
> That lingers in the garden there.

The old Anstruther Church stands on a rocky promontory above the Dreel Burn. Its tower is yet another sixteenth-century bell tower that imposes its strong and three-feet thick walls onto our twentieth-century eyes as structures that can offer hope to those who are all too aware of the transitional qualities of so many of today's bland and smooth-surfaced buildings. This is not to be oblivious, in 1998, to the poor condition of the surface of the tower, but hopefully repair work will begin soon and it can be as well preserved as the Tolbooth tower at neighbouring Pittenweem.

Behind the kirk, the old kirkyard, or green, reaches out to be almost surrounded by the sea at high tides. The Dreel Burn in spate has a driving force that seems out of place alongside harbour walls. As Forbes Macgregor wrote, "no kirkyard could be nearer the sea. It seems almost as if those in their last sleep wished to hear the roar of the ocean into eternity." Out of place the Dreel may seem, but it certainly added to the excitement of a storm of 1596 described by Rev James Melville in his *Diary*,

> about noone, ther fell a cloud of rean upon Kellie Law, and the mountains besyd, that for a space covered them with rinning water, the quhilk desending thairfra, rasit sa at ane instant the strypes and burns, that they were unpassable to the travellars, whowbeit weill horsed. The burn of Anstruther was nevir sein sa grait in mans memorie, as it rase within an hour. The reid speat off fresche water market the sea mair nor a myll and a halff. That brought grait barrenness upon the land the yeirs following.

In that same year Melville recorded another "prodigius thing"—"a monstrous grait whaale, befor the hervest cam in, upon Kincrag Sandes [at Elie]."

Round from the old kirk is The Esplanade which could not be farther from what most of us envisage as an Esplanade. It is a very short street. From the short sea wall at its end the cliffs of the Isle of May seem to form a unique top-piece to the main harbour wall. Looking

64

back up the Esplanade the Dreel Burn makes a beautiful S-bend along the kirkyard wall. The Esplanade can boast some of the oldest houses in the town; and in perfect juxtaposition to each other. The Studio House, a former inn with interesting wheatsheaf panel, is a perfect companion to "The White House" on the corner that looks almost too perfect to be authentically eighteenth century, but it does date from 1760. Further along is the old manse which carries the date of 1703. That date is notable on walking along the Esplanade towards the sea. Despite the two doors on the long front side of the manse, it remains a single and undivided house. Next to it stand houses with outside stairs, with cast-iron balustrades of delicate and varied designs, of such perfect proportions that their functionalism merges easily into pleasing aesthetics.

I first knew of the manse of 1703 from Forbes Macgregor whom I knew as an Edinburgh headteacher; indeed as Headmaster of South Morningside School which may seem to be of another world from most aspects of Anster. For many years, however, Forbes, and his wife, came to stay with his sisters-in-law, the Misses Combie, in the Old Manse in The Esplanade. Forbes has recorded that "the terrible tempest of Hogmanay 1978, which caused much damage to Cellardyke and other East Fife towns, undermined and completely demolished the stone stable of the Old Manse, which had withstood the waves for so long."

The manse is a narrow building with one gable facing onto The Esplanade and it is given protection from the sea by the houses that stand between it and the seawall. Its double-doored front is detached and there is access to the garden along this frontage. The garden beyond the narrow west-facing gable, however, faces the sea. Here Forbes and his wife and sister-in-laws had their own private "sitooterie". Here also stood the old stable. From Forbes's next door neighbours, who live in one of the distinguished houses with elegant outside stair, I learned that in 1996 there was another great storm that again threatened the manse garden. No doubt Forbes would have enjoyed coming to Anstruther to work again, in his individualistic way, on the wall at the end of that most interesting house and garden.

His very distinctive sense of humour made Forbes Macgregor feel very much at home in Anster. One of his poems has the long title, "On Cementing Level the Stable Floor at the Old Manse, Wester Anstruther, St Swithin's Day, 1963",

> Bored with his stall, wanting he knew not what,
> The minister's gelding chafed here at his lot;
> Till his old age from that he was a foal
> His stamping hoof ground out this shallow hole.
>
> With some success, penned in my cramping pew,
> My soul has raged against the canting crew
> And these splenetic kicks I could not quell
> Have cut me out a hole as deep as hell.

In 1836 a new manse was built for the minister of the old kirk by the Dreel Burn. Much extended and altered, this is now The Craw's Nest Hotel on the Pittenweem road. Dreel Castle has been long demolished but it stood overlooking the shore at the end of Castle Street; this turns into Wightman's Wynd which has a high wall into which fragments of the Castle have been incorporated. A long-lived Anstruther story is that, following a meal provided for him by Sir Philip Anstruther in the tall and very narrow Dreel castle-tower,

King Charles II commented "a fine supper I've gotten in a craw's nest." The Craw's Nest Hotel has used another version of the King's words in its advertising—"I hae ne'er supped or dined sae weel as in The Craw's Nest." The King's remark is said to have encouraged Sir Philip to build a new house on a site overlooking the town which was in our day to be occupied by the buildings of the Clydesdale Bank.

Rev Walter Wood, minister of Elie from 1845 to 1865, wrote of a much earlier Anstruther of the tower of Dreel who lived in the time of King Robert I, the Bruce. This individualist was known as "Fisher Willie" because he liked to go to sea with the fishermen of Anstruther and was not averse to joining them in a competitive attitude to the men of Crail who thought themselves a cut above fishers from less important harbours. This Sir William Anstruther had also given offence to the laird of Thirdpart, who might have been a Cunninghame or even an Inglis-Tarvit, by indicating that he was against a marriage between his daughter and the laird. Mr Wood described Sir William as,

> scarcely beyond the prime of life, though constant exposure had given him the appearance of being a few years older. In figure he was tall, with a slight stoop, and the bleached and somewhat grizzled curls of his light brown hair escaped from beneath the steel cap which he wore, even in his aquatic excursions, beneath the common fisher's head gear of tarred canvas. He also invariably wore a shirt of mail beneath a warm woollen doublet (or jacket as we now call it), which was bound round his waist with a stout leathern belt. Enormous boots encased his nether man, and in his hand he carried an oaken staff which might have served for a boathook, and was on days when any affray was in the wind, exchanged for a Scottish pike with a long steel blade, the lower part of which was formed somewhat like a battle-axe, and armed on the reverse with a hook. There was, therefore, something in the appearance and accoutrements of the Knight of Dreel which, even among his contemporaries, was out of the common; but the warm kindliness of his manner made him both loved and respected among his neighbours.

The grudge that Thirdpart bore seemed to have been done with when he invited Anstruther to dine at Thirdpart. Pleased to accept, Sir William duly set out but on his way to Crail was warned by a gaberlunzie, or licensed beggar, that Thirdpart had set a trap for him and he returned home from where he invited his neighbour to dine with him at Dreel. When Thirdpart arrived Sir William met him, with the gaberlunzie, in the courtyard and challenged him to deny the man's warning. Anger flared on both sides, and Thirdpart accused the gaburlunzie of being a traitor. As told by Mr Wood the encounter continued, "'Traitor is he?' roared the Knight; 'nay thou art the traitor,' and with one step backward he reached his trusty poleaxe from the wall, and with a single blow clove his opponent's skull on his own threshold." Taking no chances with the King's justice, Sir William fled to the Bass Rock where he remained until pardoned by the King. It is said that this is when the Anstruthers received new heraldic bearings; the crest being two hands holding a poleaxe and the motto, *"Piriissem ni periissem"* or "I had perished had I not gone through with it".

Since the building of their new house in the town in 1663, the various members of the Anstruther family have not been short of grand mansions of which I shall mention three only in Fife. They also married well, as did all such families. When recently researching my book *Splendid Lanarkshire,* 1997, I was surprised to learn that a branch of the Anstruthers inherited a good part of the estates of the Earl of Hyndford at Carmichael, and Mauldslie Castle on a most beautiful stretch of the Clyde; the fortunate man being Sir John

Anstruther, a grandnephew of a daughter of the second Earl and Sir John Anstruther of Anstruther, Bart. The earldom had become dormant but Anstruther took the name of Carmichael and when he died in 1818 was succeeded by another Carmichael Anstruther.

In Fife, Elie House was built by Sir William Anstruther in 1697; and in 1698 Sir Robert Anstruther bought Balcaskie, north of St Monans, which remains in the family today. Balcaskie was the first work of Sir William Bruce, whose clients were Moncrieffs, and the date around 1629, but a fortilice there is mentioned long before that date. In 1665 Bruce bought the house and estate for himself and had it extended. He also created a large garden in the Italian style. When he was created a baronet in 1668 he was of Balcaskie but, having bought the Kinross estate, he sold Balcaskie to Sir Thomas Steuart in 1684 from whom the Anstruthers bought it. When Sir Walter Scott visited Balcaskie in 1827 with Anstruther Thomson from Charleton he saw it as "much dilapidated; but they are restoring the house in the good old style, with its terraces and hedges." The building was worked on by William Burn in the early 1830s and, almost inevitably, by David Bryce in the 1850s. In 1912 Robert Lorimer provided wrought-iron gates for the North Lodge. Today Balcaskie is the home of Sir Ralph Anstruther, Bart.

In the 1830s William Burn also worked on Charleton, which stands north-west of Colinsburgh, and after Lieutenant-Colonel Charles Anstruther inherited the estate in 1904 he employed Robert Lorimer to make more alterations and others have followed, including some by the Anstruther family themselves. There is now a Charleton Golf Course with a club house and restaurant which is open to non-golfers.

Sir William Bruce has been described as the father of the architectural profession in Scotland. When he bought the Kinross estate Bruce built a new mansion which focused on Loch Leven Castle as Balcaskie's garden faces out over the Forth to the Bass Rock. Bruce also remade Leslie House and, having been appointed royal architect, had the Palace of Holyroodhouse rebuilt. Much of Holyrood was destroyed by Cromwell's soldiers and the King regarded the building as having been poorly done although Cromwellian repairs and new buildings were usually very well done, as those at Burntisland show. We can see other reasons why the restored King might wish to be rid of reminders of the Cromwellian years. The Royal Warrant instructed Bruce, "Wee doe hereby order you to cause that parte thereof which was built by the usurper, and doth darken the court, to be taken down."

Another major project of Bruce was Hopetoun House which he designed for Charles Hope, later first Earl of Hopetoun; building began in 1699 and was completed in 1707, some three years before Bruce's death in 1710. The next phase of building at Hopetoun was designed by William Adam; the work began, in 1721 and was to span twenty-five years with William's sons John and Robert continuing the work. William Adam, who became, in 1729, Surveyor of the King's Works in Scotland, was born in Kirkcaldy in 1689 where he was living when his son Robert was born in 1728. Robert made the Grand Tour in the entourage of Charles Hope, younger brother of the Earl of Hopetoun.

William Adam worked on Elie House, which has a complicated history that dates back to the late seventeenth century, but the plans he drew for a new house came to nothing. All who travel along the A915 beyond Lundin Links can see the derelict, but still imposing and impressive, walls of the magnificent Largo House which was probably designed by John Adam in 1750. The eagle gates show where one of the avenues approached the house. I was told in Upper Largo that the house was occupied by Polish soldiers during the 1939-45 war and that the roof was later taken off to save taxes. In 1998 new trees were planted alongside the stumps of those that had been planted when the house was built but it seems that there are no plans for its restoration.

To return to Anstruther, we have travelled some way in time since the Anstruthers were in the old Dreel Tower but the Dreel Burn flowed on then as now to merge with the sea that never seems to be boringly calm when I stand east of the burn, on the shore by the harbour. The burn marked the boundary of the Royal Burgh of Anstruther Easter from the equally Royal Burgh of Anstruther Wester. This is another burn associated in local memory with King James V travelling *incognito* as the Guid Man o Ballengiech. The burn being in spate he was carried over it by a well-nourished beggar woman whom the King thanked by giving her his King's Purse. A plaque on the interesting Dreel Tavern, which stands high above the burn, tells this story. The Inn served us very good haddock and chips—very obviously *not* the flat frozen breaded variety of haddock that is served in too many bars at lunchtime!

Off the west end of High Street is the house in which Thomas Chalmers was born in 1780. He was to become almost as famous a preacher as John Knox. Following the Disruption of 1843 he became the first Moderator of the General Assembly of the Free Church of Scotland and also principal of the new Church's theological college. Chalmers had previously been Professor of Moral Philosophy at St Andrews and Professor of Divinity at Edinburgh. His collected works make 34 volumes and a memoir of his life needed four volumes. I doubt if many in Anstruther, or Kilmany where he ministered, now read this voluminous literary achievement. Professor William Wilkie, whose "great" Homeric work is now unread, wrote that Ossian's deathless strains,

> With modern epics share one common lot
> This day applauded and the next forgot.

The old Anstruther kirk by the Dreel Burn is now known as the Hew Scott Church Hall, taking its name from the second minister who lived in the new manse of 1836. He seems to have been a most stable, not to say dogged, man as he is the compiler of the truly monumental *Fasti Ecclesiae Scoticanae* in which are recorded the details of each minister, his family and achievements, in each parish in Scotland; not the incumbents but the complete list from the Reformation to the date of Scott's visit to the kirks. He travelled each summer and visited more than nine hundred parish kirks. In December 1871 Scott said, "My work is done"; and died the following summer. Scott's is a noble work of field research—and it is still used by scholars in the updated editions.

Time and again whilst walking around Anstruther and Cellardyke the cliffs of the Isle of May come dramatically into view. I have long intended to take one of the small boats from Anstruther to the Isle but, although I have been to Inchcolm with its ruined but well-preserved Abbey, I have not yet stood on May where, typical of the interesting but historically inaccurate stories attached to the early Celtic saints, it is said St Adrian lived and was killed by Norsemen. Some centuries later the monks of the Benedictine Abbey were forced by genuine raiders to retreat to a priory in Pittenweem. It is said that a hermit remained on May to be visited by many a pilgrim including, in 1499, Mary of Gueldres who was on her way to become the Queen of James II. Just before his death at Flodden, James IV gave lands to the famous admiral Sir Andrew Wood of Largo on condition that he would transport the King and his successors in pilgrimage to May Isle.

I associate the view of the Isle of May from Anstruther with the poet Alastair Mackie who for many years taught English in Waid Academy and lived right by the sea, west of the Craw's Nest Hotel. It was in Anstruther that he wrote his most important poetry which I was privileged to encourage him to write and to publish for him. Born in Aberdeen in 1925, and educated there at Robert Gordon's College and the University, he taught for a few years in Orkney before he arrived in Anstruther in 1959.

Many of Alastair's best poems deal with tragic situations; the very best of these poems are in *Clytach,* 1972, including "Pietà", and "Mongol Quine", but Mackie could also be a witty poet as in "Back-Green Odyssey" where he gives us a prospect from his home in Anstruther by the sea,

> The sun's oot. I sit, my pipe alunt and puff.
> The claes-line's pegged wi washin. They could be
> sails. (Let them) Hou they rax and thraw, and yet
> caa naethin furrit. Gress growes on my deck.
>
> Thro the wheep-cracks o my sails the blue
> wine o the sea is blinkin to the bouwl rim
> o the horizon whaur my classic tap
> the Berwick Law hides oor nothrin Athens.
>
> Nae watters for an odyssey ye'll think
> whaur jist tankers, coasters, seine-netters ply.
> Still ablow this blue roof and burst o sun
>
> my mind moves amon islands. Ulysses—
> dominie, I cast aff the tether-tow
> and steer my boat sittin on my doup-end.

alunt: ablaze   rax: reach   tether-tow: moorings rope   doup-end: backside

As a dominie at Waid Academy Alastair Mackie encouraged several of his pupils who became published writers. These include: Andrew Greig, mountaineer on the north-east ridge of Everest, who is a poet and novelist; John Lloyd, who was editor of the *New Statesman*, a very successful London journalist and for a time Russian correspondent of the *Financial Times*, and who has this year published a very fine book *Rebirth of a Nation: An Anatomy of Russia;* and Christopher Rush, teacher of English in Edinburgh, poet and short story writer who is best known for the film *Venus Peter* which, although not filmed in Fife, is based on one of his stories set in an East Neuk fishing village—probably St Monans, his birthplace. From Harry D. Watson, however, I learn that Peter Murray, a Cellardyke skipper of the late-nineteenth century, was known as "Venus Peter" after his boats "Venus" and "Venus Star". A younger poet who was taught by Alastair Mackie is Andrew McNeil whose parents still live in Anstruther. Andrew Greig wrote a poem sequence, *A Flame in Your Heart*, 1986, with Kathleen Jamie, who currently lives in Fife, in Newburgh, but was born in Renfrewshire, educated in Balerno and, like Greig, at Edinburgh University. Jamie travels widely to contribute, in verse and prose, to the again fashionable genre of literary travel books.

Billy Kay, a poet who is well known for his television series on Scottish cultural history and the Scots language, has lived for a good few years in Newport-on-Tay. The actor Tom

Watson has lived for many years in the East Neuk, and he has been writing poems for most of these years, although only in 1997 were they published in his collection *Dark Whistle*. The poems cover a wide range of subjects and have many tones, as does that entitled "East Neuk",

> This huddle wracked aboot
> But tidy—some hooses there
> Wi' blindet een tae hide
> Stramash or see aff strangers.
>
> A man can bide inside
> The kernel o' the corner
> Winds, an' skliff braced up
> Tae sniff the sixpenny sea—
> Breathcatchin' whiles.
>
> A ticht turf keeps things ticht,
> But cacklers at the cemeteries,
> The slee-slung gulls, scream
> Oot the heroes, a' the shilpit an'
> The obdurate shauchlin' through
> Dead drunk an' roarin' fu'
>
> Hard bitten rocks still bite,
> An' auld yins that have seen
> The hale thing backyairds sine
> Stane coffins oan the Fisher
> Dykes, gang cleekin' oot
> The partins, hard as hell,
> Yet lichtsome whiles, lik'
> Weasels dancin'.

> blindet een: blinded eyes   stramash; trouble
> shilpit; thin and insipid   shauchlin: shuffling
> sine: since   cleekin': hooking   partins: crabs

The very name Pittenweem rings with abstract sounds that stimulate my interest. It may be that the name comes from a Celtic word meaning settlement, or place, of the cave. There are many such "places" in north-east Fife including Piterthy and Pitkeirie. Also, the four Pitcorthie farms of days past may each have been a "place of the standing stone". "Corthy" may be very old indeed as it could be a very early Pictish name for the circular, roofless building where religious and other ceremonies were held. A map in the Abbot House, Dunfermline, which introduces Pictish Fife, shows what I guess to be about forty place names that begin with "Pit" including, of course, Dunfermline's own Pittencrieff. Our inability to know anything of these peoples of pre-history prompted my poem, "The Very Old Ones",

> The Picts who spoke in awe of the Very
> Old Ones?
> The nameless Ones?
> And at once a white-washed wall.

Not even that.
Nothing? Naethin? The licht
gone?
Yet, yet, the awe.

Memories owre auld to say.

Some Pittenweem memories have retained the story of the two smugglers, Andrew Wilson and George Robertson, who robbed an excisemen, or tax-gatherer, in an inn which stood in Marygate along from the Tolbooth tower. A well-designed shield-shaped plaque informs interested passers-by, "Near this spot stood the Inn where the Tax Gatherer was robbed by smugglers giving rise to the Porteous Riots, 1736. Sir Walter Scott has immortalised the event in The Heart of Midlothian." The two smugglers were taken to the old Tolbooth in Edinburgh where they awaited execution. When Wilson was hanged in the Grassmarket the mob almost rioted and were fired on by the City Guard, commanded by John Porteous, killing three men. Porteous was found guilty of murder and condemned to be hanged. When he was reprieved the mob took him from the Tolbooth and hanged him in the Grassmarket from a dyer's pole. As the plaque says, the story has continuing life thanks to its retelling by Sir Walter Scott in The Heart of Midlothian.

There is a headstone erected in Andrew Wilson's memory in Kirkcaldy in the Pathhead Feuars' Graveyard which runs alongside the grounds of Braehead House, the former head offices of Nairn, linoleum manufacturers, with access from Commercial Street, if you can scramble over the wall. The inscription reads: "Erected by public subscription to mark the grave of Andrew Wilson whose name associated with Sir W. Scott and the Porteous Mob has obtained a distinguished place in Scottish history. He was a native of this town and executed at Edinburgh 1736". In the winter of 1997 Wilson's headstone could be identified by being the only one in this well-tended graveyard with a flourishing green plant growing at its base.

Coming along Pittenweem's peaceful High Street, past the more spacious Market Place, we can hardly miss the late-sixteenth-century Kellie Lodging which was the town house of the Earls of Kellie. Like Fordell's Lodging in Inverkeithing, this building of rugged but well-crafted stone overcomes any crude resemblance to nineteenth-century Scottish Baronial à la Bryce by revealing, or imposing on us, its honest and almost raw functionalism. Today's architects of open-structure buildings have found this more difficult to achieve. I must admit that I have not usefully learned to use in my thinking the technical terms for parts of these buildings. Stair turret and crow-stepped gable are within my grasp but terms such as corbelled, chamfered, fore-jamb and cap-house are not in my thoughts as I look at such aesthetically pleasing buildings.

Even more noticeable from Market Place is the robust square tower of the Tolbooth which visually commands the end of the street. Angled to the tower is a gable of the Parish church within which a circular window completes this most pleasing composition of lines and circle. As we get closer to the tower we can see that the harling is very well maintained and that set against the tower is the very worn Mercat Cross which dates from 1736. It is almost as if a passerby had casually left it standing against that most sober and civic of walls and, over the years, it had attached itself to the tower.

The church building has a history as old as any Tolbooth, with remnants of a thirteenth-century building surviving into one of 1532 which was extended sideways in 1882. But considerable dramatic interest is added to the church by the sixteenth-century Tolbooth tower (1588) which has been visually metamorphosed into a west tower of the church. The tower was heightened in the seventeenth century but restraint was shown in that it projects only enough to mark the change of materials. Similarly the balustrade adds interest without undue fussiness and the spire is an elegant method of linking the old Christian church to the civic Tolbooth. When going through Pittenweem on the main through road I always look out for a side-on view of the church. These glimpses do not equal that of Tolbooth and kirk from the High Street but they do show another aspect of the church to very good advantage. That same through road passes Christ the King Church which catches the eye with a powerful piece of sculpture, "Our Lord" by Hew Lorimer whose smaller mother and child sculpture adorns Tayport's Church of Our Lady Star of the Sea

Down Cove Wynd, with its steep steps, and eye-catching pink-walled Binny Cottage, is the harbour at East Shore. Unlike at Anstruther, here the Bass Rock seems to me to be more prominent than May Isle. Here the fishing sheds can be busy; each time I visited Pittenweem in 1997 and 1998 the catch being boxed was prawns—for scampi. Again, however, we have a picturesque East Neuk harbour scene enhanced by the changing northern light, whether bright and sunlit or grey and overcast, that many artists have struggled to transmit, via oil and water-colour paints, to paper and canvas.

The cave from which Pittenweem may take its name is that of St Fillan who may have been a native Fife Abbot of Pittenweem. St Ninian, who may have died in 432 AD, could have established a religious cell here. That would make Pittenweem a Christian Centre before Canterbury and before Columba came to Iona in 563. A more cautious date for a church at Pittenweem would be 640. This ancient cave of St Fillan is on Cove Wynd. It now has a grilled and locked gate and a neat and well-maintained porch of modern design that, I must admit, suggests a public convenience. Above the slabbed roof of this modern structure, however, towers a wall of bedrock. Also, an inspection of the actual cave can banish this unflattering association. A notice at the top of Cove Wynd informs where to go on the High Street for the key to the cave which was re-dedicated in the 1930s for Christian visitors.

Above the cave stands Pittenweem Priory and the cave was provided with a steep stair that gave access to a vaulted underground chamber from which another stair gave access to the garden of the Priory. Today the stair is blocked off and the garden is private. The Great House of the Augustinian Priory has been excellently restored for use as residential flats; initially, I was told in Pittenweem, as residences for Episcopal ministers—a church of some influence in these parts where the landed gentry have sought Anglicisation. Gradually, however, the flats were sold by the church and are now private residences. Other Priory buildings in this complex area by the kirkyard of the Parish Church and Cove Wynd are also private homes. Some of the Priory buildings can be seen by going along Marygate to pass the Episcopal Church and into Priory Court but a gate carries a notice which properly informs, "private".

In days long gone, the grounds of the Priory were infamous as an arena for cruel treatment of women suspected of being witches. Tradition has it that some of these unfortunates were taken the three Scots miles to Kinneuchar (or Kilconquhar) loch for execution. As the rhymster put it, using a version that hangs on the wall of Kinneuchar Inn,

They tied her arms ahint her back,
And twisted them wi a pin.

They tain her tae Kinneuchar Loch
And threw the limmer in
And a the swaans tak tae the hills
Scared wi the unhaley din.

Witches still fascinate many a sober-seeming man but in recent years few have gone so far as the early-nineteenth man who defended an irresponsible outing by blaming it on witches taking him from Old Hag's Hill between St Monans and Elie to carry him seven times around Kinneuchar Loch; ten airborne miles before he was dropped back to firm earth. Indeed an experience almost as sobering as Tam o' Shanter's encounter with witches in Alloway Kirkyard.

I may have no literary hooks on which to hang the walk along the shore line from Pittenweem to St Monans but I do have many memories: of the May Isle seen as an imposing silhouette topped by an archetypal lighthouse; of the thousands of varied shells, the lucid water of rock pools and the always pleasing sound of waves whether rippling or rolling surf; and there are the views both ways to unique groupings of buildings. Almost at St Monans, there is a small burn that is so rich in iron that it extensively stains the rocks on the shore. I was delighted to find it as rich in iron in the 1990s as it was when, almost sixty years ago, I first stepped over it as a child. In 1997 a Canadian visitor explained to me that it flowed from a Chalybeate well of St Monans. I had to ask him "What does it mean?" I was able, in turn, to show some specialised knowledge when I explained to him that the smooth grassy area by the old swimming pool was once a putting green for holiday visitors. Ahead are the crowstepped gables cluttering into a pleasing pattern and the unequalled spire of the auld kirk. I can remember at Harvest Thanksgiving the walls of its tight but unoppressive walls hung with fishing nets.

I have to admit that I do not remember noticing as a boy the ruined windmill that stood above the path that runs alongside the seaward aspect of Miller Terrace, but the ferns that grow on the edge of the terrace are as fresh today in my memory as when I touched them as a very small and sometimes homesick boy—and their descendants are thriving there some sixty years on. From the terrace the broad panoramic expanse of the Forth glimmers with light that no child can respond to as does an old brain stored with memories and a lifetime's experiences.

Today the old windmill is superbly restored and there is a helpful noticeboard which my Canadian acquaintance used to explain to me the working of the windmill. The board gives the history of the salt pans, and also allowed me to identify a man-made cutting in the rocks that had also eluded that child who had scrambled over them. The unobtrusive and indeed natural-looking cutting through the sea-battered line of rocks is as much an industrial artifact as the remains of a colliery. That cut through these dark rocks continues to surprise me, even annoy me that, as a child, I did not recognise it as man made.

The kirk of St Monans is a classic and not only for its architecture but also its situation right by the sea. I do not find it a building that reminds me of my mortality; indeed I have happy memories of boyhood holidays when I guddled in rock pools below its walls. A decaying wreck of a fishing boat lay hereabouts. I remember the harbour, then still busy with fishermen and their boats, with nets hung on the magnificently rugged wall that faces the huddle of harbour-side houses. I remember especially the long breakwater. We boys climbed up the long ladder to the harbour wall, then down another to jump a gap to the breakwater. When the tide was high the waves broke over the breakwater and we added to the excitement of that great stone wall by judging a gap between the waves to return to the safety of the harbour. Perhaps I was more afraid than I realised. Perhaps there is something sinister in the small squat kirk with its short steeple that I do not admit with my conscious mind as, although I have not attended a funeral in St Monans, my only poem on the village, "Homer Country", involves a graveside scene,

> This is Homer country.
> Here by the seaside in cemetery in Fife.
>
> *Then death will drift upon me*
> *from seaward, mild as air, mild as your hand.* *
>
> The meenister's words into the wund
> aulder than time they seem.
> And pop sang birlin in my heid,
> *Through the graves the wind is blowing.*
> And him of perfect physique
> and not quite twenty
> being lowered to be at ane wi the mool
> as his stane in time
> carved in immemorial leid
>
> *from seaward, mild as air, mild as your haund . . .*
>
> *Odyssey, Book XXIII   birlin: spinning   mool: earth of a grave
> leid: language

From the Castle of Newark at St Monans it is no great distance along the Elie road to the promontory on which stands the much-diminished ruin of the Castle of Ardross. There is a downhill section of the road from which the full extent of the promontory, and of what remains of the castle, can be appreciated. This was the stronghold of the powerful Dishington family, one of whom may have married a sister of King Robert I, the Bruce, and so was a cousin of David II. Tradition has it that when King David II (1329-71) and his Queen, Margaret Drummond, widow of Sir John Logie, were crossing the Forth to visit Ardross Castle they were shipwrecked but unharmed. Whilst in danger, the King thought of St Monans and vowed that if they reached land safely he would have a church built to the saint. So, this story goes, he had his votive chapel dedicated to St Monans and the lands of Abercrombie, Inverie and Newark were to have a new name, St Monans, although the Inverie Burn still flows below the kirkyard. As a boy I found the burn, with its many currents and stones, almost as interesting as the rock pools on the shore beneath the kirk and crossing it a more interesting way to approach the steep, narrow paths and wynds of the village than the proper road nearer the top of the kirkyard.

It has been suggested that St Monans may be a corruption of St Ninian but I cannot quite see any probable phonetic progression. Forbes Macgregor, perhaps a quarter of his tongue in cheek, followed Rev Archibald Scott, who wrote a book on the Pictish Church and Nation, in suggesting that St Monans was originally dedicated to an Irish lady of noble birth who was educated at Candida Casa, or Whithorn, in Wigtonshire. This lady, christened Darerca, had a familiar name Mo'enna or Mo'ninne. The early Culdee or Pictish church had a cell near Fife Ness and a map of 1645 gives this as Kilmonen—the

74

cell of Monan. Forbes suggested that to prove this St Monans was a woman we had only to look at the records of old Edinburgh. In the Old Town a St Monans Wynd, says Forbes, takes its name from a chapel there dedicated to "St Monan or St Mennan and the Close was named Lady Minnan's or Lady Menzies or Lady Minnes Close." Forbes Macgregor was putting his faith in what knowledgeable eyes can learn from the stones that form the walls, harbours, buildings and the wynds of the East Neuk of Fife when he praised the work of the preservation societies and said, "What can't speak can't lie."

Less controversially, we may accept that a royal chapel was built on the site of today's church, that it was rebuilt in the 1360s by David II and only became the Parish Church of St Monans in 1646 when the village was moved from Kilconquhar parish to merge with the small parish of Abercrombie. Only the choir was re-roofed in 1646, but a major restoration by William Burn in 1828 included the roofing of the north and south transepts. General Sir David Leslie, Lord Newark, who owned Newark Castle, was buried in St Monans in 1682, but architect Burn had the floor lowered as part of his restoration and the tomb of Leslie may have been one of those removed and his bones thrown over the kirkyard wall into the sea. The model ship which hangs in the kirk may have been first placed there in 1800 but Burn also had it removed and only luck led to its being found many years later in Edinburgh. A spiral stair leads to the tower where, as Rev James Melville related, in the time of James VI Bothwell's soldiers took refuge. Witches were held in the tower before execution and their ashes may have been scattered in the tower room known as the "Brunt Loft". Or again, the room could take its name from a burning by the English in 1544 when the original spire may have been damaged. We owe the current simple spaces of St Monans Kirk to a restoration of 1955.

From the St Monans to Elie road, above and beyond Partan Craig and Long Shank, the ruins of Newark Castle can be seen over where once the railway line ran; the line closed in 1969. The castle was long held by the family of Sandilands who include the James Sandilands who was knighted and then raised to the peerage as Lord Abercrombie. In the mid-seventeenth century a riotous young Sandilands, Lord Abercrombie, sold Newlands to General Sir David Leslie, who became Lord Newark and, perhaps two generations on, Newark Castle passed via marriage to the powerful Sir Alexander Anstruther. In the 1890s Sir Robert Lorimer drew up grandiose plans for the restoration and extension of Newark Castle but the project came to nothing despite the client being Sir William Burrell. Think of the tourists who would be parking their cars along from St Monans kirk if the Burrell Collection had come to a rebuilt Newark Castle.

General Sir David Leslie of Newark Castle was, like his uncle Sir Alexander Leslie, first Earl of Leven, a professional soldier, and some historians have had difficulty in distinguishing the two men. Physically they were more easily recognised as the Earl of Leven was small and, in the terms of his time, physically "crooked". Although born about 1580, Sir Alexander learned his soldiering after the wars of chivalry. A veteran in the Swedish service of a master of the new warfare, Gustavus Adolphus, Leslie rushed home to take command of the Covenanting army that faced down King Charles I at Duns Law. In 1641 Leslie was given a coronet by the King against whom he had led troops; he was made Earl of Leven. In 1644 the Earl of Leven was at Marston Moor. In 1646 he was besieging Newark when King Charles came to the French ambassador, Montreuil, who was in the Scottish camp. A story is told that the old warrior diplomatically offered the King his sword but, when it seemed that Charles might take it, he told the King, "I am the older soldier, sir; your Majesty had better leave the command to me." Newark surrendered at the royal command. On 30th January 1649 King Charles I was beheaded "at Whytehall gate, in England" as the Lyon King, Sir James Balfour of Denmylne, near Newburgh, wrote when Charles II was proclaimed King at Edinburgh Cross.

Sir David Leslie also had experience in the army of Gustavus and in 1644 he was in the army of his uncle that went into England. At Marston Moor Sir David achieved more there than did his uncle. It was Sir David Leslie who achieved, in 1645, a Covenanting victory over Montrose at Philiphaugh near Selkirk, and then allowed a butchering of the prisoners. It was the Earl of Leven who was made King Charles II's general against Cromwell, but it was his nephew, Sir David, who achieved some successes around Edinburgh. However, at Dunbar disaster came to the army led by Sir David who regrouped to made a show of generalship at Stirling. The reckless advance by the King and his army into England, truly an escape route, followed, as did Cromwell's concluding victory at Worcester. Sir David spent almost a decade in the Tower of London but, on the Restoration, Charles II ennobled him as Lord Newark. His father, a bitter royalist, remembering his son's former campaigns as leader of the Covenanting army, half-jokingly told him, "he should rather have been hangit for his *auld wark*."

6

Elie & Earlsferry, Lower Largo and around Kilconquhar & Colinsburgh

MY FIRST memory of Elie is as a small eight-year-old boy. Fifty-five years on the High Street of Elie must have changed but I can easily merge my first memory with what I see today. Elie remains for me a haven of holiday peace, long sunny days and warm sands where space is not at a premium.

The caves at Kincraig Point and the soaring and dangerous cliffs, even with their manufactured chain walk, make a dramatic contrast to the sands of the beautifully enclosed Shell Bay that await round the Point. I have not ventured onto these intimidating cliffs, but I was less than ten tears old when I first walked over the extensive lands behind them to reach the magnificent sands beyond Shell Bay and Ruddons Point to walk round to Lower Largo and on to Leven. This was not a planned walk; the stony-faced conductress of the last bus from Elie to Leven had stretched out a hand with the words, "Sorry, full up!" I can remember seeing then, and also in the 1970s, thousands of small perfectly formed shells edging long stretches of the bay. These white and golden sands remain, as does the absence of all but a very few fellow human beings. Walking round that long curving bay, from Kincraig Point past the harbour of Lower Largo and round to Leven, we are likely to meet no more than a dozen fellow walkers. Leven now has a small caravan site but even the far western end of the beach now lacks the semblance of a beachful of sun worshipers, castle-builders and paddlers in the cold but gentle sea. The days when hundreds of Glaswegians came on holiday to Leven are long gone.

The harbour of Lower Largo is pleasingly small and enhanced by the slow-flowing Hatton Burn that has none of the dramatic fierceness of Anstruther's Dreel. There is now a domestic air to Lower Largo and all the more so since the fishermen have been forced into other work. Alexander Selkirk, who became the model for Daniel Defoe's Robinson Crusoe, was born in 1676 in Lower Largo in a thatched cottage on the main street. The house which now stands on the site of his cottage carries a statue of Selkirk as he might have appeared when on the island of Juan Fernandez. He had no Man Friday on the island and he seems to have been a troublesome and unpleasant man. Certainly in Lower Largo he was the rebellious son of a shoemaker, although that could indicate not an obnoxious attitude but a brave and independent radicalness.

Aspects of Daniel Defoe's career were, in relation to Scotland, more decidedly dubious. From the autumn of 1706 to the spring of 1710, he was working in Scotland as an underground propagandist for the Union of 1707. Openly, during 1708-09, he wrote a *History of the Union* but he also worked as an agent, and from 1716 to 1720 he seems to have been a secret agent who worked with a Jacobite publisher and passed information to the Hanoverian Whig ministers. But a new Defoe emerged following the end of his career as a political propagandist in 1717. In April 1719, when he was almost sixty years old, the first part of *Robinson Crusoe* was published. It is something of a continuing surprise to me to remember that Alexander Selkirk lived until 1721, although he died in his middle forties.

The statue in the niche was made in 1885 by Stewart Burnett. The Crusoe Hotel by the harbour houses a small "Crusoe Visitor Centre".

Selkirk was drowned off the West African coast and some seventy years later in the section on the Parish of Largo in *The Statistical Account of Scotland*, published in 1792, Rev Spence Oliphant gave Selkirk's history, divested of Defoe's creative fictions, although Mr Oliphant may have added a religious assumption,

Having gone to sea in his youth, and in the year 1703, being sailing master of the ship "Cinque Ports", Captain Stradling, bound for the South Seas, he was put on shore on the island of Juan Fernandez, as a punishment for mutiny. In that solitude he remained for four years and four months, from which he was at last relieved and brought to England by Captain Woods Rogers. He had with him in the island his clothes and bedding with a firelock, some powder, bullets and tobacco, a hatchet, knife, kettle, his mathematical instruments, and Bible. He built two huts of Pimento trees, and covered them with long grass, and in a short time lined them with skins of goats which he killed with his musket, so long as his powder lasted (which at first was but a pound); when that was spent he caught them by speed of foot. Having learned to produce fire by rubbing two pieces of wood together, he dressed his victuals in one of his huts and slept in the other, which was at some distance from his kitchen. A multitude of rats often disturbed his repose by gnawing his feet and other parts of his body, which induced him to feed a number of cats for his protection. In a short time these became so tame that they would lie about him in hundreds, and soon delivered him from the rats, his enemies. Upon his return, he declared to his friends that nothing gave him so much uneasiness as the thoughts, that when he died his body would be devoured by those very cats he had with so much care tamed and fed. To divert his mind from such melancholy thoughts, he would sometimes dance and sing among his kids and goats, at other times retire to his devotion.

The poet Sydney Goodsir Smith (1915-75) came regularly from Edinburgh to Lower Largo, including visits to review exhibitions at the small Loom Gallery, and he wrote several poems on the village including the one simply entitled "Largo", one aspect of which is angrily concerned with the decline of fishing out of Largo,

> Ae boat anerlie nou
> Fishes frae this shore,
> Ae black drifter lane
> Riggs the crammasie daw,
> Aince was a fleet, and nou
> Ae boat alane gaes out.

My "Traivellin Man" sequence has a poem "Progress in Largo Bay" which is headed by a verse from Goodsir Smith's "The War in Fife",

> "By the 'Crusoe', backs tae the rain-straikit waa,
> Auld jersied men staun hauf the day,
> The fishin killt bi trawlers, nou
> They drink the rents the tourists pay."
> Sydney Goodsir Smith

> I'm a tourist steyin no in auld fishermen's hooses
> but at the "Crusoe" itsel
> on the very herbour

and richt up agin the sea
lappin dramatically at high tide
agin the waw ablow the lounge windae.
It couldna be better for the bairns
if near ayont oor means.

And in the "Crusoe" baur,
standing half the day,
trendy men and their wives
talkin o their catamarans,
the fishermen's houses
they hae convertit,
and the life back in Edinburgh
durin the week.

The fishermen's tourist tred killt
by weekenders. Nou
twa jersied men alane are to be seen.
They trap lobsters
for the "Crusoe's" à la carte tables
famed in the *Good Food Guide*

and the reason why we're here!

Uphill from Lower Largo, on the Ladies Golf Course of Lundin Links, stand an elegant group of standing stones. When, in 1760, the Right Rev Dr Richard Pococke, Bishop of Meath, made the last of his three tours of Scotland, he wrote of the stones as being, "from four to six feet broad, and about fifteen feet high; there seems to have been two or three more, so as to form rather an oblong square than a circle, and were doubtless an ancient Druid temple." The Bronze Age cists that were found at nearby Strathairly date from c.1500 BC. What I like about the stones is the angles that have been formed on their faces and their position in relation to each other. Henry Moore would have been hard pressed to match the aesthetic qualities of these survivals from ancient times.

I think of Kilconquhar, prounouced locally as Kinucher, as at the centre of an area with many acres of fertile fields that, in their varied sizes, shapes and crops, offer an ever-changing landscape that defies categorisation. Here the fields are well farmed but not to such an extent that the only criteria is profit. Often the stone walls, the fences, the pasture and the single specimen trees reveal this to be what I call estate land owned by families who are rich enough not to be forced to count the yield from every fraction of a hectare. The big houses are usually well screened by plantings of good hardwood trees. As Elie is approached from Kilconquhar, the red poppies can be seen to have been given their space amongst the commercial crops.

The loch at Kilconquhar can hardly be said to be typical of this part of Fife, being truly special with the tower of the parish church adding its 80 feet to the sparkle of the landscape as does the eighteenth-century Kinneucher Inn which is now especially busy with so many holidaying in the nearby complex built around the restructured Kilconquhar Castle. A late-sixteenth-century tower, with eighteenth-century additions, the castle was remade by William Burn for Sir Henry Bethune in the 1830s. David Bryce, the master of Scottish baronial turrets and other decorative features derived from an earlier functionalism, may have added more embellishments to the castle. There was a fire in 1978 and much of the castle was demolished or reduced in size before being converted into flats.

In Kilconquhar kirkyard are buried descendants of Cardinal Beaton, now spelled Bethune, although female succession adds many complications to the Beaton line. Sir Henry Beaton (by then Bethune) was created a baronet in 1822. His wife was a daughter of John Trotter, and his heir, Sir John Trotter Bethune, Bart., successfully claimed "the honours and dignitaries of Lord Lindsay of The Byres, Earl of Lindsay and Lord Parbroath, and of Viscount Garnock and Lord Kilbirny, Kingsburn and Drumy".

In this inland area of the Lindsays is the cottage of Robin Gray, a herdsman on the Balcarres estate, who was given fame by Lady Anne Lindsay through her poem, "Auld Robin Gray",

When the sheep are in the fauld, and the kye a' at hame,
When a' the weary warld to sleep are gane,
The waes o' my heart fa' in showers frae my e'e,
While my gudeman lies sound by me.

Young Jamie lo'ed me weel, and sought me for his bride;
But saving a croun he had naething else beside.
To make the croun a pound, my Jamie gaed to sea,
And the croun and the pound, they were baith for me.

He hadna been awa' a week but only twa,
When my mither she fell sick and the cow was stown awa';
My father brak his arm—my Jamie at the sea;
And auld Robin Gray cam a-courtin' me.

My father couldna wark, my mither couldna spin;
I toil'd day and nicht, but their bread I couldna win:
Auld Rob maintain'd them baith, and wi' tears in his e'e,
Said, "Jeanie, for their sakes, will ye marry me?"

My hear it said na—I look'd for Jamie back;
But the wind it blew hie, and the ship it was a wrack;
His ship it was a wrack—why didna Jamie dee?
And why do I live to cry, Wae's me?

My father urged me sair; my mither didna speak,
But she looked in my face till my heart was like to break.
They gied him my hand—my heart was at the sea;
Sae auld Robin Gray, he was gudeman to me.

I hadna been a wife a week but only four,
When, mournfu' as I sat on the stane at the door,
I saw my Jamie's wraith—I couldna think it he,
Till he said, "I'm come hame, my love, to marry thee."

O sair did we greet, and meikle did we say:
We took but ae kiss, and I bade him gang away.
I wish that I were dead, but I'm no like to dee;
And why was I born to say, Wae's me?

I gang like a ghaist, and I carena to spin;
I daurna think o' Jamie, for that wad be a sin.
But I'll do my best a gude wife to be,
For auld Robin Gray, he is kind to me.

kye: cattle   saving: apart from   stown: stolen   sair: forcefully   gudeman: husband
sair: sorely   greet: weep   meikle: much   ae: one   like: likely

Lady Anne Lindsay (1750-1825) was a daughter of the Earl of Balcarres. The cottage of Auld Robin is to be seen in Colinsburgh, or so I was told, but his cottage would have been well into the Balcarres estate. Balcarres House is the home of the Earl and Countess of Crawford and Balcarres and has a history going back to a late-sixteenth-century tower house built by the Lindsays. Like Kilconquhar Castle, Balcarres was given major extensions by William Burn and Scottish baronial embellishments by David Bryce.

When Colin, third Earl of Balcarres, who was fully committed to the exiled Stewarts, returned from exile to Balcarres he had Colinsburgh, formerly known as Nether Rires, built as a small village for his unemployed soldiers. The date is 1705 and the stone used for the buildings is dark whinstone which does not add to the cheerfulness of those who take a bus journey along its truly Main Street, being almost the only one.

This is not only Lindsay country but, for other reasons, Lorimer territory. One of the finest rescue acts for a north-east Fife building is that involving Kellie Castle, which stands north of St Monans and Pittenweem. As its saviour had justly inscribed above its entrance, the castle was "snatched from rooks and owls". Kellie has a history dating from the days of the tower castles, with the very earliest parts, of the mid-fourteenth century, merged into structures that belong to the sixteenth and seventeenth centuries. Today the castle, gardens and some 16 acres of land are in the care of the National Trust for Scotland.

The Oliphant family had Kellie for two centuries from 1361 when it passed to them from the Siwards who were also at Pitcorthie. The fifth Lord Oliphant considerably altered his castle in the early years of the seventeenth century but this may have stretched his finances and he sold the estate in 1617 to Thomas Erskine, Viscount Fentoun, later first Earl of Kellie. He adorned the castle with his coat of arms but the panel we see today was carved by Hew Lorimer. The ninth Earl of Mar inherited both title and house in 1829. All too often when a great family, with their own grand mansions, inherit extra lands and house, the building is surplus to their requirements and is allowed to deteriorate. That is what happened to Kellie Castle. A saviour came along in 1879 when Professor James Lorimer took a lease on the castle and commissioned John Currie to repair but not restyle the building. Lorimer's young son Robert (born in 1864 and knighted in 1911) made valuable contributions but there was no egotistical redesigning of the exterior. Professor Lorimer's daughter has described the state of the castle when her father started restoration,

Dandelions, grass and nettles grew in the turrets and trees rooted themselves in the walls, where large cracks rapidly extended. The tenant of the farm, left to his own devices, rooted out shrubs, ploughed up the approach, and even cut down several acres of wood. The garden, still encircled by a tumble-down wall, was a wilderness of neglected gooseberry bushes, gnarled apple trees, and old-world roses, which struggled through the weeds, summer after summer, with a sweet persistence.

In 1915 Sir Robert Lorimer bought Gibliston House, east of Balcarres and near Arncroach, as his own home. Interestingly Lorimer, when working for himself, mostly resisted any temptation he may have had to embellish this classically plain house, of the early 1820s, with Arts and Crafts structures and objects. A Sir Alexander Martin was at Gibliston in the seventeenth century and he was among the train of noblemen and eminent gentlemen that escorted the newly-inaugurated Archbishop Sharp from Leslie House to St Andrews. A little later there were Sibbalds at Gibliston, including Dr George Sibbald who was an uncle of Sir Robert Sibbald, father of Fife historians. Sibbald's *The History Ancient and Modern of the Sheriffdoms of Fife and Kinross* was published in 1710.

The Lorimer family's burial ground is in the kirkyard of the ruined Newburn Old Parish Kirk which lies between Colinsburgh and Upper Largo and not far from Charleton House, owned by the Anstruthers, which Sir Robert Lorimer worked on. A long-distance, but evocative, view of the broken walls of the kirk can be seen from the A917. The ruined kirk sits off a minor road behind the A917, and close up the central memorial to Professor James Lorimer reveals the influence of the Arts and Crafts Movement on Robert Lorimer's design. These Lorimer memorials, which include that of Sir Robert, combine to make this corner of a country churchyard an interesting contribution to the history of modern design. Out on the Forth the simple and bold shape of the Bass Rock provides a contrast to the considered fussiness of the Lorimer inscriptions.

Margaret Oliphant Wilson (1828-97), who married her cousin Francis (or Frank) Wilson Oliphant, is reputed to have set her novel, *Katie Stewart*, 1853, at Kellie Mill and the book, set in the time of the press gangs of the Napoleonic wars, certainly reveals the author's familiarity with the area around Anstruther. In her novel *Sylvia's Lovers*, published ten years after *Katie Stewart*, Elizabeth Gaskell perhaps reveals her familiarity with the young Oliphant's novel. Margaret Oliphant was initially sceptical of her mother's claim to be descended from the Oliphants of Kellie but later wrote of the old family as "a race to which I also belong, both by birth on the mother's side and by marriage." She may also have been related to the Katie Stewart, a daughter of John Stewart the miller, who was an adult women in the 1740s. Katie's sister may have married Philip Landale of Kilbrachmont and it is a Landale, who may have married an Oliphant, whose daughter was the novelist's mother. Her husband and full cousin, Frank Wilson Oliphant, was an artist who died young of tuberculosis leaving Mrs Oliphant with three young children. She supported the family by writing over 100 best-selling novels and, as John Blackwood's daughter said of Mrs Oliphant at Strathtyrum, she was nothing if not hard working.

To the east of Kellie Castle stood a cottage in which lived Thomas Constable. He had succeeded his uncle who had been factor to two Earls of Kellie one of whom, Thomas, the sixth Earl, was known in Pittenweem as "Fiddler Tam", rather as Sir William Anstruther had been "Fisher Willie" in Anstruther. In 1774 in that cottage on the Kellie estate was born Archibald Constable who is important as an early publisher of works by Sir Walter Scott. He was to be described by Lord Cockburn as "the most spirited bookseller that has ever appeared in Scotland." And Scott was to write, "he knew, I think, more of the business of a bookseller in planning and executing popular works than any man of his time." In these days bookseller also meant publisher and Constable was a great and innovative publisher. It is to be regretted that Scott did not remain with this fine publisher rather than entering into ventures with James Ballantyne that proved to be financially disastrous. The return of Scott to Constable resulted in, as John Sutherland has written, a partnership "forged anew in 1813-14" that "was to be glorious."

$$\boxed{7}$$

Coastal Castles, MacDuff (and Macbeth), Earls of Fife and Wemyss and Wemyss Caves

FOLLOWING the coast line from St Monans to Aberdour, which has its own castle a little way from the sea, we are never far from a ruined castle or tower: These include: castle of Newark or St Monans; Ardross east of Elie; MacDuff Castle at East Wemyss; the superb repaired ruin of Ravenscraig at Pathhead, Kirkcaldy; and Seafield between Kirkcaldy and Kinghorn. There is also Wemyss Castle at West Wemyss which remains an inhabited home owned by the Earl of Wemyss who may be descended from a MacDuff.

The MacDuffs who became "Thane of Fife", or earls, may go far back into Celtic and pre-Norman times and may have had a stronghold near Markinch, at Dalginch, which seems likely to have been one of the capitals of Fife in Pictish times. The name of MacDuff, Thane of Fife, is well known world-wide thanks to William Shakespeare's creative retelling of the story of Macbeth. This "mythical" rather than historical Macbeth was given to Shakespeare via Raphael Holinshed's compilation *Chronicles of England, Scotland and Ireland,* first published in 1577 and enlarged in 1586. William Harrison contributed not only the *Description of England* but also the *Description of Scotland.* Harrison was agin all foreigners and very nationalistic, and so gave Shakespeare, and many another Englishman, a stimulating panegyric of their country. For his Scottish *Description* Harrison drew on an early history of Scotland by Hector Boece (or Boyce) (c.1465-1536) as translated in 1536 by John Bellenden. Boece had drawn on a work by John Mair (or Major), *Historia Majoris Britanniae,* that included English as well as Scottish history and advocated a union of the two kingdoms.

Before these historians, however, there was Andrew of Wyntoun (c.1355-1422) who tells the story of MacDuff and Macbeth in his pioneering *Orygynale Cronykil of Scotland.* Wyntoun was a canon regular at St Andrews and from the 1390s to 1413 he was Prior of St Serf's Inch, the island on Loch Leven where Mary, Queen of Scots, was later imprisoned. Wyntoun followed the example of the great poet John Barbour in his epic *Bruce* by using rhyming couplets of eight syllables. At Dunsinane Macbeth has been informed that MacDuff, the Thane of Fife, has left and he decides to move against him into Fife,

> Yit MacDuff nevertheless
> That set be south the water was
> Of Erne, then past on in Fife
> Till Kennawchy, where then his wife
> Dwelt in a house made of defense,
> And bad her with great diligence
> Keep that house, and gif the King
> Hither come and made bidding,
> There ony felny for to do,
> He gave her bidding then that sho`
> Suld hald Macbeth in fair trety

83

A bate, while sho suld sailand see,
Fra north to the south passand,
And fra sho saw that bate sailand,
Then tell Macbeth the Thane was there
Of Fife, and till Dunsinane fare
To bide Macbeth, for the Thane
Of Fife thoucht or he come again
Till Kennawchy then for till bring
Hame with him a lauchful king.
Till Kennauchy Macbeth come soon,
And felny great there wald have done,
Bot this lady, with fair tretty,
His purpose letted done to be,
And soon fra sho the sail up-saw
Then till Macbeth, with little awe,
Sho said, "Macbeth, look up and see,
Under yon sail forsooth is he,
The Thane of Fife, that thou has soucht.
Trow thou well and doubt richt noucht
Gif ever thou sall him see again
He sall thee set in till great pain,
Syne thou wald have put his neck
In till thy yoke. Now will I speke
With thee na mare, fare on thy way,
Outher well or ill as happen may."
That passage syne was commonly
In Scotland called the Erles-Ferry.

Editors of Wyntoun's work have identified the Kennawchy Castle as being that which stood on the Maiden Hill at Kennoway. The site of a mediaeval motte can be seen by all who travel between Windygates and Kennoway. This long-gone Maiden Castle is traditionally associated with MacDuff, Thane of Fife. Distance or chronology need not be taken too literally in early histories or epic poems, but historians of the East Neuk have been keen to suggest that Kennoway is rather far from Earlsferry for it to be the castle where MacDuff's wife dwelt when Macbeth followed the Thane to Fife. Another option could be an earlier fortified house on the site at East Wemyss where there now stands the ruined remains of what is generally known as MacDuff Castle. The Castle of Creich was in early times in the possession of the Earls of Fife, as was Rires Castle which stood near Balcarres. Ardross Castle, near Elie, is ruled out by local historians as not old enough, with Sir William Dishington building it about 1390. Almost four centuries later, Lady Janet Anstruther had a summer house built near the castle, known as the Lady Tower, where she changed for bathing. The folk of Elie were warned by a bellman to stay indoors whilst her ladyship bathed. Thomas Carlyle saw the lady as "a coquette and a beauty".

Rires Castle (or Riras) has been favoured by some East Neuk historians as the fortified house to which MacDuff came. Rires has gone, but stood on high ground between Balcarres and Charleton (once Wester Rires). In the 1930s James Wilkie gave a lyrical description of Rires' situation,

A deserted road by a burnside, gay with white hawthorn in early summer and red with haws in autumn, marks out the track which the Maormars and Earls of Fife and their successors traversed on their impetuous pilgrimage. It is quiet now—the sound of a bird among the leaves, the note of a robin, alone break the September stillness. The corn grows thick above the foundations of Riras; but the moat is distinctly marked, and without question dungeons and a subterranean way lie deep below the ground.

The lands of Rires were by 1393 in the hands of Sir John Wemyss who was empowered to build a castle on the site of an early MacDuff structure. The fun-loving Margaret Beaton of Creich, aunt of Queen Mary's Marie, Mary Beaton, lived in this turreted building. We are told that she lacked, "the golden-haired, dark-eyed perfection of her niece" and that in her more mature years she had become, "very heavy, baith by unweildy age and massie substance". Near the castle stood "The Chapel of Marie, Rires" which was swept away by the Reformation although the graveyard continued to be used by the several owners of Rires. According to the *Statistical Account,* nearby there stood for centuries a great tree fourteen feet in circumference. For no properly explained reason it was known as "The Bicker Tree'. One tradition is that the lairds gathered around it for "convivial gatherings". That seems too obviously literal. Another contrasting theory is that it was a "hanging tree" used by the Thane when he "executed" his right of "pit and gallows". In his *Annals of Colinsburgh,* 1896, Rev Robert Dick tells of coffins being turned over by the plough and that a local doctor suggested that the skeletons of the men indicated death by hanging. The Ordnance Survey map of 2½ inches to the mile that I used in the 1950s indicated the historic sites of Tree, Castle and Chapel. The road-path that led to the Castle and Rires Farm also had branches to both Balcarres and Charleton. The slopes of Flagstaff Hill, although not a competitor to Largo Law to the west, are a good backcloth to these historic walls and whatever events took place by the Bicker Tree.

We shall never know where MacDuff's family were when he was on the run from Macbeth, but Rires is not far from Kincraig cave (named on some maps as MacDuff's Cave) where the Thane of Fife is said to have hidden from Macbeth until a boat was able to sail and carry him across the Firth and south to England where he hoped, like many another noble before and after him, to enlist help against his Scottish enemies. Those who favour the MacDuff Castle at East Wemyss have also suggested that the Thane escaped down an underground passage to the Well Cave from where he travelled to Earlsferry for a crossing to North Berwick. We know that such a passage existed and that the steps that led into it from the East Tower of MacDuff Castle were seen in recent years.

At East Wemyss I went down School Wynd to pass the War Memorial with its vigorously sculpted marching soldier, to turn left to the sea. It was almost high tide, and a day of roaring, surfing seas when I was there in March 1998. The massive black stones, six feet square within their rugged edges, are obviously essential to give protection from the powerful seas. To the east the houses of Buckhaven can be seen topping the slopes above the beach with the cranes of Methil rising above the lines of flats. Near, edging the last houses of East Wemyss, are the red sandstone cliffs with the mouth of the first cave just discernible—it is the Court Cave. To the west Wemyss Castle sits as a massive, but ragged, edge on the skyline. As so often on this coast, Arthur's Seat adds its distinctive shape to the view, but that day in early March, the dominant feature was much closer—the roaring, pounding and breaking waves.

A few yards towards the caves there is an excellent display of panels giving an introduction to the caves. These are first-rate not only for the excellently lucid text but as examples of an exemplary use of good illustrations and typography. There is also one of the most useful Fife Coastal Path information boards. All the caves are marked with boards indicating the dangers of entering them. The Court Cave has larger open entrances than the others but the intimidating brick columns that have been built to support parts of the roof of the cave show well enough how threatened the cave is not only by the sea but by faults in the rock, both natural and due to past coal mining. Beyond the Court and Doo caves, a great concrete "walkway" goes round alongside a sea wall, but a broken section reveals the power of the sea at this stretch of the often quiet and peaceful bay that stretches from Ruddons Point, beyond Shell Bay, to Kinghorn. The section of concrete, with central drainage pipe, must have weighed many, many tons yet it had been thrown round, and away from its original position, as if a single brick.

There is a large grassy area in front of the Well Cave which has a very low entrance under the sandstone cliffs on which stands one of the lesser walls of the ruined MacDuff's Castle. The small gate in the grill across the entrance to the cave had been forced open but I had not one second of thought of entering what is now a very dangerous place. From the Well Cave the eroding path continues round to the two gaping entrances to the Jonathan Cave. Both entrances are grilled but again the gate had been forced open and, unlike at the other caves, the warning notice had been ripped from the cliff face. Here the sea wall is some ten feet above the surging sea and grass and plants grow profusely around this most significant cave. To the west, below Wemyss Castle, the village of West Wemyss can be seen edging out into the great bay. As I wrote these words by Jonathan's Cave a great cracking sound made me jump. I thought it gunfire but it was a great wave crashing against a broken sea wall by a promontory. Potentially this is a beautiful place, with the large expanse of sea—but at high tide in March the sea presents an excitingly fierce aspect, even on a mild and sunny day.

By Jonathan's Cave an easy, but sometimes muddy, path goes through a break in the cliffs to a rougher track that runs along the edge of a ploughed field and up to MacDuff Castle. A more direct path, involving less scrambling, goes up near the Well Cave. The view out to sea from the ruined castle is yet another superb one with the sun creating, on the sea, a dazzling path of light. Trees cut off the eastwards view and West Wemyss is the only sign of human habitation on the Fife coast, but over the Forth, are the familiar shape of Arthur's Seat and the outline of Inchkeith. The large red sandstones of the seaward castle wall show signs of continuing erosion and a crack runs a fair length of it. The west-facing wall has almost completely gone but much could still be saved.

A path goes round the back of the tower and follows the line of a long, low wall, with old and large eroding sandstones, and the fence of MacDuff Cemetery to the main road where a sign indicates the Fife Coastal Path and also Buckhaven. The larger path goes down to the caves and the narrower path is the one alongside the cemetery fence. In MacDuff Cemetery are the graves of a wide range of men and women; fishermen lost at sea, captains, miners killed in accidents and others living to good old ages, merchants, a climber killed on Glencoe, farmers, blacksmith, doctors and ministers including Rev Alexander Orrock Johnstone whose headstone was designed by Charles Rennie Macintosh but seems to carry only the stone mason's name on the foundation stone, McGilvray Ferrets & Co.

Most of the Wemyss Caves are now too dangerous for anyone to enter them and I regret that I missed the opportunity of seeing them in the 1950s. Of course, they have been well described by others, including Frank Rankin whose *Guide to the Wemyss Caves* was published in 1996. There are three Well Caves below MacDuff's Castle but one is an entrance hollow and it has been gradually filled in. It is the double Well Cave that interests us here. The low-set entrance cave is 13 metres and it gives access to a low 5 metre underground passage to the Well Cave. This cave is 20 metres long by 17 metres wide. The roof of this great dome is some 10 metres above the sandy floor. The cave takes its name from a well that was near the back of this now dangerous cavern. It may have been of religious significance to the Picts. As was their custom, the early Christians took over such places; this became St Margaret's Well. Until the end of the last century the people of East Wemyss went in a torchlight procession to the cave to sing hymns and songs and eat and drink cakes and wine and to drink from the well which was famed for its curative powers. This took place on Handsel Monday, the first Monday in the New Year. Like many other Scots, the folk of East Wemyss did not like the "new calendar" of 1752 which involved the "loss" of eleven days. My grandfather, who was born in 1864 and a farmer, said I was born on Auld Ne'erday, the old New Year's Day—the 11th January—and that by then you could see a lengthening of the days—the sun was on its way back. In East Wemyss the Handsel Monday procession was moved to the first Monday after 11th January. If there is one thing about folk memory it is that it is very long and can go back to pre-Christian ceremonies.

The Well Cave had its well but no pre-historic drawings have survived in it. The cave with by far the most drawings is Jonathan's Cave but the amount of vandalism that it has suffered and the continuing neglect by those who could save this and the other caves is a national disgrace and cultural tragedy. The Save the Wemyss Ancient Caves Society needs all the support it can get.

Along from the well on the back wall of the Well Cave is the entrance to the passage that went up to the East tower of MacDuff's Castle. Sir Walter Scott accepted Wyntoun's account of MacDuff's castle being at Kennoway rather than Wemyss, but took the view that Macbeth, on learning that MacDuff had escaped, saw his castle as too strong to be easily taken and returned to Dunsinane without attacking and causing further bloodshed. Shakespeare, following Hollinshed, gives a more bloody account and one that demanded revenge,

> *Ross*: Your castle is surprised; your wife and babes
> Savagely slaughtered; to relate the manner,
> Were, on the quarry of these murder'd deer,
> To add the death of you.
> *Malcolm*: Merciful heaven!
> What! Man; ne'er pull your hat upon your brows;
> Give sorrow words; the grief that does not speak
> Whispers the o'er-fraught heart and bids it break.
> *MacDuff*: My children too?
> *Ross*: Wife, children, servants, all
> That could be found.
> *MacDuff*: And I must be from thence!
> My wife kill'd too?
> *Ross*: I have said.
> *Malcolm*: Be comforted:
> Let's make us medicine of our great revenge,
> To cure this deadly grief.

With the Normanisation of Celtic Scotland came feudalism and the old Celtic chief or king of Fife became a feudal earl. The Celtic ceremony of placing a new King on the Stone of Destiny at Scone was given to the MacDuffs and they also retained some Celtic privileges that involved the MacDuff Cross, the very much reduced remains of which stand, I like to believe, on a superb site on a hill above Newburgh. This may have been not only sanctuary for MacDuff's kinsmen who committed hot-blooded murder but also some form of compensation. The King of Scots may have been making a diplomatic gesture not only to the proud MacDuffs, who had provided Celtic Fife with its kings, but also to the proud men of "the kingdom". That the term survives today is surely a tribute to the long memories of "the folk". The use of the idea of "the kingdom" of Fife harms no-one today, but becoming involved in old traditions in a world that wants to know nothing of them can be dangerous as Isabella, Countess of Buchan, learned in the fourteenth century.

When King Robert, the Bruce, was raised onto the Stone at Scone, it was Isabella, Countess of Buchan, who took this hereditary privilege of the MacDuffs when her brother, Duncan, Earl of Fife, avoided this dangerous ceremony. The Countess was to be hung in a cage from the walls of Berwick. The last time an Earl of Fife took this privilege was when James I was placed on the Stone by his cousin, Murdoch, Duke of Albany, who was also Earl of Fife. This act certainly did not bring luck to the once powerful Albany; he was beheaded for treason, and the Fife earldom reverted to the Crown. The old "kingdom" had lost the right to even a great feudal overlord. Falkland Tower, which may have had its beginnings as a hunting lodge of the MacDuffs, was also taken by King James I. Not that the king favoured it. He would be all to well aware that his older brother, the Duke of Rothesay, died there whilst held by the Duke of Albany. The murder of James I at Perth gave that place an even worse name for other Stewarts, and they were to prefer not only Linlithgow, Holyrood, Stirling, and Dunfermline but also Falkland.

The MacDuff line may have continued, perhaps through a younger son, into that of the Wemyss family although Andrew Wyntoun, who would have wished to pay full tribute to his patron, makes no mention of Sir John of Wemyss being descended from the Celtic earls of Fife. It may have been Sir John of Methil and Wemyss (Muckle John of the Caves) (c.1203-65) who built the first stone castle on the site by East Wemyss.

Another branch of the family, in the person of Sir John of Wemyss, Rires and Kincarldrum, had in 1393 a charter to the lands of Rires, Myrecairnie, Newton, Markinch and Nether Cameron with permission to build a castle on the lands of Rires. It could be that this Sir John also built the earliest part of Wemyss Castle which, much extended and altered, still stands above West Wemyss. The descendants of this Sir John Wemyss include the Earls of Wemyss who for a time moved from Wemyss Castle to the now-ruined MacDuff Castle at East Wemyss. The builder of these castles, Sir John of Wemyss, Rires and Kincarldrum was also the patron of Wyntoun who wrote in his *Cronykil*,

> this tretise simpillie
> I made at the instance of ane larde
> That hade my service in his warde,
> Schir Johnne of Wemys be rycht nayme,
> Ane honest knycht and of gude fame,
> Suppose his lardschip lik nocht be
> Till gretar staitis in equalitie;
> He man of nede be personeir
> Of quhat kynd blame, that I suld beir;
> Sen throw his biddin and counsall
> Of dett I spendyi my travale;

In addition to the caves below MacDuff Castle, there were at least two caves further west; the large Glass Cave and the Michael Cave. Both were near the Michael Colliery and both were, in effect, destroyed by the mining. The Glass Cave collapsed in 1901 and was filled up. The Michael Cave was discovered in 1929 because a new boiler was being installed at the Colliery but, after photographs had been taken of the ancient wall drawings, the cave was filled in with concrete.

The Glass Cave takes its name from an early Scottish glass works that Sir George Hay established in it in 1610. Both Lord Kinnoul and David, second Earl of Wemyss, had glass made in the cave which was described, in 1790, by the parish minister as being 200 feet long, 100 feet broad and 30 feet high. The poet John Brewster, who was born in Methil in 1957, has written a sequence of short poems entitled "The Wemyss Caves" which includes "The Michael Cave",

> Aince hairts wur circled
> an staur-keepers ringed i stane:
> nou coal girds thaim baith.

John Brewster is one of the poets included in the anthology, *Four Fife Poets: Fower Brigs ti a Kinrik* which was published in 1988 by Aberdeen University Press. The other poets are William Hershaw, Harvey Holton and Tom Hubbard. William Hershaw, who was born in Newport in 1957 has recently published a collection of poems entitled *The Cowdenbeath Man*. Harvey Holton was born in Galashiels in 1949 and has travelled the world but lives in north-east Fife. Tom Hubbard was born in Kirkcaldy where his grandfather, who had worked in Fife pits, was Provost and MP for Kirkcaldy Burghs. Tom Hubbard, who took his Ph.D. at Aberdeen University and qualified as a librarian at Strathclyde University, was first librarian of the Scottish Poetry Library, but in recent years he has been lecturing in universities in Scotland, Europe and the USA. In 1991 Tom Hubbard edited the anthology *The New Makars* in which he printed William Hershaw's "Januar Winds o Revolution" in which the poet mixes political revolution with descriptions "o a seaside toun" in Fife where the poet lives,

> A cauld, sleety wind angles doon the High Street
> It blaws aff the Forth and ower the Links,
> Past the butcher's, the bookies, the pub and the Store.
> It rattles the lichts on the toun Christmas tree,
> It birls the newsagent's sign aroond,
> It blaws like a wild Blake picter
> On this mirkfu januar efternin.

One of the poems by Tom Hubbard in *Four Fife Poets* is concerned both with the medieval history of the ruined Seafield tower, which dates from about 1500, and stands on a promontory between Kirkcaldy and Kinghorn, and all the mine workings that have taken place below and around that stretch of the coast. The poem is entitled "At Seafield, Fife" and starts with these direct and emotive lines,

> I staun at the tour,
> The mines are ahent an ablow me.
>
> Here I'm maist intimate wi oor nation's past:
> Minstrels made music within thae waas
> Whaur noo the wind sings; deep, deep in the erd

Hae coalliers warslt ti create, as nou—
But sall they jyne the minstrels in oblivion?

Here I'm maist intimate wi oor nation's present:
Dame Scotland nurtures coalliers in her wame
That they maun nurture us, an bards unborn:
A process as organic as the cleckin
o that rich gress that growes aboot this tour's
Lang-tummilt stanes
                    —Oh ay! Are we sae shair o't?
Heid-makars still an on fail ti tak tent
o haun makars:

ahent: behind   erd: earth   warslt: wrestled, struggled   wame: stomach
Lang-tummilt: long ruined (fallen down)   tak tent: take notice, pay attention

Also in the *Four Fife Poets* anthology is Harvey Holton's "The Weather Braks an Hard Storms Come In" which could be set almost anywhere on this superb coast,

Syne awe airts breingin bulge
wi claitterin cloods. Sea-bree streaman,
storman strecht high owreheid
wi joukan jaggit breikit blasts.

airts: directions   joukan: jinking   breikit: broken

8

Methil and Buckhaven, the three Wemyss villages, and Dysart

BEACH WALKING has to temporarily end at Leven where the river Leven enters the sea, and the power station and then Methil docks are serious obstacles. At Buckhaven the way is open again, to go past the ruin of MacDuff Castle, the caves at Wemyss with their very early works of art, under the high walls of Wemyss Castle, and past the shortened but restored old harbour, to what can be a very difficult scramble round to Dysart over rocks and the dramatic and large concrete blocks that have to be negotiated when the tide is in. The walk from Dysart, through the well-restored harbour with its many leisure boats, passes another cave and carries on along the walled coastal section of Ravenscraig Park to the mighty ruin of Ravenscraig Castle. This is one of the finest sections of the Fife Coastal Path. The views over the Forth to Edinburgh or, in the other direction, to the Bass Rock and Berwick Law, are in constant change even when the weather is fine. The May Isle can also be seen given the right light.

Today the skyline above Methil is decorated with tall cranes that are employed to assist with building structures for the oil industry. When I first knew Lower Methil it was a darker place and dominated by the large and busy docks that served the coal industry. Then the nearby streets pressed in on the arched dock gate. Today many docks have been filled in and those that do remain seem almost out of place with the gates gone, as are the ships, and with new houses and flats, with a spacious if geometric air, angled to what remains of the docks. I have a memory of fishing, in the 1950s, a Methil dock with a multi-hooked line and pulling four mackerel out as often as I retained interest in this variety of fishing. The closed dock was boiling with fish and we were putting fish back as quickly as we took them out.

Methil took over from West Wemyss as the major coal-exporting port of Fife and both were inaugurated by the Wemyss family. It was in 1883 that Randolph Wemyss began the construction of the modern docks at Methil. With much new building, it is not always easy to see the routes of the mineral railway lines but they were well laid down to go from the Wemyss collieries to the docks. A railway line ran behind Bayview, the ground of East Fife Football Club, but I cannot now remember which pit or works it served. East of Methil Brae a line of lock-up garages indicates a section of the line's route.

From Methil and Buckhaven to Dysart, via East Wemyss and Coaltown of Wemyss, the coal seams were as important as any in Fife. A good many of the collieries took their names from members of the families of the Earl of Wemyss, including Wellesley, Rosie, Michael and Randolph. The individual who was "Rosie" escapes me but others are: Captain Michael Wemyss (1889-1982); Lady Eva Wellesley Wemyss was the second wife of Randolph Erskine Wemyss. The Lady Blanche and the Frances collieries at Dysart took their names from the Sinclair family. The Seafield colliery, on the west side of Kirkcaldy not far from the old castle-tower, was opened in 1954 and closed in 1988. In its later years seams of the Michael and Frances collieries were worked from this new pit. The Frances opened in 1850 and, following a fire, was closed in 1985; the Michael was worked from

1892 to 1967 when it was shut down. A fire at one of the Michael faces cost nine lives and the closure of the pit. A memorial has been erected in East Wemyss at Michael Place. Nationalisation came to the Scottish coal industry in 1947 but it has been recent governments' policies which have ended the underground workings. No doubt the fires and floodings were tragedies in economic as well as the more important human terms but no-one has convinced me that the Michael or the Frances or the Seafield collieries, and Balgonie, and perhaps also the new Rothes colliery, would have closed without preference being given, in government policies, to oil and gas and to nuclear power.

The sum total of all this is that all the pits from Methil to Kirkcaldy are closed; and there is little to be seen, above ground, of their remains. The fragile-looking structure of the winding tower at the Frances colliery still stands. It can be seen from the Wemyss to Dysart road and it makes a dramatic and emotive statement against the sky and the sea beyond—no sculptor creating an abstract or figurative work in memory of coal mining and the miners could match this functional structure. I hope that it is preserved. Open-cast mining has recently begun close to Dysart and Thornton and not far from where the towers of the failed Rothes Colliery once stood. The bulldozed landscape looks as if has come out of a scene from Dante's Hell.

The new Rothes colliery at Thornton was sunk as part of the creation of the New Town of Glenrothes and it was planned that miners from several areas, including the West of Scotland, would be rehoused in Glenrothes. When the *Third Statistical Account of Scotland* was published in 1952, the writer on the Parish of Markinch wrote, "The Balgonie Colliery, in spite of the gloomy forebodings of the writer of the *Old Account*, is still operating, and the reserves are estimated at 15 million tons, which should keep the pit working for a further 50 years. . . Now in process of sinking is a shaft for a new pit at Thornton, which will work some 80 million tons in the Limestone Coal group. The pit will be the most modern in Scotland and should last for more than 100 years." The now-demolished twin towers at Rothes became a symbol of a failed concept and, eventually, of the end of the age of underground coal mining in Fife. The village of Coaltown of Balgonie remains very neat and tidy and the villages of East Wemyss and Coaltown of Wemyss, with the miners' rows excellently preserved and modernised, have already acquired a picturequeness that would surely surprise the old miners' families. The might even be amused! In some respects, the cottages look even more charming when viewed over the fields that line the Standing Stone road that runs from Kirkcaldy's Boreland to Windygates (A915).

Once Kirkcaldy had a whaling fleet, West Wemyss and Dysart were coal ports and once Buckhaven was a fishing village with golden sands. A boat or two goes out from Dysart to lay lobster pots but this is not full-time work, and the harbour is a recreational centre for many boat owners. The fishing industry of the Fife coast has shrunk to near extinction and the docks, from Kirkcaldy eastwards, have followed the mining industry into nearly terminal decline. The future lies in healthier and cleaner work in the new light industries of smart industrial estates. We live also in a time of Heritage Centres and industrial museums and, like tourism, these provide work in the coastal towns and villages of Fife.

It is only a little over a century since, in 1891, there were 155 fishing boats in the harbour and 360 fishermen living in Buckhaven, or Buckhyne as we can still hear the place named by those who live in the village. Ten years earlier, in 1881 there were 198 boats and 410 fishermen. That compares with 221 boats at Anstruther and Cellardyke; 91 at

Pittenweem; 47 at St Monans; 34 at Crail; 34 at Largo; and Dysart which had only 18 boats and 27 fishermen. At that time St Andrews had 57 boats and 145 resident fishermen.

The past of Dysart, Wemyss, Buckhaven, Leven and Largo can be heard in old songs and ballads. Robert Burns gave us a spirited version of a song which begins,

> Up wi' the carls of Dysart,
>   And the lads o' Buckhiven,
> And the Kimmers o' Largo,
>   And the lasses o' Leven.

> CHORUS
> Hey ca' thro' ca' thro'
>   For we hae mickle a do,
> Hey ca' thro' ca' thro'
>   For we hae mickle a do.

> We hae tales to tell,
>   We hae sangs to sing;
> We hae pennies to spend,
>   And we hae pints to bring.
>   Hey ca' thro' &c.

> carls: fellows   kimmers: gossips   mickle: much
> ca' thro': get the work done

There is an anonymous song, sung to the same tune, that varies the first verse,

> Here's to the dance of Dysart
> And the kimmers of Largo
> And the brides of Buckhaven
> And the gossips of Leven.

> CHORUS
> *Hey ca' thro' ca' thro,'*
>   *For we hae muckle to do,*
> *And hey ca' thro' ca' thro'*
>   *For we hae mickle to do.*

> And Johnnie Geordie rose
> And he put on his clothes;
> When he bang'd up his trumps
> The lasses came in by the lumps.
>   *Hey ca' thro'&c.*

> And they had muches and rails
> And aprons wi' peacock tails
> And a' sic busks sae bonnie—
> Come dance wi our Johnnie.
>   *Hey ca' thro' &c.*

Maggie she kiss'd the piper,
There could naebody wyte her;
She had nae siller I trow,
But she gae kisses anow.
    Hey ca' thro' &c.

We have sheets to shape,
And we have beds to make,
And we have corn to shear,
And we have bairns to rear,
    Hey ca' thro' &c.

bang'd: struck   trumps: musical instrument   muches: caps
rails: neckerchiefs   busks: finery   wyte: blame   trow: believe   anow: enough

The well known "The Boatie Row" is set in Largo bay,

I cust my line in Largo Bay,
    And fishes catch'd nine,
There were three to boil and three to fry,
    And three to bate the line.

O well may the boatie row,
    And better may she speed;
And lees me on the boatie row,
    That wins the bairns' breed.

cust: cast   lees me on: blessings on

A rather different tone is struck in a poem entitled "Coming Home" which is the work of Mrs Dinah Craik who was once famous for *John Halifax, Gentleman,* 1857. For almost fifty years the painter Sir Noel Paton, Queen Victoria's Limner for Scotland, spent the summer in a cottage by the sea near Lower Largo, down from Strathairly House. It was after visiting the artist that Mrs Craik wrote these no doubt well-intentioned lines,

The lift is high and blue,
And the new moon glints through
    The bonnie corn stooks o' Strathairly.
My ship's in Largo Bay,
And I ken it weel, the way
    Up the steep, steep brae o' Strathairly.

In my 1940's schooldays in the West of Scotland the lively sounds of "The Wee Cooper of Fife" made it popular with primary school teachers. One of my classmates even had the honour of being chosen to sing it on the BBC's "Children's Hour".

There was a wee cooper that lived in Fife,
    Nickety-nackety, noo, noo, noo;
And he has gotten a gentle wife,
    Hey Willie Wallacky, how John Dougall;
        Alane, quo' Rushity, roue, roue, roue

94

She wadna bake, nor she wadna brew,
  Nickety-nackety, noo, noo, noo;
For the spoiling o' her comely hue,
  Hey Willie Wallacky, how John Dougall;
    Alane, quo' Rushity, roue, roue, roue

And so on for another lively eight verses without us giving any thought to the significance of Willie Wallacky, and John Dougall beyond the sounds of their names. More interpretative admirers of the song have seen them as "old sweethearts" of the gentle wife—"the useless limmer o' a lassie"—who had been bested by the superior courting of the clever cooper, who soon had a hard working wife and was a man from whom others could learn,

A' ye wha hae gotten a gentle wife,
  Nickety-nackety, noo, noo, noo;
Send ye for the wee cooper o' Fife,
  Hey Willie Wallacky, how John Dougall;
    Alane, quo' Rushity, roue, roue, roue

The Fife Coastal Path is being continually extended and, as one who walks a short section of it almost daily, truly a matter for considerable celebration. Looking eastwards from Kirkcaldy, the village of West Wemyss looks a perfect model of a Fife fishing village but many of the buildings seen from that viewpoint are awaiting restoration and the street they stand on is depressed by their fake windows. But, they do still stand and can be made habitable again. The tall square bell tower of the Tolbooth, with a nicely angled roof, gives considerable interest to what could almost be a simple domestic building. The prospect of Dysart from the west is equally picturesque and, unlike West Wemyss, close up no less so with the shore cottages either restored or eye-deceiving replacements built to a very high standard of vernacular design. Although Dysart's Tolbooth has a basic square tower, the overall effect is of a heavy and complex building. This is due to the stair tower, the forestair, and a bell area that is octagonal and topped by an ogee roof.

For all its good proportions, the heavy St Serf tower close to Dysart harbour does not have the look of being the remains of a church but that is what it is. The conversion of Fife to Christianity has been rather generously credited to St Serf who was steered towards Fife by Adamnan, biographer of St Columba and ninth Abbot of Iona who died in 704. One story has St Serf meeting Adamnan on Inchkeith. The Culdees of Loch Leven took St Serf as their patron, he is associated also with Creich, and tradition has it that he founded a church at Culross where he died and was buried. For centuries 1st July was St Serf's day in Culross when a procession involved carrying green boughs through the burgh, but this was replaced by a Riding of the Marches. Like all the Celtic saints, St Serf has been delightfully humanised by the faithful with various stories. Prior Andrew Wyntoun, writing his Chronicle on the Island of St Serf, tells us that,

This holy man had a ram,
That he fed up of a lam;
And oysit him til follow ay
Quherever he passit in his way,
A theyf this scheppe in Ackham stale
And ey hym up in pecis smalle.
Quhen Sanct Serf his ram had myst

Quha that it stal was few that wist,
On presumption, nevertheless,
He that stal it arestyt was;
And til Sanct Serf syne was he broucht.
That sceppe he said that he stal noucht;
And tharfar, for to swer an athe,
He said that he wolde nocht be laythe;
But sone he wertthit red for schayme,
The scheppe that bletyt in his wayme.
Swa was he tynctyt schaymuly,
And at Sanct Serf askyt mercy.

There is also the tale that the devil had taken up residence in one of the Dysart caves and that St Serf was enlisted to cast him out. The story can be continued westwards as the devil has been said to have moved on to Kirkcaldy,

Some says the Deil's daid
An burraid in Kirkcaldy.
Some says he'll rise again,
An fleeg the Hielant laudie.

Sir Michael Wemyss is credited with being the first Scottish admiral but he lacks the fame of Sir Andrew Wood of Largo whose successes were continued by the Bartons, father and three of his sons. Most of the woods (pun almost deleted!) of Fife were cut down to provide timber for King James IV's great ship, *St Michael*. Naturally the King protected the forest of Falkland where he hunted. Wood was the master of the unwieldy *St Michael* and John Barton her skipper. Four lines of doggerel celebrate a victory of Wood and John Barton in the late 1490s over the English when the English admiral, Stephen Bull, and three ships were captured behind the May Isle,

The battle fiercely it was fought
Near to the Craig of Bass:
When we next fight the English loons,
May nae waur come to pass.

The Parish Church of Upper Largo (Kirkton of Largo) stands high and forms an impressive silhouette on the skyline. The tower dates from 1628 and the chancel a little earlier but both are now part of an early-nineteenth-century building. Admiral Wood was buried in an earlier Largo church and I am told that traces can still be seen of a canal he constructed to be able to go to it by an eight-oared barge.

Much more recently, Lord Wemyss was Admiral of the Fleet and First Sea Lord at the end of the 1914-18 war. He is buried in Wemyss Chapel in the Chapel Garden, to the west of West Wemyss harbour. The garden has wall panels and an iron gate by Robert Lorimer. Over the walls can be glimpsed a ruin that could be sixteenth-century but overall has something of the look of a nineteenth-century folly. A few centuries earlier David, the second Earl (1610-79) was decidedly a man of action. In 1640, whilst still Lord Elcho, he commanded a regiment of Fifeshire infantry. In 1644 he suffered complete defeat by Montrose at Tippermuir and he was also present, on the losing Covenanting side, at Kilsyth in 1645 where many Fife women were widowed and, for several generations, made Fife a poor recruiting ground for any army.

Many of the Earls of Wemyss were as interested in trade and business as war. They were enterprising as developers of not only the salt industry and coal mining of their estate but also the harbours at West Wemyss and Methil. David, the second Earl, kept a *Diary* and I think he was rather proud when the first boat came into his new "Methil Herbure",

On 15 September 1664 Andrew Thomsone in Leiven did leade his Botte in the new Herbure of Methil wt colles from the colle of Methil being 60 leads of colles and he did tak them to Leith one 17 of Sepr. 1664. Which was the first Botte yt did leade wt colles att yt Herbure. The colles was well loved att Leith & since thorrow all sea ports in Scotland. I sould them att 5li the 12 lodes & 2 sh. to the grive. I give 22d for mining them to the coller and 1sh. 2d. tot he caller of them from the colle pit to the Herbure.

Almost twenty years after the Earl had settled into Wemyss as a manager of the estate, and developed a first-rate understanding of working its mineral resources, some military excitement came back into his life when the Dutch fleet sailed into the Forth. The entry in his diary is, however, as precise in numerical details as are his wages book and business entries,

On the last day of Aprill 1667 The hollands flitte inveadded Scottland & cam up yt day to Bruneiland wt 30 good ships sum of 60 sum of 80 gunes a peisse Beseids 10 littill ones. They did offer to land to have brunt all the Ships in Bruneiland but was beatten back and they shott above 1000 gritte sott att itt sum of 24 li. Balle and did not kille man wife or child. Shott att noe other Toune or pleasse killed one man in off Buickheavin yt day the Botte being att fishing and they would not cum abourd of them so they shott att the Botte & killed one Alex. Chirsstie. . . . The flette went away one I May 1667 and did littill more only tuek one privattire belonging to Leith Shoe ridding in Brunelland Rode when they cam up. They head out Inglish Cullers. 3 of the Kings ships was ridding in Leith Rode whoe weayed & went above the Quinis ferrie when I shotte 3 Cannone aff the housse of Wemyss to warne them.

Wemyss Castle stands high on a superb site at a centre point of the great bay that curves round many a mile from Ruddons Point, west of Elie and Earlsferry, to Kinghorn. Again the ridge of Edinburgh's Old Town can be seen stretching along behind the Lothian coast with the island of Inchkeith adding its outline as does the interesting hump of the Bass Rock and the slopes of Berwick Law. Wemyss Castle is a proper mixter-maxter of styles and dates that start about 1420 with a tower built for protection from passing armies. The seventeenth-century additions were more domestic and the Victorian work merely fashionable vulgarisations and they were removed in the 1930s. From below on the beach Wemyss looks sombre, heavy, and rather barrack-like, in the manner of later parts of Edinburgh Castle, but it retains an imposing presence and some grandeur. Somewhere within that complex structure is the room where Mary, Queen of Scots, first met Darnley on 16th February 1565. The courtier and diarist, Sir James Melville, of Halhill, recorded his impressions, "Her Majestie tuk weill with Darnley, and said that he was the best-proportioned lang lad that she had seen, for he was of heich stature, land and small, even and brent up, weill instructed from his youth in all honest and comely exercises." By the time Darnley left Wemyss three days later, on the 19th, the Queen had decided to marry this right royal eyeful whose lack of mental grace was soon to be revealed to her. Thus began the tragedy that continues to fascinate sophisticated romantics worldwide.

9

Kirkcaldy

"THE BEACH of Kirkcaldy in summer twilight, a mile of the smoothest sand, with one long wave coming on, gently, steadily, and breaking into a gradual explosion, beautiful sounding, and advancing, ran from South to North, from West Burn to Kirkcaldy harbour, a favourite scene, beautiful to me still in a far off way." So wrote Thomas Carlyle and that long wave remains a fascination of light and length and movement.

To see that wave we have to be west of the harbour but, farther east, below the dark and admirably solid Ravenscraig Castle, are Pathhead sands which have had a more varied history. Pathhead village is where Adam Smith saw the nail makers hammering away day after day, and out of these small forges came a section of Smith's great *Wealth of Nations,*

> This great increase of the quantity of work, which, in consequence of the division of labour, the same number of people are capable of performing, is owing to three different circumstances: first, to the increase of dexterity in every particular workman; secondly, to the saving of the time which is commonly lost in passing from one species of work to another; and lastly, to the invention of a great number of machines which facilitate and abridge labour, and enable one man to do the work of many.
>
> First, the improvement of the dexterity of the workman necessarily increases the quantity of the work he can perform, and the division of labour, by reducing every man's business to some one simple operation, and by making this operation the sole employment of his life, necessarily increases very much the dexterity of the workman. A common smith, who, though accustomed to handle the hammer, has never been used to make nails, if upon some particular occasion he is obliged to attempt it, will scarce, I am assured, be able to make above two or three hundred nails in a day, and those too very bad ones. A smith who has been accustomed to make nails, but whose sole or principal business has not been that of a nailer, can seldom with his utmost diligence make more than eight hundred or a thousand nails in a day. I have seen several boys under twenty years of age who had never exercised any other trade but that of making nails, and who, when they exerted themselves, could make, each of them, upwards of two thousand three hundred nails in a day. The making of a nail, however, is by no means one of the simplest operations. The same person blows the bellows, stirs or mends the fire as there is occasion, heats the iron, and forges every part of the nail: In forging the head too he is obliged to change his tools. The different operations into which the making of a pin, or of a metal button, is subdivided, are all of them much more simple, and the dexterity of the person, of whose life it has been the sole business to perform them, is usually much greater. The rapidity with which some of the operations of those manufactures are performed, exceeds what the human hand could, by those who had never seen them, be supposed capable of acquiring.

For some now-forgotten reason the folk of Pathhead seem to have been angered by those who recited a two-line rhyme to them. The Feuars Arms, off Commercial Street, with its long 1890's bar, stained glass, and fine tile pictures of a shepherdess and fool by Doulton, might have been the scene of such a provocation,

> Pickle till him in Pathhead;
> Ilka bailie burns another!

Adam Smith was born in Kirkcaldy in 1723 and educated at the school there before going first to Glasgow University and then to Balliol College, Oxford, in 1740 with a Snell Exhibition. Following some lecturing in Edinburgh, and the Chair of Logic and Professor of Moral Philosophy in Glasgow, Smith was in Paris and Geneva as tutor to the third Duke of Buccleuch. The publication of his *Theory of Moral Sentiments* in 1759 made him famous. In 1767 he returned to his mother's house in Kirkcaldy where, on a building facing Kirk Wynd on Kirkcaldy's High Street, a plaque informs that his mother's house stood on that spot and that it was there he spent the years 1767-1776 completing *The Wealth of Nations,* published in 1776. The house was demolished in 1834.

The nail makers who worked in Pathhead could have stretched their eyes by looking over the Forth and they could also walk on the beach below the towering dark mass of Ravenscraig Castle which was started by James II in 1460. The King died five months later, killed while beseiging Roxburgh Castle when one of his own cannons exploded, having been, in Robert Lyndsay of Pitscottie's memorable words, "mair curious nor becam him or the majestie of ane king". Work continued on Ravenscraig and it became the home of Queen Mary, of Gueldres, in whose name the land was acquired. The Queen had only a few years to enjoy the view from her new battlements as she died on 1st December 1463. The widow may have enjoyed more than the view over the Forth to Edinburgh. Certainly this is so if we accept the words of Lyndsay of Pitscottie.

> This quene was werie wyse and werteous in her husbandis tyme, bot sune efter his deid sche knawand hirself to be regent and gydder of the realme, seing all men to obey hir and nane to controll her wther waysis, scho became leichorous of hir body and tuik Adame Hepburne of Haillis quho had ane wyffe of his awin and committit adulltrie witht him, quhilk caussit hir to be lichtliet witht the haill nobilietie of Scotland that scho saw sa money nobill men in Scotland, lordis souns and barrouns fre of marieage that scho wald not desyre them to have susteinit hir lust, bot tuik ane uther wyffis husband to satisfie hir gredie appetyte.

On the Queen's death the castle passed to her son, King James III, but he soon granted the castle and lands to William Lord Sinclair in exchange for rights in Orkney where the Sinclair family had acquired the earldom in 1379. The castle remained with the Sinclairs until 1896. In addition to Sinclairtown, the Kirkcaldy districts of Boreland and Gallatown owe their names to being outposts of the castle. Boreland seems to have been the Bordland of Ravenscraig, that is to say the "board-land", the farm that supplied the table of the castle; and Gallatown the Gallowstown of the feudal Lord Sinclair who could also hold his court in Dysart which was in the mid-sixteenth century the most important port in Fife with much European trade.

Many dreadful scenes were witnessed from Ravenscraig on its rocky promontory with sheer 80-foot cliffs. Another form of Ravenscraig was Ravensheugh, to be used by Sir Walter Scott, with "heugh" Scots for high, rugged and sheer cliff. In May 1544 many must have stood on Ravenscraig's high battlements and looked over the Forth to witness the burning of Edinburgh by the English. In 1548 the horrors were much closer—in Kirkcaldy which was burned by an English fleet. At this time the islands of Inchkeith and Inchcolm were in the hands of English garrisons and English ships were marauding from the islands through the narrow waters of the Forth. Following the defeat of the army of the Covenant and the King, Cromwell's soldiers are likely to have taken up at least temporary residence in the castle. In 1592, following his murder of the "Bonnie Earl of Moray" at Donibristle near Dalgety Bay, the Earl of Huntly sought refuge at Ravenscraig.

The castle also saw great royal feastings including one in the early Spring of 1598 when King James VI took his brother-in-law, the Duke of Holstein, on a grand tour which played havoc with both the royal stomach and purse. The King's wife, Anne of Denmark, was only fourteen on her marriage in 1589 and, unlike other formidable spouses of the Stewart kings, Anne was not a political influence on the King or the nation. I presume that the twenty-four year old Queen was part of the cavalcade in which the King, "maid progres out of Halyroudhouse ower the water of Forthe to Rewinsheuche the first nicht, from that to Balcomie, Pittinweem, St Androis, Leucheris, Dundie, Foulis, St Johnstoun, Sterling, Linlithgow and Edinburgh, quhairre he was bancketted all the way."

That is recorded history, but Sir Walter Scott romanticised Ravensheuch in his "Lay of The Last Minstrel" when telling the story of Rosabelle Sinclair (or St Clair) of Rosslyn,

> Sad is the note, and sad the lay
> That mourns the lovely Rosabella
>
> . . .
>
> Moor, moor the barge, ye gallant crew!
> And, gentle ladye, deign to stay!
> Rest thee in Castle Ravensheuch,
> Nor tempt the stormy firth to-day.
>
> The blackening wave is edged with white:—
> To inch and rock the sea-mews fly;
> The fishers have heard the Water-Sprite,
> Whose screams forebode that wreck is nigh.
>
> Last night the gifted Seer did view
> A wet shroud swathed round ladye gay:
> Then stay thee, Fair, in Ravensheuch:
> Why cross the gloomy firth to-day?

The names live on in Rosslyn and St Clair streets in Sinclairtown and Gallatown, with Boreland sweeping round above Dysart. Dysart House was the home of the Earl of Rosslyn until 1889 when he sold the Dysart estate to Michael Barker Nairn (later Sir Michael) son of Michael Nairn, founder of the floorcloth industry in Kirkcaldy. Previously Sir Michael had bought Rankeilour estate, near Bow of Fife, as his summer home and he was being driven to Kirkcaldy from that open country in the Howe of Fife when he died aged 78 in 1915. I presume that it was Sir Michael who chose the peaceful old rural kirkyard at Monimail as the place where he wished to be buried. Today it is Sir Robert A. Spencer Nairn, Bart. who lives at Rankeilour Mains Farm.

In 1929 Sir Michael Nairn, the second baronet, having bought Elie House, presented the grounds of Dysart House, including Ravenscraig Castle, to the Town Council of Kirkcaldy and it remains one of the finest public parks in Scotland with a splendid coastal path that includes the steps down to the beach below Ravenscraig Castle. The thirty-nine steps of the novel by John Buchan are said to be based on one of the stairways that go down from Ravenscraig although I am not confident that I have found these famous steps, and Buchan's wife is reported as saying they were at Broadstairs where the Buchans were living in 1914. The youthful Buchan certainly knew the Pathhead area as his father was minister there. The first chapter of Buchan's *Prester John* is clearly set on Pathhead sands. His sister Anna, who wrote novels as O. Douglas, was born in Pathhead.

Great battles between armies are fought by men who mostly remain nameless and similarly the small-seeming tragedies that were of major concern to the men and women involved mostly die with the memories of those immediately involved. Andrew Wilson, whose memorial is in a Pathhead graveyard, is remembered because of the Porteous riots and Sir Walter Scott's retelling of them in a well-known novel. Facing the Wilson headstone is that of Thomas Alison, a Pathhead merchant and candlemaker. It is a large monument with interesting eighteenth-century lettering. The memorial stone also records some details of a tragedy that happened in the cave immediately below the castle on Pathhead sands. On 7th January 1770 at least nine boys were with Thomas Alison, a young son of the merchant, who died "through fatal fall of stones from the upper part of the cave that is on the south side of this town and of his age yrs 7, candlemaker in Dunikeir."

In the graveyard of Kirkcaldy Parish Church there is a long, narrow stone that once carried the inscription, "1842 M.N." Not many men who founded a great industry and a dynasty of millionaires have such a simple headstone over their grave. This is the grave of Michael Nairn (1804-58), who, as a plaque placed beside the stone by the Kirkcaldy Civic Society informs, was the "First Scottish Floorcloth Manufacturer." Nairn bought the plot in the graveyard when his father died in 1842.

The first printed mention of Michael Nairn is as a linen manufacturer in Links; the date was 1825 and Nairn was then 21 years old. He had his first factory for the manufacture of floor covering in Pathhead in 1847 although previously, in 1828, he had founded a canvas factory in Coal Wynd. Nairn's was to be the only linoleum manufacturer who made their own canvas. The site of Nairn's first Pathhead factory at Nether Street is marked by a mounted plaque recently re-set inside a nicely curved stone wall from near which there are splendid views over the bay to the promontory on which stands Seafield Castle and beyond, across the Forth, to Edinburgh and Arthur's Seat. It is difficult now to envisage that very large factories rose from these sands, and not only Nairn's factory. There were whale oil boiling sheds used by owners of the whaling ships that brought the blubber from Greenland; linseed oil was used for making linoleum only when it became difficult to get enough whale oil. Here, on Pathhead sands, were chemical works and R. Hutchison & Sons had a malting establishment. At their premises at Eastburn Mill, close to the harbour, R. Hutchison & Co set up a company, Youma Ltd, which made a malt-flavoured baking floor that was to be used by bakers in most parts of the UK. Some readers may remember the Youma loaf. Only Hutchison's mills still stand east of the harbour and large sections of their older works are being demolished as I write. All these industrial concerns were in sight from Ravenscraig Castle.

The story of the Nairn family's success with linoleum is as impressive as, for example, that of Jesse Boot with his herbal shop in Nottingham that grew into the great chain of chemist shops. The linoleum factories by the harbour have gone, as have those that ran parallel to Pathhead's Commercial Street and hard by Factory Road, but beyond the smart, new houses of Pathhead Village can be seen what is still a large works, owned by Forbo-Nairn Ltd, producing floorcovering.

To smart-alec outsiders Kirkcaldy was the town of a famous smell associated with linoleum manufacture. The revival of the demand for linoleum as an environmentally friendly product that contains linseed oil means that the vapour can sometimes still be inhaled from the clean air of the town. The new waiting area of Kirkcaldy railway station is well clad in good linoleum and a panel of the floorcloth hangs on a wall imprinted with Mrs M. C. Smith's jaunty poem, "The Boy in the Train",

> Whit wey does the engine say *Toot-toot*?
>   Is it feart to gang in the tunnel?
> Whit wey is the furnace no pit oot
>   When the rain gangs doon the funnel?
> What'll I hae for my tea the nicht?
>   A herrin', or maybe a haddie?
> Has Gran'ma gotten electric licht?
>   Is the next stop Kirkcaddy?
>
> There's a hoodie-craw on yon turnip-raw!
>   An' sea-gulls!—sax or seeven.
> I'll no fa' oot o' the windae, Maw,
>   It's sneckit, as sure as I'm leevin'.
> We're into the tunnel! We're a' in the dark!
>   But dinna be frichtit, Daddy,
> We'll sune be comin' to Beveridge Park,
>   And the next stop's Kirkcaddy!
>
> Is yon the mune I see in the sky?
>   It's awfu' wee an' curly.
> See! there's a coo and cauf ootbye,
>   An' a lassie pu'in' a hurly!
> He's chackit the tickets and gien them back,
>   Sae gie me my ain yin, Daddy.
> Lift doon the bag frae the luggage rack,
>   For the next stop's Kirkcaddy!
>
> There's a gey wheen boats at the harbour mou',
>   And eh! dae ye see the cruisers?
> The cinnamon drop I was sookin' the noo
>   Has tummelt an' stuck tae ma troosers . . .
> I'll sune be ringin' ma Gran'ma's bell,
>   She'll cry, "Come ben, my laddie."
> For I ken mysel' by the queer-like smell
>   That the next stop's Kirkcaddy.

In Bennochy Cemetery there is a very large marble kist which informs "In Memory of Catherine Ingram, widow of Michael Nairn. Died 3 May 1891 age 76 years." The white marble of the kist has weathered to produce a pleasing surface which contrasts very well with the polished marble of the base. Like her husband, Catherine Ingram's family had been involved in weaving. I am told by one of her descendants that she was "a formidable woman" who kept the business going, and expanding, until her sons were old enough to continue the development of the company. Other Nairns are buried in Bennochy, including John Nairn, younger brother of Sir Michael Barker Nairn, whose only son Ian Couper Nairn was killed in the 1914-18 war. It was John Nairn who presented Kirkcaldy War Memorial to his native town. This includes the Art Gallery and Museum which was built in 1922-24 and when it was opened in 1925 Mr Nairn saw the completion of the Memorial as it was first planned. He presented some paintings from his collection to the new Gallery. Almost as soon as the Gallery was completed an extension was planned to create the Public Library on the ground floor and three new galleries above it. John Nairn lived at Forth Park and, in 1934, his daughter, Mrs Wemyss Honeyman, gifted the house and grounds to the Town Council for use as a Maternity Hospital.

There is a superb group of paintings by William McTaggart in Kirkcaldy Art Gallery and other significant paintings, by Scottish Colourists (Cadell, Fergusson, Hunter, and Peploe), came to the Gallery from the collection of John Waldegrave Blyth who owned the Hawklymuir linen factory. The factory building still stands on the corner of Park Road and Lawson Street with the name above the door. John Blyth's nineteenth-century kinsfolk are buried in Sinclairtown Feuars' Cemetery near Ravenscraig Castle. Another descendant of these linen manufacturers is the wife of Michael Portillo who so dramatically lost his seat in the House of Commons at the 1997 election. Another politician with links to Kirkcaldy is Gordon Brown, currently Chancellor of the Exchequer, who was educated at Kirkcaldy High School whilst his father was minister of St Brycedale Church.

In the far corner of the newer part of Bennochy Cemetery is the grand sandstone memorial of the McIntosh family who established the prestigious furniture company. The centre feature is an almost life-size sculpture of a classical thinker, in red sandstone; today the figure is shattered and continues to disintegrate. The McIntosh factory in Victoria Road has been demolished but ESA McIntosh Ltd are manufacturing furniture in Mitchelston Industrial Estate. The new industrial estates on the edge of Kirkcaldy show that the town continues to prosper and that not all new companies go to the very successful industrial and business estates of Glenrothes—or Dunfermline.

The now unread English historian of the Victorian age, J. A. Froude, wrote a sentence that swelled the chests of those who were proud of what was then referred to as North Britain, "the Covenanters fought the fight and won the victory, and then, and not till then, came the David Humes with their Essays on Miracles, and the Adam Smiths with their political economies, and steam engines, and railroads, and philosophical institutions, and all the other blessed or unblessed fruits of liberty." Froude became an admirer and biographer of Thomas Carlyle, who taught in Kirkcaldy in the burgh school when it was in Hill Street. A plaque in Kirk Wynd informs that Thomas Carlyle "lodged here 1816-1818" and that "his school is opposite". The house has gone and the school closed in 1843. A plaque on its site informs that the school building was erected by the Town Council in 1725; and that Thomas Carlyle "was schoolmaster 1816-1818". We also learn that Adam Smith was a pupil 1729-1737; that Robert Adam, "eminent architect and designer, court architect to King George III" was "born in Gladney House, Links", in 1728, that he "attended this school 1734-1739" and was buried in Westminster Abbey in 1792. Another distinguished son of Kirkcaldy who attended the old school in Hill Street was Michael Barker Nairn (later Sir Michael). Admittedly the six-year-old Nairn attended the school for one day only as he immediately took part in the procession, led by Rector John Lockhart, from Hill Street to a new building. Dr Lockhart's headstone in Bennochy Cemetery informs that he taught in, and superintended, the school from 1840 to 1873. He was born in 1798 and died in 1882, and his descendants remained in the town he served so well.

Distinguished biographers of Robert Adam have omitted his years at school in Kirkcaldy and have him going straight to Edinburgh High School in 1734. Such writers can also misplace the old High School building which was in High School Yards near today's Infirmary Street facing Edinburgh University's Old College designed by Robert Adam. Robert Adam's father, William, was born in Kirkcaldy in 1689 and he was still living there when, in 1716, he married Mary Robertson whose family lived at Gladney House, which may have been built for William Robertson in 1711. Principal William Robertson of Edinburgh University, who wrote a best-selling *History of Scotland*, is the great architect's cousin. We may wonder what Robert Adam would think of the light-weight William Robertson building that the University built, between the David Hume and Appleton Towers, when they destroyed half of George Square.

By perhaps 1910 Gladney House had become a lodging house for tramps and other homeless men and women and was generally regarded as an unsavoury place until it was demolished in 1931. The Adam brothers designed Viewforth Tower, also in the Links area, and it was demolished as recently as 1960. In Hunter Street, St Brycedale House, which became Hunter Hospital and is currently unused, is thought to have been built by George Heggie to a design by one of the Adam brothers. Robert Adam died at his London home in 1792 and the place of his burial in Westminster Abbey is the south transept in Poets' Corner. I do not know of any poems by Robert Adam but his father William Adam is mentioned in a very fine poem by Robert Fergusson.

William Adam died in 1748 and is buried in Edinburgh in Greyfriars Kirkyard. In Fergusson's poem, "The Ghaists: A Kirk-yard Eclogue", the two ghosts are George Watson and George Heriot who both founded schools in Edinburgh. The ghost of Watson refers to Heriot's School, which stands alongside the kirkyard, and which he sees over the tomb of William Adam. Heriot laments the decline of Scotland since King James VI went south to London and sees his own school with sunken towers, his lands barren and his fame and honour withered like the flowers that students place each year on his statute in the courtyard of his school. But Watson replies,

> Sure Major Weir, or some sic warlock wight,
> Has flung beguilin' glamer o'er your sight;
> Or else some kittle cantrup thrown, I ween,
> Has bound in mirlygoes my ain twa ein,
> If ever aught frae sense cou'd be believed
> (And seenil hae my senses been deceiv'd),
> This moment, o'er the tap of Adam's tomb,
> Fu' easy I see your chiefest dome:
> Nae corbie fleein' there, nor croupin' craws,
> Seem to forspeak the ruin of thy haws,
> But a' your tow'rs in wonted order stand,
> Steeve as the rocks that hem oor native land.

104

Major Weir confessed to incest, sorcery and murder, and was burned at the stake in 1670; his sister Grizel was hanged in the Grassmarket as his accomplice.
kittle cantrup: mysterious charm, witch's trick   mirlygoes: illusions or fancies
ein: eyes   seenil: seldom   corbie: raven   Steeve: firm

From St Clair Street, above Pathhead, there is a magnificent view not only of the Forth but also, to the west, of the pastoral hills that stand above Kirkcaldy and Kinghorn. When the light is right the white farm steadings, set amongst these green upland acres, seem to belong in a drawing in a realistic picture book yet also to be of a distant world that can never be reached. Not that the magic has gone when the hillside roads are walked, but it is of another order; the view is outwards to the sea and down to the town as well as uphill to a more work-a-day view of the farm buildings.

I remember these back roads of the inland area west of Kirkcaldy, south of Auchtertool and north of Kinghorn, when vehicular traffic on them was so insignificant that walkers gave no thought to it. Nowadays I pass this way on the roads taken by the Glasgow bus, which can go via Auchtertool and Dunfermline, and the Edinburgh bus, which takes the inland road to Dalgety Bay, but the minor roads remain rural, almost surreally so. It's not only a hilly area between the coast and Auchtertool, but delightfully freakishly so with ridges and gullies coming in at so many bizarre angles. Of course this is not solely the work of slow passing glaciers and centuries of surges of water; humans have also had their brief day, and I guess that there have been more quarries hereabouts than those that can still be clearly seen.

The standing stones at Glassmount are close to what I regarded as the middle road from Kirkcaldy—"two down" from the Auchtertool road and "one up" from the road that goes round by Kinghorn! Here also have stood what seems to be more than a fair spread of castles and tower houses: Seafield (very early sixteenth century) is on the coast, but inland stood: Balwearie (see below); Pitteadie (late fifteenth century with a gateway dated 1686); Balmuto, near Auchtertool (early fifteenth century with 1797 battlemented parapet of 1797 and eighteenth-century additions which were removed when the house was reconstructed between 1974 and 1984—see below), Halyards (see below) and, a good bit further west, Knockdavie (another phonetically pleasing name).

There is a poem, or song, by James Hogg entitled "The Witch o' Fife" that could have been written for this part of Fife. It was first printed as part of a work entitled "Dr David Dale's Account of a Grand Aerial Voyage" which was published in 1830 in *The Edinburgh Literary Journal*. The good Doctor Dale is accompanied on his hugely improbable journey by the Ettrick Shepherd, a character played by Hogg throughout much of his literary career, who sings this song as the balloon rises. The poet gives a note which explains that this is "another balloon song, notable for nothing save its utter madness". So it may have been, but there is much sense in these joyful words. Today I envisage the quiet and colourful balloon rising from the high ground above Kirkcaldy and Kinghorn. It is a splendid Fife morning; the sky glows to the east with the varied reds of the recently risen sun and the northern light of a May morning enhances the varied lengths and breadths of Fife,

> Hurray, hurray, the jade's away,
>   Like a rocket of air with her bandalet!
> I'm up in the air on my bonny grey mare,
>   But I see her yet, I see her yet.

I'll ring the skirts o' the gowden wain
    Wi' curb an' bit, wi' curb an' bit;
An' catch the Bear by the frozen mane—
    An' I see her yet, I see her yet.

Away, away, oe'r mountain an' main,
    To sing at the morning's rosy yett;
An' water my mare at its fountain clear—
    But I see her yet, I see her yet.
Away, thou bonny witch o' Fife,
    On foam of the air to heave an' flit,
An' little reck thou of a poet's life,
    For he sees thee yet, he sees thee yet.

From various viewpoints on the inland roads above Kirkcaldy and Kinghorn the solid large mass of Raith House, with its tall chimney stacks, can be seen on the skyline. Raith House has a history going back to the late-seventeenth century. The design is by James Smith who, having worked for him, succeeded Sir William Bruce as Surveyor of the King's Works in Scotland. Smith had also married into the dynasty of great masons to the Kings—the Mylne family whose importance and wealth may be judged by their memorial in Greyfriars Kirkyard, Edinburgh. One of the masons who worked on Raith was a John Adam who could be William's father and so grandfather of Robert Adam. The important mason was Alexander Gavinlock. A few years after his work at Raith, James Smith may have competed with Bruce to be commissioned to design the grand and classical Melville House, near Monimail, for the First Earl of Melville. In the late eighteenth century James Playfair redesigned parts of the interior of Raith and also some new buildings, including the lodge and the gateway near Beveridge Park.

In forty years much has changed around Raith but I remember the grounds as almost tropical. To lie in Raith facing south on a wooded bank high above the town and the sea was luxury indeed when the grass was warm, the breeze light, and the sun was high on a June day. And down in the town my work was waiting for another day. Once the main avenue into Raith was close to the gates of Beveridge Park; today the avenue is blocked by a retirement home and a private housing estate. Other houses have been built off what is a new Oriel Road but behind these, as in days past, the estate's farm lands remain extensive and the slopes around the house impressive, with sweeping grassy banks and innumerable trees. The view from the main ground-floor windows of the house remains an everchanging delight with Edinburgh's Arthur's Seat setting off the Firth and the much nearer island of Inchkeith especially attractive because it is just in view over the small rolling hills above Kirkcaldy and Kinghorn. Also, from the main door there is still a good prospect, over the avenue, to the front of the stable court with its niches and classical busts.

The Sir John Melville referred to by John Knox in relation to the suppressions of Cardinal Beaton as "the faithful laird of Raith" is the fifth laird of Raith. He was executed on 14th December 1548 aged 46. Not unexpectedly in a writer who approved of the Reformation, Robert Lyndsay of Pitscottie saw this as an injustice and a product of a time when

> . . . nether dreadand sin nor schame heirin bot to fulfill thair lustis ussit thair awin appietyte. For at this tyme ane auld barroun of the contrie callit the laird of Raith was taine be the bischope of Sanctandrois in Fyfe quhair he was for the tyme and

had to Edinburgh and justifieit this to say, he was heidit and his head sett upoun the tolbooth of Edinburgh and his landis forfalit and gevin to the governouris freindis, and this was done all for sending of ane missive bill in Ingland.

Two of Sir John Melville of Raith's sons are Sir Robert Melville of Murdocairney who became the first Lord Melville in 1616, and the courtier and diarist Sir James Melville of Halhill, near Collessie and Monimail, but I leave their story till a later chapter on the Howe of Fife. In 1643 George, fourth Lord Melville, took Raith into the barony of Melville; he became Earl of Melville in 1690. The Earl, who died in 1707, outlived his son, the Lord Raith who built Raith House, and the next Earl was David Melville who also became Earl of Leven on the death of his mother, Katherine Leslie, a grand-daughter of General Leslie. It was this third Earl of Leven and second Earl of Melville who, in 1725, sold the Raith estate to Robert Ferguson whose family became very influential in Kirkcaldy. They also bought, in 1782, lands in the Parish of Penicuik, previously owned by the Sinclair (or St Clair) family of which the Earl of Rosslyn was the head.

Three members of the Ferguson of Raith family were MPs for Kirkcaldy Burghs through most of the years 1806-62. The first was Lieut-General Sir Ronald Crawford Ferguson of Raith, son of William Ferguson, who was born in 1771, married Jean, daughter of General Sir Hector Munro of Novar, County Ross, fought in the Peninsular Wars, and died in 1841. The second was General Ferguson's brother Robert Ferguson, Lord-Lieutenant of Fife, who died in 1840. The third MP was Lieutenant-Colonel Robert Munro Ferguson, son of General Ferguson, and Deputy-Lieutenant of Fife who died in 1868. A fourth laird of Raith, Ronald Crawford Munro Ferguson, born in 1860, followed his father and uncle into parliament and had a most distinguished career. He was MP for Leith Burghs for almost thirty years, Provost of Kirkcaldy from 1906 to 1913 and Governor-General of Australia 1914-20 when he was knighted. Shortly after his return to Kirkcaldy, when a large crowd at Kirkcaldy Station welcomed him, Sir Ronald was created Viscount Novar and in 1922 became Secretary of State for Scotland. He died in 1935 aged 75 and, as with other members of his family, a memorial plaque was placed in Abbotshall Church. In 1998 the Raith estate remains with the Munro-Ferguson family.

Abbotshall Church stands close to the old entrance to Raith estate and from 1769 the Ferguson family of Raith were the patrons who presented ministers to the kirk. One of the ministers of Abbotshall was Bruce Beveridge Begg, a grand-nephew of Robert Burns. Rev B. B. Begg came to Abbotshall in 1865 and when he celebrated twenty-five years of ministering in Kirkcaldy it was the thirty-year-old Mr R. C. Munro Fergusom, M.P. (later Viscount Novar) who presided. One of the speakers was Rev Dobbie, an old friend of Mr Begg, who cleverly regretted that he had not known Begg when they were boys so that he could quote parts of two verses from "Auld Lang Syne", in the version by the poet to whom Mr Begg was "not very distantly related",

> We twa hae run about the braes,
> And pou'd the gowans fine; . . .
> We twa hae paidl'd in the burn,
> Frae morning sun till dine;

Marjory Fleming, the child author (1803-11), is buried in the kirkyard of Abbotshall with a pretty, life-size, seated figure, of 1930, by the sculptor Pilkington Jackson (1887-1973) and the words, "The Youngest Immortal in the World of Letters". Set into the back of the very well crafted seat on which the figure of Marjory sits, with an open book on her lap, is the simple stone erected when she died; it says, "M.F. 1811". A stone surround to Marjory's grave forms a little garden planted with small flowers.

Named "Pet Marjorie" by Dr John Brown, Marjory's fame was promoted, by those who wrote of her, as a friend of Sir Walter Scott but he is not mentioned in her journals, nor she in his. Nevertheless her journals are a notable achievement by a ten-year old. The diary which covers the last 18 months of her life also includes a number of poems. My own favourite is her sonnet on a charming pug,

> O lovely O most charming pug
> Thy graceful air and heavenly mug
> The beauties of his mind do shine
> And every bit is shaped so fine
> Your very tail is most devine
> Your teeth is whiter than the snow
> You are a great buck and a bow
> Your eyes are of so fine a shape
> More like a christians than an ape
> His cheeks is like the roses blume
> Your hair is like the ravens plume
> His nose cast is of the roman
> He is a very pretty weomen
> I could not get a rhyme for roman
> And was obliged to call it weoman.

Against the wall of Abbotshall Church, and facing over the Forth, are the graves of the Burt family who were booksellers in Kirkcaldy from the 1880s to the 1970s. The kirkyard of Abbotshall is kept immaculately and the church is one of the most pleasing buildings in Kirkcaldy. Always it raises my level of optimism when, unexpectedly, I see its tower and spire on the skyline. I have been inside Abbotshall once but have to confess that I was distracted from looking at details of the excellent renovation by becoming involved in the minister's memories of Cumnock, in Ayrshire, where he had been minister, and where, from her great-great-grandfather's time, my mother's folk had a smiddy. I do, however, remember a most pleasing circular arrangement of pews of light wood.

The name Abbotshall may, for once, mean just what it says—the Hall used by the Abbot of Dunfermline for relaxation by the sea. Before it was merged into the Raith estate, Abbotshall was part of the estate of the Scotts of Balwearie. The castle of Balwearie, on the western edge of Kirkcaldy, was built about 1460, in the reign of King James III, by William Scott. He may have been descended from Scotts who were feudal lords at Strathmiglo. A Sir William Scott was taken prisoner at Flodden and paying his ransom ate into the Strathmiglo estate. The castle of Strathmiglo stood near the village on the lands of Cairney. Sir William Scott of Balwearie is said to have had the castle built hurriedly to impress the King when he was at Falkland. King James V did come to dine but was not impressed by Balwearie's new home and, sensing its insecure structure, named it "Cairney Flappit". The castle was ruined by the 1730s.

Balwearie has been taken to be the birthplace of Sir Michael Scott, the famous wizard and philosopher who wrote learned works on astrology, medicine and alchemy, but it seems that there were no Scotts at Balwearie before 1235 when a Sir Michael Scott married Margaret, the heiress of Balwearie, whose father was Sir Richard Balwearie of that ilk. It has been theorised that the "wizard" was a son of this couple. If this is true then the wizard was born not earlier than 1236. I have not attempted to disentangle the various biographies of the Michael Scott who appeared in so many literary works; many experts have already tried and, it seems to me, failed. The myth of the man is more influential than any documented biography.

He gets a mention in Dante's *Inferno;* in Boccaccio's *Decameron,* "You must know that lately there was a necromancer in this city called Michael Scotus, because he was a Scotsman"; he is mentioned by Giovanni Villani, historian of Florence who died in 1348, as a successful foreteller of the future; Picus de Mirandola in attacking astrology attacks Scott's system; Thomas Dempster (1579-1625) said his name was to identify him as a Scotsman and that he had nothing to do with Balwearie; John Laylande (1506-52) who searched for *Englande's Antiquitees,* said Scott was an Englishman born in Durham; Folengo (1491-1544) praised "renowned Scotus" in macaronic verse; and the Scottish historians, Hector Boece, George Buchanan and Bishop Lesley, repeated stories about him; Sir Walter Scott, knowingly I presume, continues the tradition of the Wizard in "The Lay of the Last Minstrel"; and in "Anster Fair" William Tennant writes in good high spirits,

> With her resided that famed wizard old,
>   Her uncle and her guardian, Michael Scot,
> Who there, in Satan's arts alignly bold,
>   His books of dev'lish efficiency wrote.

Scott's appearance in Dante is amongst those who practised astrology and divination,

> The other one, about the loins so spare,
>   was Michael Scot, who in good sooth well knew
> all juggling tricks and was their cunning player.

Tom Hubbard has written poems and a play in which he explores the Faustian theme in literature and within these works can be discerned the shadowy figure of Michael Scott. In his dramatic poem of eleven verses entitled "Mephistophelean Ballant-Scherzo On Ane Fife Legend" the action takes place on a Fife beach. Two verses give a hint of the tone of the work,

> I tak the doktor doun the shore
>   An scoop inti his haund
> Whit's cheengeless as the fowk theirsel—
>   An common tae—the saund.

> "Look there," says I, "fir nae twa grains
>   'll ever byde thegither;
> Ilkane will think itsel unique
>   Though we canna tell ane fae the t'ither."

One advantage the long length of the Esplanade confers on Kirkcaldy is space for the annual Links Market—all the fun of the Fair. When I was a young man it was the custom, and it may still be, for us to invite our girlfriends to the Links Market as we would also invite them to an annual dinner-dance. Another of my "Traivellin Man" poems, entitled "By the Sea", is about a return visit to the Market,

"I had a luve walked by the sea"
Sydney Goodsir Smith

We're back in the Lang Toon for the Links Market
for oor bairns, we say.

I mind takin you aince a year
in oor courtin days. An annual celebration
we walked haund in haund the haill lang length
and were on awthing.

The steamboats near swingin richt owre
and the dive-bombers daein juist that. The dodgems
to show what a deevil I was at the wheel
haein nae caur to drive you hame. And elaborate
new-fangled stomach-turners
noo forgotten. I shot an air-gun at wee pipes being
a crack-shot and threw
pingpong balls into gold-fish bowls nae bother at aw.
We bought candy floss and hot dogs
and rolled pennies doon wee slides
till aw oor money was gone.
Still we *were* laden wi prizes!

Prizes soon forgotten as we walked by the sea
and stood close thegither in the daurk
doon by the sea-waw.

Noo the bairns canna be kept back. I face the horror
o the steamboat but aince, and disgrace mysel
being seik ahint a caravan. I'm grounded.
I dinna quite live up to my Buffalo Bill image
and suspect the hot-dog stall to be unhygenic.
Still I'm a whizz-kid on the dodgems
and I can cairry aw the prizes the bairns are winnin.
The trouble is their money disnae seem to be runnin oot
and we'll be back themorrow nicht.

They can cairry their ain prizes.
Wan thing husnae cheynged
—we can still walk by the sea!

10

Auchtertool, Lochgelly and Bowhill

THE BOSWELLS of Balmuto have been major landowners in the parish of Auchtertool for many centuries. This is the family of Marjory Boswell who married a Beaton of Balfour and was mother to an Archbishop, grandmother to a Cardinal who was murdered, and to another Archbishop who survived to die in Rome. James Boswell, the biographer of Samuel Johnson, is related to the Boswells of Balmuto. King Robert, the Bruce, granted a charter of lands to John de Glen, the second son of a Sir David de Glen who had been involved in a heroic defence of Stirling Castle in 1304 when it was besieged by King Edward I. These lands were of Balmutache (Balmuto) in Fife, and they remained with the Glen family until early in the fifteenth century when Mariote, heiress of Sir John Glen, married Sir John Boswell of Balgreggie in Fife. The house at Balmuto dates from a fifteenth-century tower house with later additions and alterations.

Balmuto is another castle-tower saved from the crows and owls. In Burntisland in 1998 I met Mr Norman Mackie who, as a boy, had lived in Auchtertool in the 1940s. The Boswell family had gone to the USA, and each time the young Mackie went into parts of the tower he was, indeed, startled by an owl fluttering around him. He found the old stable more surprising—and a sad sight. It was as if the occupants had left in an emergency as, indeed, the war might be so regarded. The saddles and bridles and other tack were still hanging on their hooks, but rusting and tattered at the edges. Fortunately members of the Boswell family returned and the tower was saved. The restoration work, implemented by The Appleton Partnership of Edinburgh, took ten years from 1974 to 1984.

In 1722 Andrew Boswell sold Bulmuto to a distant kinsman, John Boswell of the family in Auchinleck. The new owner of Balmuto was an uncle of Lord Auchinleck of the Court of Session and a grand-uncle of James Boswell, Johnson's biographer. The heir to Balmuto was Claude Boswell, another judge who took the judicial title of Lord Balmuto. When Alexander Boswell was raised to the bench in 1754 he took the title of Lord Auchinleck. This is the father of Johnson's biographer, James Boswell. The biographer's son, Sir Alexander Boswell, instigated the Burns monument on the banks of the Doon and set up a press at Auchinleck to print his own works and also fine books.

In 1822 Sir Alexander Boswell was involved in a duel with James Stuart of Dunearn, who had a house, Hillside, near Aberdour, where many literary men were entertained. The duel was held in a field at Wester Balbarton Farm, Auchtertool, because the authorities in Edinburgh had made duelling illegal. Stuart's second was Lord Rosslyn. The mortally wounded Boswell was taken first to a farm cottage and then to Balmuto, the home of his octogenarian cousin, Claude Boswell, Lord Balmuto, where he died. Boswell was taken from Balmuto to Auchinleck for burial. Sir Alexander's verses are hardly significant but "Jenny Dang the Weaver", which tells of a courting at a country wedding, has a certain liveliness,

In ilka countra dance and reel
Wi' her he wad be babbin'
When she sat doun, then he sat doun,
An till her he wad be gabbin'.
Where'er she gaed, or butt or ben,
The coof wad never leave her,
Aye clackin' like a clockin' hen,
But Jenny dang the weaver.

It has been suggested that Thomas Carlyle first met his wife Jane Welsh in the manse at Auchtertool where Jane's cousin, Rev Walter Welsh, was minister, but they were married in 1826 and Mr Welsh did not arrive in Auchtertool until the 1840s. The old church stands high, and perhaps three-quarters of a mile out of the village. Auchtertool House, where the Carlyles also stayed, sits on the edge of the village and there is a good view of the church from its western wall. Uphill from the village is Puddledub road end from where the church can be seen high on the skyline open to the Auchtertool side but sheltered to the west by trees. Far over towards where Lochgelly lies, and edging a planting of evergreens, there stands the ruined tower of Halyards. Looking back down over the village, Camilla Loch can be seen and further round, through a gap in the hills, Berwick Law and the Bass Rock stand out on the distant-seeming Forth. Nearer, down in a small plain south of the village, the elegant tower of Balmuto can, in winter, be glimpsed through its surrounding trees. This is an upland place with surrounding hills that can be bleak indeed in winter but in summer Jane Carlyle must have enjoyed the soft, warm breezes and the rural quietness that is still there today.

The large manse stands alongside the kirkyard with a large open garden and two smaller hedged gardens. I can envisage Mrs Carlyle, holidaying with her three cousins, the minister and his two sisters, sitting in the larger of these enclosed gardens perhaps writing to her husband. The largest area of the garden is now much simpler and less colourful than when Jane Carlyle was coming here. When Rev Welsh moved into the manse his father, John Welsh, was generous in having the garden landscaped and many trees and shrubs planted. There was a summer house where the great Thomas Carlyle went, with Rev Welsh and any male visitors, to smoke his long church-warden pipe. The Misses Welsh were ahead of their time in not permitting smoking in the manse. Behind the summer house there was a sheltered walk, running north to south and lined with screens of holly, which came to be known as "Carlyle's Walk." The minister's father was generous beyond the garden as he, with Rev Guild, signed a bond giving the Presbytery security for Rev Welsh's stipend. The Earl of Moray, despite still being patron of the church, did not add his signature to this surely unusual piece of paper.

When Rev Welsh first went to Auchtertool he was assistant to Rev David Guild. In July 1846 Jane Carlyle wrote to her husband from Liverpool where she was visiting her Uncle John, "Jeannie writes to me from Auchtertool that the old minister is suddenly dead, so Walter is now in possession of the appointments of his office. There is something rather shocking in one person's death being necessarily a piece of good fortune for another; but it is all one to the old man himself now whether they make sad faces at his departure or gay ones."

Mr Guild was 82 years old and had never married. In his later years a widowed sister and her family lived with him in the manse. His memorial plaque is on the wall of the kirk below the very evocative belfry. Indeed the bell chain and rope is tied to a hook between

112

Guild's memorial and that of the important Liddell family who were at Auchtertool House in the time of Jane and Thomas Carlyle. I am told that the bell is still rung at Christmas and other special occasions. The old manse is now in private ownership and the Sunday morning services are conducted by the minister of Linktown Church in Kirkcaldy.

Most Victorian ministers may not have had a large stipend but, as the rather grand manse in Auchtertool suggests, they could live in some style. Auchtertool manse was built in 1812 and designed by J. Gillespie Graham who was also responsible for both kirk and manse at Dalgety Bay; and for the small "Gothic" kirk at Dunino.

There was still patronage when, in 1800, Mr Guild was presented to the parish by the Earl of Moray. The new minister had been schoolmaster at Wemyss and he was the son of the parish schoolmaster of Auchtertool. The Rev Guild may have previously tutored members of the families of both the Earl of Moray and Mr Wemyss of Wemyss. It seems that on coming to Auchtertool the minister continued to spend most of the week at the houses of his patrons. Each Monday, fashionably dressed, as always, in knee-breeches and black silk stockings, the minister mounted his pony to ride out of the village, and Auchtertool had neither sight nor sound of him till the end of the week.

From a letter from General Alex Campbell to General Wemyss, M.P., Wemyss Castle, Dysart, dated 16th Sept, 1815, and written from Monzie, we learn that General Wemyss dined with Mr Guild at the manse in Auchtertool. The letter also allows us to glimpse another hilarious level of snobbery involving David Monypenny, Lord Pitmilly, the judge whom Lord Cockburn wrote about in his *Memoirs*. Robert Burns visited John Ramsay at Ochtertyre and was advised by him to write in English and not "coarse" Scots. Sir Walter Scott also visited Ochtertyre and modelled Jonathan Oldbuck in *The Antiquary* on Ramsay whose extensive journal was edited, after his death, into a book, *Scotland and Scotsmen in the Eighteenth Century*, which in my youth I rather admired. I am presuming that the Sir Peter of General Campbell's letter is a Ramsay.

> My dear General, I dined yesterday at Ochtertyre, and Sir Peter told me that he had lately received a letter from you, intimating your intention of being soon in this country, which gave me much joy, when up spoke a thing they call a Lord, by the name of Pitmilly, *ci devant* [formerly] Davy Moneypenny, and emitted the following evidence—viz., "that the said Wemyss had been overturned, coupt, or whumled in his carriage, to the great damage of his person, on his return from dining with a reverend clergyman, whose name he could not recollect, nor could he testify to the exact amount of damage the person of the said General actually received." On being cross-examined, he admitted that the Parish of Auchtertool might be that of your entertainer, and I immediately called to mind the sage person who came upon our flank at the end of the engagement at Wemyss Castle, as Blucher did at Waterloo, and I believe, with the same success. But, seriously, I will be obliged if you will let me know how you are, and whether you are much hurt; above all, I hope you will be able to make out your purpose of visiting this country. The parsons here do not ask people to dinner, so you will be safe that way. My best wishes to all at Wemyss Castle. Believe me, yours faithfully, ALEX CAMPBELL

In 1842 Mr Welsh was appointed by the Earl of Moray as assistant and successor to Mr Guild. The Disruption was about to send shattering tremors through the Established Church and opposition to patronage was central to the new thinking. Although some 40 parishioners, individually, petitioned the Presbytery, Rev Walter Welsh was ordained minister of Auchtertool on 13th September 1843. He remained there until his death in 1879, unmarried but with two sisters living with him. When Rev Andrew Miller succeeded Mr Welsh in 1880 he was elected by the vote of the people who had heard the candidates preach.

It is likely that Jane Welsh was introduced to Carlyle by her tutor, Edward Irving, in Haddington, East Lothian, where she was born and her father was a doctor. Irving became a famous preacher who attracted large congregations. Indeed, when he preached in Kirkcaldy in 1828 the church was so full that the gallery collapsed, killing 28 of the congregation. Irving and Carlyle were friends in Kirkcaldy between 1816 and 1818 when both were teaching there. Mrs Carlyle was at the Auchtertool manse more often than her husband and her letters to him, and others, allow us to glimpse other aspects of life in this part of Fife in the mid-nineteenth century. On 5th November 1844 she wrote to her cousin Mrs Russell about her other cousins,

> Jeannie and Maggie are at Auchtertool with Walter, leading a good-for-nothing life there, according to their own account of it—engaged in perpetual tea-drinkings with "people whom they take no pleasure in," and "making themselves amends in sitting at home with their feet on the fender talking over the absurdities of the said people." Whereupon I have written Jeannie a very scolding letter, which it is to be feared will share the common fate of all good advice in the world—make her angry at me without putting a stop either to tea drinkings with people "we can take no pleasure in" or the idle practice of sitting with her feet on the fender, and still worse practice of laughing at one's neighbours' absurdities rather than one's own.

On 7th August 1856, from Edinburgh, she wrote to her husband,

> The day before yesterday I bathed at Kirkcaldy and walked to Auchtertool after, and the fatigue was too much, and I was up to nothing but lying on the sofa all the evening, which delayed my packing till yesterday morning; and I got up at half after six to leave time for a letter, and it was not till "prayers" were over and breakfast ready that I was ready to sit down. Immediately after breakfast the dogcart came round to take me to the half after eleven boat . . .

Whilst in Kirkcaldy in 1849 Jane Carlyle was stung by a wasp at Whytehouse but she went out to Auchtertool to see her Uncle John who was staying at the manse and whom she had described as "John, sole uncle of my house and heart!". A letter describes the suffering that wasp imposed upon her,

> I suffered horribly in silence and all night; the trophies of the world would not let me sleep—not one wink. However, I went next day to Auchtertool with my hand in a poultice, being still determined to come out of that on Monday, and unwilling to go without saying farewell to my poor uncle, whom it is likely enough I shall never see again.

It could be that she did never see the poor man again, but he did live another four years! The Auchtertool letters perhaps show that holidays did not truly agree with Jane Carlyle, but then letters written for one's husband and not public reading must always give only a partial view. In August 1856 she went to Edinburgh to hear Dr Guthrie preach and wrote to her husband,

I was well to a wonder; hadn't one hour of my sickness nor one wholly sleepless night since I left Chelsea; and the idea must needs take me that Sunday I was in Edinburgh to have out my humour to hear Dr Guthrie. So for two hours I slowly simmered as in one of Soyer's patent stewpans (the crush to hear him being as great in Edinburgh as in London), and then I had to walk to Morningside in a cutting east wind. . . . The consequence of all this bad management was a cold on my nerves, which the crossing next day and the blowy drive in the dogcart brought to a height. And I have been two whole days in bed . . . and am still very poorly, though today I can sit up and write, as you can see. Indeed last night I never once closed my eyes. Nothing could be more ill-timed than this illness, two dinner parties having gone off "without effect" so far as I was concerned. . . . Poor Walter, his poor little stipend must be dreadfully perplexed to meet all the demands his munificent spirit makes on it. Besides these dinner parties, we have a house chock full. Jeannie and her husband came over to see me chiefly, and Sofie from Liverpool with Jackie, a remarkably stirring little gentleman of three and a half years, and another human mite that rejoices as yet in the name of Baby. And in the dead watches of the night there will arise a sound of "infants weeping in the porch", and on the whole it is not now like paradise here as it was in my first two weeks. I should have stayed on here while the coast was clear, and only been going on my Haddington visit now.

A year later her Auchtertool visit again included some bad health,

Oh heaven! Or rather, oh, the other place! I am degenerating from a woman into a dog, and feel the inclination to bark—bow-bow!wow! Ever since I came here I have been passing out of one silent rage into another at the things in general of this house. Viewed from an invalid point of view they are enough to make one not only bark but bite, were it not that in other people's houses one has to assume the muzzle of politeness. . . . Is it possible that the change of a cook can make the difference betwixt now and last summer, or is it the increased irritability of my nerves that makes it? Or are my cousins getting stupefied for want of something to stir their souls, on this hill-top? The devil knows best how it comes, but I as one solitary individual find no satisfaction in the arrangements here, though there be "no reflections of want of roses" and "beautiful views" and "pure air". . . . But then "that damned thing they call the milk of human kindness" not being all gone to sour curd in me, I would not show my unfeeling impatience to be gone where I am treated (though God knows how injudiciously) most kindly according to their light and ability.

Both Mr and Mrs Carlyle were at Auchtertool House in August 1859 which, as Jane explained in a letter of August 1859 to George Cook, had been "lent by Mr Liddell",

Whether it be that the air of Auchtertool suits me better than that of Aberdour, or that my having my kind little cousins within cry is a wholesome diversion, or that I required a continuance of country air to act upon my feebleness, I am not competent to say, nor is it of the slightest earthly consequence what the cause is, so that the effect has been as I tell you.

Of course, these extracts from private letters review only part of a not-too-well Jane's view of her cousin and his sisters, and writing to her husband from Craigenvilla,

Edinburgh, in September 1862 she shows something of both sides of her attitude to visiting the manse,

> I find I cannot get off from Auchtertool. . . . After all, I have no kinder relative or friend in the world than poor Walter. Every summer, when invitations were not so plenty, his house and all that is his has been placed at my disposal. It is the only house where I could go without an invitation at any time that suited myself.

In what was perhaps her last letter from the home of Rev Walter Welsh and his sisters, dated 8th September 1862 and to her cousin Mrs Russell, the great writer's wife reveals again appreciation of their kindness and that her cousins lived in a world rather different from that of Chelsea, London,

> Everywhere that I go I am warmly welcomed and made much of . . . and here though I am cousin—their one cousin of whom their naturally hospitable and kindly natures are doubly hospitable and kindly—still I miss that congeniality which comes of having mutually suffered and taken one's suffering to heart! I feel here as if I were "playing" with nice, pretty, well-behaved children! I almost envy them their light-hearted capacity of being engrossed with trifles.

The brougham in which Mrs Carlyle died in Hyde Park was sent, with its horse, to Mr Welsh and they "grew old in his service." Mr Welsh died on 17th December 1879, as his headstone says, "in the 65th year of his age" which was the 37th of his ministry in Auchtertool. The third minister after Mr Welsh was Rev William Stevenson and he, having previously written on Markinch and *The Presbyterie Booke of Kirkcaldie*, wrote the first history of *The Kirk and Parish of Auchtertool* which was published soon after his death in July 1908. This remains a very readable work which I have gratefully drawn on for this chapter. Mr Stevenson's dignified memorial is on an outside wall of the kirk.

Having quoted from Jane Carlyle's letter to Mrs Russell, Mr Stevenson wrote, "that was written fifty years ago, and 'the pretty well-behaved children' with their 'light-hearted capacity of being engrossed with trifles' are now in the old kirkyard, as near to the Manse as it was possible to lay them, and there in spring their graves are covered with snowdrops as pure as the whitest snow."

The kirkyard remains well cared for but the snowdrops now seem to be confined to the old manse's garden and the headstone beside that of Rev Walter Welsh had, in the Spring of 1998, fallen face down. I am optimistic that soon it will be upright again.

Sometimes when Thomas Carlyle came to Auchtertool he brought a riding horse with him. He and the minister took long rides and he may have been regarded as something of an eccentric. Carlyle wrote most appreciatively of his wife's Uncle John, who was the Rev Walter's father and who did much to improve the manse's garden. Indeed, in his later years, John Welsh lived with his son and died there in 1853. A memorial stone was erected in his memory in Auchtertool but he is buried in Liverpool where he spent most of his life, and of which Thomas Carlyle wrote,

> He was cheerful, musical, politely conversible; truly a genial, harmonious, loving nature; but there was a roar in him too like a lion's. He had had great misfortunes and provocations; his way of life in dusty, sooty, ever noisy Liverpool, with its dinnerings, wine-drinkings, dull evening parties issuing in whist, was not his element, few men's less, though he made not the least complaint of it (even to

116

himself, I think): but his heart, and all his pleasant memories and thoughts, were in the breezy hills of Moffatdale, with the rustic natives there, and their shepherdings, huntings (brock and fox) and solitary fishings in the clear streams.

Carlyle also wrote with enthusiasm of Walter Welsh, his wife's and Rev Welsh's grandfather, who farmed at Capelgill, near Moffat. It is as fine and warm a piece of descriptive prose as the great man wrote,

> I really liked old Walter heartily, and he was a continual genial study to me over and above; microcosm of old Scottish life as it had been, and a man of much singularity and real worth of character, and even of intellect too if you saw well. I have hardly seen one of hotter, more impatient temper. Sudden, vehement, breaking out into fierce flashes of lightning when you touched him the wrong way. Yet they were flashes only, never bolts, and were gone again in a moment, and the fine old face, beaming quietly on you as before. Face uncommonly fine, serious, yet laughing eyes, as if inviting you in, bushy eyebrows, face which you might have called picturesquely shaggy, under its plenty of grey hair, beard itself imperfectly shaved here and there; features massive yet soft (almost with a tendency to pendulous or flabby parts), and nothing but honesty, quick ingenuity, kindliness, and frank manhood as the general expression. . . . He had the prettiest laugh (once, or at most twice, in my presence) that I can remember to have seen, not the loudest, my own father's still rarer laugh was louder far, though perhaps not more complete, but his was all of artillery-thunder, *feu de joie* from all guns as the main element, while in Walter's there was audible something as of infinite flutes and harps, as if the vanquished themselves were invited or compelled to partake in the triumph. I remember one such laugh (quite forget about what), and how the old face looked suddenly so beautiful and young again. "Radiant ever young Apollo," etc, of Teufelsdröckh's laugh as a reminiscence of that.

After Jane's death in 1866 the dyspeptic author blamed himself for neglecting his wife; for being "gey ill to live wi". Froude made more than something of this in his biography of Carlyle, and a host of a second form of "Janeites" emerged to see their heroine as a genius who had been kept down by the self-centred son of his father—a classic example of the dour, dense and humourless Scot! This of the man who wrote *Sartor Resartus: The Life and Opinions of Herr Teufelsdröckh,* the title of which alone sweeps away such a characterisation. North of Aberdour is Humbie where Carlyle is said to have come to work on a book, and to have brought with him a donkey for his wife's phaeton. The book he is said to have worked on is *Frederick the Great* a copy of which I once owned—a large-format edition in six volumes which I bought in a dark shop near Holyrood Palace—but never read. But, like Walter Welsh's laugh, *Sartor Resartus* is of another world all together,

> "Perhaps the most remarkable incident in Modern History," says Teufelsdröckh, "is not the Diet of Worms, still less the Battle of Austerlitz, Waterloo, Peterloo, or any other Battle; but an incident passed carelessly over by most Historians, and treated with some degree of ridicule by others; namely, George Fox's making to himself a suit of Leather. This man, the first of the Quakers, and by trade a Shoemaker, was one of those, to whom, under ruder or purer form, the Divine Idea of the Universe is pleased to manifest itself; and, across all the hulls of Ignorance and earthly Degradation, shine through, in unspeakable Awfulness, unspeakable Beauty, on their souls: who therefore

are rightly accounted Prophets, God-possessed; or even Gods, as in some periods it has chanced. Sitting in his stall; working on tanned hides, amid pincers, paste-horns, rosin, swine-bristles, and a nameless flood of rubbish, this youth had, nevertheless, a Living Spirit belonging to him; also an antique Inspired Volume, through which, as through a window, it could look upwards, and discern its celestial Home. The task of a daily pair of shoes, coupled even with some prospect of victuals, and an honourable Mastership in Cordwainery, and perhaps the post of Thirdborough in his hundred, as the crown of long faithful sewing,—was nowise satisfaction enough to such a mind: but ever amid the boring and hammering came tones from that far country, came Splendours and Terrors; for this poor Cordwainer, as we said, was a Man; and the Temple of Immensity, wherein as Man he had been sent to minister, was full of holy mystery to him.

The hero of Carlyle's book is one of the great idiosyncratic individuals of literature. The Fife lairds have been seen, collectively, as unusually idiosyncratic. Set apart between Forth and Tay, Fife had a reputation for being *different*. We can see this in Lady Nairne's song "The Fife Laird". The reference to Inchkeith suggests that the laird took the ferry from Pettycur. Like Rev James Melville, he had a difficult crossing which is blamed on a storm raised by some witches who lived about St Andrews toun,

> Ye shouldna ca' the Laird daft, though daft like he may be;
> Ye shouldna ca' the Laird daft, he's just as wise as me;
> Ye shouldna ca' the Laird daft, his bannet has a *bee*—
> He's just a wee bit Fifish, like some Fife lairds that be.
> Last Lammas when the Laird set out to see Auld Reekie's toun,
> The Firth it had nae waves at a', the waves were sleepin' soun';
> But wicked witches bide about gude auld St. Andrews toun,
> And they steered up an unco blast, our ain dear Laird to droun.
>
> Afore he got to Inchkeith Isle, the waves were white an' hie—
> "O weel I ken thae witches wud hae aye a spite at me!"
> They drove him up, they drove him doon,—the Fife touns a' they pass,
> And up and round Queensferry toun, then doun unto the Bass.
> The sailors row, but row in vain, Leith port they canna gain—
> Nae meat or beds they hae on board, but *there* they maun remain;
> O mirk and cauld the midnight hour, how thankfu' did they see
> The first blush o' the dawnin' day, far spreadin' owre the sea.
>
>   Ye shouldna ca' the Laird daft, etc.
>
> "Gae hame, gae hame," the Laird cried out, "as fast as ye can gang,
> Oh! rather than wi' witches meet, I'd meet an *ourna-tang*;—
>
> A' nicht and day I've been away, an' naething could I see
> But auld wives' cantrips on broomsticks, wild cap'ring owre the sea.
> I hae na' had a mouth o' meat, nor yet had aff my claes—
> Afore I gang to sea again, some *folk* maun mend their ways."
> The Laird is hame wi' a' his ain, below the Lomond hill,
> Richt glad to see his sheep again, his dookit and his mill!
>
> Ye shouldna ca' the Laird daft, tho' daft like he may be;
> Ye shouldna ca' the Laird daft, he's just as wise as me:

Ye shouldna ca' the Laird daft, his bannet has a *bee*,—
He's juist a wee bit Fifish, like some Fife Lairds that be.

The lairds of Fife are probably no more peculiar than those in other parts of Lowland Scotland, but not many lairds have come together to attempt a *coup d'état* by murdering a Cardinal as did: Sir James Kirkcaldy of Grange and his son William; the kinsfolk of Sir James's wife who was a Melville; and members of the Leslie family, with Norman Leslie amongst the ringleaders. Today's Grange Farm is inland from Seafield castle-tower, between Kirkcaldy and Kinghorn, and its round white-walled tower, with conical roof, attracts my eyes each time I pass below it on the A921.

The church at Dunkeld held the lands of Auchtertool and the bishops came to a castle within the parish for relaxation and the fresh air from the Forth. So it could be that poet and bishop Gavin Douglas spent relaxing hours hereabouts. In 1539 the church lands were feued to Sir James Kirkcaldy who moved from nearby Grange to Halyards. His wife was Janet Melville, a daughter of Sir James Melville of nearby Raith who introduced his son-in-law to the Court of King James V. Sir James became Treasurer of the Kingdom and never lost the trust of the King. After the battle of Solway Moss when the distraught James V was making his way through Fife to Falkland he spent a night at the Halyards. The next morning the young William Kirkcaldy accompanied the King to Falkland where he was joined by his father Sir James. Both men were at the bedside of the dying King. When Cardinal Beaton became even more powerful following the King's death, Sir James not only lost office but plotted to take the life of Beaton. The Earl of Hertford, reporting to King Henry of England on the plottings against Beaton, suggested that "the Larde of Grange, late Thesaurer of Scotland, wolde attempt either to apprehend or slee him at some time when he sholde gow through Fyfeland, and in case he colde so apprehend him wolde deliver him unto his Majesty." The plotters were neither slow in looking to Henry for support nor adverse to accepting cash from him.

Beaton had his spies also, and Kirkcaldy, and his son Sir William, were on the Cardinal's hit list, as was the laird of Raith, Sir John Melville. On the day of the Cardinal's murder Sir James Kirkcaldy was at Halyards but he and Norman Leslie were major plotters. Also, as John Knox wrote, his son, "William Kirkcaldy of Grange, younger, was in the town [of St Andrews] before, awaiting upon the purpose". As I have written above, the purpose was to murder Cardinal Beaton, and when it was under way Knox reported, "The first thing that ever was done, William Kirkcaldy took the guard of the privy postern, fearing that the fox should have escaped. Then go the rest to the gentleman's chambers, and without violence done to any man, they put more than fifty persons to the yett. The number that did this was but sixteen persons." Following the murder of Beaton, Sir James Kirkcaldy, laird of Grange, came to St Andrews Castle accompanied by his other sons and his brothers and also his Melville in-laws.

Following the fall of the Castle to the French, eight Kirkcaldys and four Melvilles were named as conspirators in a proclamation read at the Mercat Cross of Cupar. They were imprisoned or exiled in France as were Norman Leslie and other members of his family. Sir James returned to Scotland to die peacefully at Halyards about 1556. Norman Leslie died fighting in Europe but Sir William Kirkcaldy, now laird of Grange, returned to Halyards in 1557 and was to be very involved in many of the nasty intrigues surrounding Queen Mary. He had a command with Regent Moray's army against the Queen at the battle of Langside and showed excellent tactical awareness and leadership. He was rewarded with the governorship of Edinburgh Castle and he used this command when, during the years of Mary's imprisonment in England, he changed sides to hold Edinburgh Castle for the Queen.

The Regent Morton had the support of an English army which besieged the Castle. Despite Kirkcaldy's brave defence of it, Sir William Drury and his English artillery destroyed the Tower of King David II. The ruins of this great keep became part of the Half-Moon Battery which Morton had built. When the Castle fell, Kirkcaldy surrendered to the English who handed him to the Regent Morton. The vindictive Morton had Sir William tried and condemned to death on 3rd August 1573. He was hanged in the afternoon of the day sentence was passed. A realistic description has been given of these few minutes at the Mercat Cross, by St Giles Kirk, on the High Street of Edinburgh. The time was about four "the sun being in the west, about the north-west corner of the steeple, when Sir William was thrust off the ladder. As he was hanging, his face was set toward the east; but within a prettie space turned about to the west against the sun, and so remained." Another version of these deliberately dreadful and fear-inspiring events was given by Robert Lyndsay of Pitscottie,

> Upone the thrid day of august the year of god mccclxxiii yearis the laird of graunge foirsaid captane of the castell of Edinburgh with his broder James Kirkcaldy quha was tane at the blacknes as I have schawin and eftir none thay war hangit schamfullie as traittouris to the kings grace. The laird of graung himsellff was brocht furth of the abbay backwart in ane cok-cairt to the mercat croce quhair the scauffauld was and thair asked god forgivenes for his rebellioun bayth aganes god and the king and so was hangit with his broder Mr James Kirkcaldy with ane that struik the cunyie [coins] callit Cok and syn thay war heiddit and quarterit and thair heidis and quarteris set upone sindrie portis, and also the secretar was tane furth of the stipill of leith quhair he lay deid the space of fourtie dayes and was brunt and quarterit be requeist of the quein of Ingland.

Yet another report says that another goldsmith, James Mossman, was hanged that day with Sir William Kirkcaldy, the laird of Grange, and that his brother James Kirkcaldy and Cock or Cockie, the goldsmith whose first name I do not know, were hanged later in the day. The two Edinburgh goldsmiths had been busy in the Castle minting coin with the Queen's head on it. Ironically James Mossman owned what is now named "the John Knox House" in Edinburgh's High Street. A plaque to Kirkcaldy of Grange was placed on the soaring wall at the approach to the portcullis gate of Edinburgh Castle.

I do not know if Sir William followed the example of earlier professional commanders of armies in the days of chivalry, including the great Montrose, in regarding poetry as an aspect of civilised behaviour. What we do know is that one poem by him has survived and that he described it as a "rowstie" rhyme. This poem was written when Kirkcaldy was pleased with his defence of the Castle. It is an attack on his enemies, blaming them for the sad state of Scotland. They are also the enemies of the Queen to whom Kirkcaldy is newly loyal. It is also a proud proclamation of his achievements as Captain of the Castle in defending his fortress on the rock of Edinburgh. It is entitled "Ane Ballat of the Captain of the Castle" and runs to ten angry verses, in one of which he predicts that Morton's turn would come for execution, which it did in June 1581.

Though God, of his just judgment,
Thole them to be ane punishment
To her, their supreme heid,
Yet, sen they were participant
With her, and she now penitent,
Richt surely they may dreid.
As wicked scourges has been seen
Get for the scourging hire,
When sinners repents from the spleen,
The scourge cast in the fire:
Sae Morton, by fortune,
May get this same reward.
His boasting, nor posting,
I do it not regard.

Sir William Kirkcaldy of Grange was the subject of a poem by Robert Sempill entitled "Hailsome Admonition" in which the balladeer surveys Kirkcaldy's fine career, and discusses the English involvement, but ends by threatening the defector from the party of Knox and the Presbyterian ministers with Divine vengeance. First the biographical praise then the warning,

O Lamp of licht and pierless Perill of pryse!
O worthy Knicht, in martiall deidis most ding!
O worthy wicht, most valizeant, war, and wyse!
O Captaine, ay constant to the King!
O lustie Lord, that will na wayis maling!
O Barroun bauld, of Chevalry the floure!
O perfyte Prouest, but maik into this Ring!
O gudely Grange, but spot unto this houre!

. . .

Thocht at this tyme thow haif that warlyke craig,
And is in hart curagious and bald,
God will nocht mys to scurge the with a plaig
Gif in his caus thow lat thy curage cald.
As thow may se, thick scugis monyfald
Lich upon thame that proudly dois disdane.
Except the Lord be watche man of the hald,
Quha walkis the same, thair labour is in vaane.

Most ding: most worthy
but maik into this Ring!: without equal in this Kingdom!

Halyards, the greatest house of the Kirkcaldys of Grange, was to pass through several members of the Skene family to the Earls of Moray and it remained occupied by members of the Earl's family until at least the early 1740s. Sir Walter Scott believed it to be a ruin by 1793 and it may have been virtually demolished in the late 1840s when its walls were plundered for stones for dykes and other estate works. The Earl of Moray changed the name of Halyards to Camilla which, the writer of the *Statistical Account* stated, "was so called after one of the Countesses of Moray, whose name was Campbell." This has been described as absurd on the grounds that there is no record of any such Countess. Still we can think of a fair Camilla when we look from above Auchtertool to Loch Camilla (once known as Lochourisburne) and walk round from the village, past the farm where the remnants of Halyards stand, to Lochgelly.

Jenny Lee, wife of Aneurin Bevan, was as formidable a woman as any real, or fictional, Countess of Moray. Jenny was born in Lochgelly in 1904 but her family moved to Cowdenbeath where her grandmother, and later her mother, ran a small hotel. Her father, James Lee, had escaped from the pits to manage the local theatre which was owned by her great-uncle. When her mother moved out of the hotel business the family returned to Lochgelly where her father returned to the Nellie Pit. Reputedly the Dux of Beath High School, Jenny went to Edinburgh University. When she married Aneurin Bevan in 1934 she was a much more famous figure than he. After Bevan's death she resumed her own more public role and, with the support of Harold Wilson, fought hard to establish the Open University in which she, as Baroness Lee of Asheridge, life peer, took a well-earned pride.

Joe Corrie, dramatist and poet, was born in Bowhill in 1894 and worked in Fife collieries. He began writing whilst still going down the pit but his success as a contributor to *The Miner*, and an allowance from the Reform Union, encouraged him to become a full-time writer. He is best known for his plays, with *In Time of Strife* particularly successful. Few poems are worthy of the mining communities but Joe Corrie's "The Image o' God" is an exception,

> Crawlin about like a snail in the mud,
>   Covered wi clammy blae,
> ME, made after the image o' God—
>   Jings! but it's laughable, tae.
>
> Howkin awa 'neath a mountain o' stane,
>   Gaspin' for want o' air,
> The sweat makin streams doun my bare back-bane
>   And my knees aa hackit and sair.
>
> Strainin' and cursin' the hale shift throu,
>   Half-starved, half-blin, half-mad;
> And the gaffer he says, "Less dirt in that coal
>   Or ye go up the pit, my lad!"
>
> So I gie my life to the Nimmo squad
>   For eicht and fower a day;
> ME! made after the image o God—
>   Jings! but it's laughable, tae.

clammy blae: blue mud   howkin: diggin   hauckit: hacked
hale: whole   gaffer: foreman   the Nimmo squad:

The poet Hugh MacDiarmid was an honorary member of Bowhill People's Burns Club and he came regularly to its Burns Suppers. W.R. Aitken, the scholarly editor of MacDiarmid's *Complete Poems*, and also of the poetry of William Soutar, was a son of the manse in Cowdenbeath and attended Dunfermline High School before going on to Edinburgh University. Following a very successful career as a librarian, Dr Aitken taught librarianship at Strathclyde University. His wife, Betsy, is the daughter and grand-daughter of Fife policemen and her brother, Robert Murison, born in Star in 1919, and who died in 1998, became Chief Constable of Fife and also a Deputy Lord Lieutenant of the county.

11

Kinghorn, Burntisland, Aberdour, Dalgety and St David's Bays, Inverkeithing, Rosyth, Limekilns, Charlestown, Torryburn & Culross

THE PEACE of Kinghorn was disturbed on 6th August 1332 by the landing of an invading army that aimed to put Edward Balliol, son of King John, on the throne occupied by the young son of King Robert, the Bruce, David II. Victory came to this expeditionary force at Dupplin, near Perth, and at Scone, on 24th September, the Earl of Fife took his traditional role of enthroning the new King, although few now remember Edward Balliol even as a Pretender to the Scottish Crown. This continuing civil war between the Balliols and the Bruces can be said to have had its beginning on the stormy dark night of 19th March 1286 when King Alexander III fell to his death whilst riding near Kinghorn. On the road between Burntisland and Kinghorn a Celtic Cross marks the spot where the King fell over the cliffs. At the side of the Cross there is a small layby and a seat from which there is a view down to the simple curve of the repaired Pettycur Harbour, to Inchkeith and over to Granton and Edinburgh.

This fatal accident to Alexander III ended what came to be seen as a golden age of peace and prosperity before the lack of an unchallenged heir to the Scottish throne led to the wars of independence. What has been seen as amongst the earliest surviving lines of worthy Scottish poetry are a lament for both the King and his Scotland,

> Quhen Alexander our kynge was dede,
> That Scotlande lede in lauche and le,
> Away wes sons of ale and breid,
> Off wyne and wax, of gamin and glee.
> Our golde was changit in to lede.
> The fruit failyeit on everilk tree.
> Christ succoure Scotlande, and remede,
> That is stad in perplexitie.

lauche: law   le: peace   sons: abundance, plenty   gamin: amusement   remede: remedy

We owe the survival of these lines of poetry to Andrew of Wyntoun who quoted them in his *Original Chronicle of Scotland*, but they are also used by John Barbour in his epic *Bruce*, when he introduced the contenders for the crown,

> Quhen Alexander the king wes deid,
> That Scotland haid to steyr and leid,
> The land sex yer, and mayr perfay,
> Lay desolat eftyr hys day;
> Till that the barnage at the last
> Assemblyt thaim, and fayndyt fast
> To cheys a king thar land to ster,
> That off auncestry cummyn wer

Off kingis, that aucht that reawte,
And mayst had rycht thair king to be.
Bot envy, that is sa feloune,
Amang thaim maid discencioun.
For sum wald haiff the Balleoll king;

        part thocht hale,
That the lord off Anandyrdale,
Robert the Brwys, Erle off Carryk,
Aucht to succeid to the kynryk.
The barounys thus war at discord,
That on na maner mycht accord;

barnage: assembly of barons   fayndyt: attempted   cheys: choose   aucht: possessed
reawte: royal blood   Anandyrdale: Annandale   aucht: ought   kynryk: kingdom

These famous words on King Alexander are also used by James Graham (Marquis of Montrose) in his poem "To His Mistress",

My dear and only Love, I pray
  This noble World of thee,
Be govern'd by no other Sway
  But purest Monarchie.
For if Confusion have a Part,
  Which vertuous Souls abhore,
And hold a Synod in thy Heart,
  I'll never love thee more.

Like *Alexander* I will reign,
  And I will reign alone,
My Thoughts shall evermore disdain
  A Rival on my Throne.
He either fears his Fate too much,
  Or his Deserts are small,
That puts it not unto the Touch,
  To win or lose it all.

The Scottish courtly tradition in verse, produced by soldier-courtiers, died on a dark May day at Edinburgh Cross when the cavalier Montrose "swung there in three fathoms of rope." The tradition of the village rhymster may lack the dignity of court poetry, and more often than not it drops into couthy doggerel, but it can be more lively than highly polished stanzas that lack enough life to dance to any tune. Also, the tradition of balladeers, such as Robert Sempill of Beltrees who gave us "The Life and Death of the Piper of Kilbarchan" or "The Epitaph of Habbie Simson", did lead into the significant poems of Allan Ramsay and the great works of Robert Burns. Ramsay wrote an elegy on Patie Birnie, a famous Kinghorn fiddler and balladeer, which he headed with Habbie Simson lines,

The famous fiddler of Kinghorn;
  Wha gart the lieges gawff and girn ay,
Aft till the cock proclaim'd the morn.

And Ramsay begins his "An Elegy on Patie Birnie" with these verses,

> In sonnet slee the man I sing,
> His rare engine in rhyme shall ring,
> Wha slaid the stick out o'er the string
>   With sic an art,
> Wha' sang sae sweetly to the spring,
>   An rais'd the heart.
>
> Kinghorn may rue the ruefou day
> That lighted Patie to his clay,
> Wha gart the hearty billies stay,
>   And spend their cash,
> To see his snowt, to hear him play,
>   And gab sae gash.

the spring: a lively tune   gart: made, compelled
gab sae gash: talk so brightly

Patie's own most famous song is "The Auld Man's Mear's [Mare's] Dead",

> *The auld man's mear's dead;*
> *The puir body's mear's dead;*
> *The auld man's mear's dead,*
>   *A mile aboon Dundee.*
>
> There was hay to ca', and lint to lead,
> A hunner hotts o' muck to spread,
> And peats and truffs and a' to lead—
>   And yet the jaud to dee!
>
> CHORUS
> *The auld man's mear's dead,* etc.
>
> She had the fiercie and the fleuk,
> The whezloch and the wanton yeuk;
> On ilka knee she had a breuk—
>   What ail'd the beast to dee?

Rossend (or Burntisland) Castle has been through many vicissitudes and it is fortunate to have survived long enough to be excellently restored by two partnerships of architects, now The Hurd Rolland Partnership, for use as their offices. The Saltire Society and other cultural organisations also meet in the castle. The road up to the castle passes the railway line as it makes its way through a cutting made into the castle rock. A little further up is a heavy two-arched gateway; even the heavier arch is, I have learned, no older then the mid-nineteenth century and the date on the other clearly says "Rossend 1932". I have not been inside the restored castle but it must be very interesting. A side path begins alongside uncared-for back gardens and goes round behind the castle to a terrace on the edge of the rock that gives a view straight into the great shed and engineering activities of the company that builds constructions for the oil industry.

I found it difficult to envisage the geographical layout here when the young Queen Mary walked by the shore of this promontory, as monks had done before her. It is easier to envisage her indoors and dancing with gentlemen of France and Scotland. In this imagined scene, the "Four Maries" *must* be seen together and taking the floor. When the Queen, not out of her teens we have to remind ourselves, returned to Scotland from the less Calvinistic French court, with her came a young poet, Pierre de Chastelard. For the Queen he played the poet and she accepted his poems. John Knox described their relationship in the worst possible terms. It does seem that the young man did hide himself in the Queen's bedroom at Holyrood and that he repeated this folly at Rossend. Execution followed in St Andrews and Knox wrote, "Such was the reward of his dancing." Another historian of the kirk, David Calderwood, wrote succinctly, "poore Chattelat was convoyed to Sanct Andrews, putt to an assize, and beheaded, the 22d of Februar 1563." Knox, who cannot be trusted in such matters, says the man confessed his guilt, but other witnesses say he rejected a religious confessor and, head held high and quite straight-backed, climbed onto the scaffold where he read a poem on death by the great Ronsard.

> Je te salue, heureuse et profitable Mort
> Des extrêmes douleurs médecin et confort.
>
> I greet you happy and profitable Death
> The healer and comforter in extreme pain.

We are also told that, looking to the place where he thought the Queen was, his last words were, "Adieu! Most beautiful and most cruel princess of the world." Or more dramatically sorrowful, "O cruelle dame."

Early in its life Rossend Castle belonged to the monks of Dunfermline who were also at Abbotshall, Kirkcaldy. The Melvilles did not confine themselves to Monimail and Raith and they were also at Burntisland. As always with early records, sorting out ownerships and individuals within a family can be difficult. Despite a take-over bid by the always acquisitive King James V, Abbot George Durie seems to have been able to pass the castle on to his kinsman Peter Durie. Documentation shows that Queen Mary rewarded Sir Robert Melville of Murdocairney by gifting him the castle but, after his forfeiture, King James VI may have returned it to a Durie. Bouncing back into royal favour, Melville may have regained the castle and, in 1591, his son, another Sir Robert, was confirmed in the Barony of Burntisland. Another version of the history of the owners of the castle has the castle being taken, during the minority of Queen Mary, from the clerical Duries and given to Sir John Melville of Raith, the father of Sir Robert Melville, and on Melville's forfeiture going to Sir William Kirkcaldy of Grange for his services at Langside against the army of Mary, Queen of Scots. On Sir William's execution, see above, Rossend Castle was given to his kinsman by marriage, Sir Robert Melville.

In the time of Charles I Burntisland was given a defensive wall, but it was not effective in keeping Cromwell out although Dundee men were drafted in. Cromwell landed at Inverkeithing on 17th July 1651 and had no difficulty in defeating mounted troops sent to intercept him. The diarist Lamont, recorded, "1651. July 29: The towne of Brintellande did render to the English armie; the garesone ther had libertie to goe forth with flieing coullers and bage and baggage." From a letter to the Speaker of the House of Commons we can see that Cromwell seems to have been impressed by the burgh,

The greater part of the army is in Fife, waiting what God will further lead us. It hath pleased God to give us Burntisland, which is indeed very conducive to the carrying on of oure affaires. The town is well seated, pretty strong, but marvellous capable of further improvement in that respect without great charge. The harbour, at a high spring tide, is near a fathom deeper than at Leith, and doth not lye commanded by any ground within the town. We took three or four men-of-war in it, and I believe 36 or 40 guns. Commissary-General Whaley marched along the seaside in Fife, having some ships to goe along the coast, and hath taken great store of artillery and divers ships. The enemy's affaires are in some discomposure, as we hear. Surely the Lord will blow upon them.

We may smile seeing God appropriated to be "on our side", and the Christian Colonel Lilburne hardly protected the people of Burntisland from the garrison he commanded. Much of the cost of repairing the streets and harbour was paid for by taxes imposed upon the burghers. In general the conquerors made sure the work was done well and part of the sea wall became known as "Cromwell's Dyke".

As late as 1587 Burntisland was referred to as Wester Kingorne and the little church, now ruined, in the Kirkton area, as *Parva Kingorne*. This old church has a history dating back to the early thirteenth century and it may be yet another Fife church dedicated to St Serf. It may have been consecrated by Bishop David Bernham in 1243 and the document to prove it may still be in the Bibliotheque Nationale in Paris. A plaque informs that part of the ruin is the Burial Ground of Ayton of Grange and inside the ruined walls are other Ayton memorials. To create a garden environment for the ruined church would not be excessively expensive and in such a setting this ivy-covered ruined would have the power to raise thoughts on small being not only beautiful but also powerfully emotive of days that have gone. In such days long gone, the parishioners of Wester Kingorne could look over the red-tiled houses of the Kirkton to the Grange of the monks and that is not something that can be restored.

The newer, and very interesting, Parish Church, St Columba's, is a four-square building, dating from the early 1590s. Approaching Burntisland by road from Kinghorn the tiered tower of the Kirk catches the eye over the Links and the rooftops. Also, like Kilrenny's "St Irnie", the tower of this most distinguished building is a sea mark although I have not heard a familiar name for it. It has been suggested that the post-Reformation design was Dutch-influenced, but the current minister, Rev John C. Duncan, who has researched the history of his church, inclines to a theory that the French Huguenots, who were familiar with square pre-Reformation church buildings in Europe, may have influenced the design of St Columba's. Although not the first Scottish church to be built after the Reformation, Burntisland is the earliest still in use. If the exterior impresses by its noble, and somewhat heavy, simplicity, then the interior dazzles with surprises. Currently, in 1998, the interior of the church is being renovated and is clothed in scaffolding and protective covers. This means that it is several decades since I was inside the building but, from talking to Mr Duncan, I do not believe that my memory has indulged in over-many distortions.

Its design echoes the democratic principles of the Reformed Kirk—all equal as each man and woman stands before God. In 1992 the Parish Church celebrated its 400th anniversary and produced a full-colour booklet to mark this historic date. In it Rev James Monaghan, who was minister from 1961 to 1967, places the architectural design in its theological context, "The Reformers declared that people should meet around the Word and the Sacrament. Our Kirk was built to enable this declaration to become a spiritual experience. Entering into this Sanctuary we stand in awe. The Word is in the midst. The Pulpit with the Bible in place. The Sacrament is in the midst. . . . So we have come and what do we see? The Parish Church of Burntisland, built around the Word and the Sacrament. The sanctuary is square with four massive pillars with soaring arches joining them together, each arch proclaiming the all embracing Love of God arched around his people."

The plain glass of the windows gives the church a purity of light and an air of simplicity, but there is no lack of colour. Around one of the massive pillars is the interesting "Magistrates' Pew", originally made for Sir Robert Melville of Rossend and bearing his coat of arms and that of his wife Joanna Hamilton in the panelling behind the pew. On the canopy of the pew is the old Burntisland coat of arms and the pew was given its present name when the lands of Rossend were taken over by the Council. The other boxed pews, of important but less knightly parishioners, have also been left in place. Further brightness is given to the church by panels on the galleries which carry the old Trade Guild Signs. These early-seventeenth-century panels were rediscovered in the early 1900s and excellently restored. A painted ceiling was also hidden under coats of paint.

The church stands on a hill overlooking the sea but it is known locally as "The Kirk of the Bible", and with good cause. When Burntisland's kirk was new, King James VI was attempting to undermine the power of ministers who interpreted the doctrine of ministerial parity to mean that each and every one of them could speak as an instrument of divine truth. With Edinburgh ministers less sympathetic to him than those in country parishes, the King asserted his authority by calling Assemblies of the Kirk in Perth, Dundee and Montrose. In 1601, an Assembly was called to meet in St Andrews but the King pled illness and changed the venue to Burntisland to shorten his journey from Edinburgh. This could have been another tactic to reduce the number of his opponents who attended the Assembly. Be that as it may, the result is that the Parish Church of Burntisland can claim to be the building in which, with King James VI present, the idea for a new translation of the Bible was first floated, even if the King of Scots trooped off to London to claim his English Kingdom; the Authorised Version of 1611 was printed after the Hampton Court Conference. If James had remained in Scotland, we can be confident that this new Bible would have been written in Scots and not English, but the many "ifs" of Scottish history have been thought about over-often without further additions to them here.

The Minute that records this important event, "See. ultima, Maii 16 1601. It being meinit [mentioned] by sundrie of the Brethern that there was sundrie errors that merritit to be correctit in the vulgar version of the Bible and of the psalms in meter, in the quhilk heids the Assemblie has concludit as follows—anent the translation of the Bible, that every ane of the bretherne, wha has best knowledge of the languages, employ their trevils in syndrie parts of the vulgar translation of the Bible that needs to be mendit, and to confer the same together at the next Assemblie." The King agreed and the Assembly unanimously approved.

This part of the history of Burntisland's church is symbolised by the open Bible incorporated into the design of the new metal gates dating from 1992. The seagoing aspect of the burgh and parish is symbolised by the anchor design which is given religious significance by pointing towards heaven. The design is by the Hurd Rolland Partnership who, with Kirkcaldy District Council, donated the gates to mark the four-hundredth anniversary.

A path follows the high kirkyard wall to a terrace, above the railway line and the docks, that gives not only a view over to Edinburgh but upriver to the two bridges at Queensferry. Leaving the Parish Church and going down Kirkgate we come to Somerville Street and Somerville Square. The latter has, on one side, a line of very interesting buildings that date from the seventeenth century. The carving of the lettering on one panel is most impressive and the words they form can also please, BLISST BE GOD FOR ALL HIS VAGES. The Square has a house significant beyond its architecture; what is in 1998 numbered 31 and 30 was the home of Mary Somerville (1780-1872) where she lived with her father, Vice-Admiral Sir William Fairfax. Her importance as an educationalist led to the re-naming of these two streets and to the naming of Somerville College, Oxford, in her honour.

I have referred to the importance of Burntisland as a ferry port and in the history of the railways in Fife but that is now old history, as is the Burntisland Shipbuilding Company which went into voluntary liquidation in the 1960s. I could, however, see construction work for the oil industry going on at the huge sheds below Rossend Castle and the aluminum works can be seen to be active from passing trains and, indeed, its American owners, Alcan, were building extensions to the works when I was there in 1998. There is still a railway station at Burntisland and the station building is an imposing surprise with Corinthian colonnade. It was designed by Grainger & Millar in 1847, as were the buildings at Cupar and Markinch stations.

The castle of Aberdour forms another backdrop to the railway line. The large ruined tower house dates from the fourteenth century and has, together with the complicated later buildings and garden, been well restored. Aberdour Castle passed to Robert the Bruce's great lieutenant, Thomas Randolph, and later to Douglases and the Earls of Morton who were at Aberdour into the eighteenth century. In the twelfth century an earlier Aberdour fortress may have been in the hands of Mortimers and, all these centuries later, a stretch of water between the coast and Inchcolm, with its ruined abbey, is Mortimer's Deep.

When the Abbey was still active, if the wind was in the right direction the people of Aberdour could hear the monastery bell and the chanting of the monks. Although I have not heard any chanting, a similar bell can still be heard daily at Dysart House which is now owned by Carmelite nuns. A traditional story relates how a daughter of a Mortimer was "awa wi the fairies" and restored to sanity by the Abbot of Inchcolm. The subject of James Hogg's "Kilmeny", which is the thirteenth bard's song from *The Queen's Wake,* is usually seen as telling the story of another woman taken by the fairies, but Douglas S. Mack, editor of Hogg, has suggested that "Kilmeny" is a religious poem dealing with heaven, not fairyland. Certainly it is a beautiful vision she has in this section of the poem which, if we count the small rocks off the coast, including those seen at low tide, and perhaps add a lake or two, could *almost* be a description of Fife, green and peaceful and enhanced by the blue Firth under a clear sky,

> She saw a sun on a summer sky,
> And clouds of amber sailing bye:
> A lovely land beneath her lay,
> And that land had glens and mountains gray;
> And that land had vallies and hoary piles,
> And marled seas, and a thousand isles;
> Its fields were speckled, its forests green,
> And its lakes were all of the dazzling sheen,
> Like magic mirrors, where slumbering lay

The sun and the sky and the cloudlet gray;
Which heaved and trembled and gently swung,
On every shore they seemed to be hung;
For there they were seen on their downward plain
A thousand times and a thousand again;
In winding lake and placid firth,
Like peaceful heavens in the bosom of earth.

Walter Bower, who became Abbot of Inchcolm in 1418, is important as a Scottish historian who extended the work of John of Fordun to cover the period 1383 to 1437. This work is known today as the *Scotichronicon*. Fordun relates how Alexander I was caught in a storm whilst crossing by the Queen's Ferry and, as the boat was being driven towards Inchcolm, vowed—like the later King David II who founded the church at St Monans—to St Columba that if he survived he would establish a place of refuge on the island. So it was that he established an Augustinian Monastery. The Monastery prospered under other monarchs and by 1178 it owned much land and the churches of Aberdour, Dalgety, Rosyth and Auchtertool. Boats sail from South Queensferry to Inchcolm where the remains of the twelfth-century Abbey are more extensive than might be thought and to be able to walk in Scottish cloisters, with enclosed walkways, is a rare pleasure. This is also a bird haven and, during the nesting season, some of the large seabirds on this isle of the peaceful St Columba can be frighteningly fierce. Seals are common enough in the Forth and they can be seen to good advantage when sailing to Inchcolm. From the shore I can regularly count over a dozen seals on rocks off Kirkcaldy's Ravenscraig Park.

In Aberdour, Hawkcraig Road is signposted as the way to the Silver Sands but it also goes to the Kirk Wynd of St Fillan's Church. This small kirk is as perfect as any in Scotland. It is protected on two sides by the high garden wall of Aberdour Castle and by the gates of the kirk a doorway gives a view of the lawn and sundial of the Castle gardens. Above the doorway is the date 1632 and the monogram of William, Earl of Morton, and his wife Lady Anne. Kirk Wynd is a delight, with a buttress that supports the garden wall forming a low arch that I incline my head under although it is a few inches over six feet in height. As the curving wynd approaches the kirkyard it is lined by twelve interesting headstones—eleven seem to be of the eighteenth century and one is certainly of the nineteenth. These were moved from within the ruined and roofless church when it was restored in 1926.

The church dates from at least 1123, and perhaps fifty years earlier, with the nave and chancel built about 1140. No-one knows for sure which St Fillan the church is dedicated to, but it could be the Abbot of the monastery in Glen Dochart and possibly the Saint linked to Pittenweem. The south light of the west window shows the Abbot of Glen Dochart with his crozier and bell which are now in the Scottish National Museum. The other, north, light shows a pilgrim making his way to the well which was believed to have the power to cure eye disorders. Inside the church the west wall rises high above the congregation but the church sits below ground level and on the outside the window is close to the ground. Between the window and the ground a panel bears what is now a worn, but mostly readable, inscription,

PANS [THINK] O PILGRIM THAT PASSITH BY THIS WAY UPON THYN END AND THOU SAL
FEAR TO SIN AND THINK ALSO UPON THE LATTER DAY WHEN THOU TO GOD MAN [MAUN
OR MUST] COONT THEN BEST THOU NOO BEGIN

130

The panel may have stood on the pilgrims' way to the Holy Well from a hospice that had been built, about 1475, to care for the pilgrims. The well was, or is, south-east of the church. Above the west wall is an interesting belfry with a pyramid roof dating from 1588. The original bell has gone but has been replaced by that of St Bridget's Church at nearby Dalgety; it is pre-Reformation and bears the inscription, "O mater Dei, memento mei [O mother of God, remember me]".

On the north wall of the church is a stained-glass window showing a Celtic missionary preaching to a gathering of local people with a background landscape that shows the Forth, Inchcolm and the Pentland Hills. The southerly view from the kirk door is directly to Edinburgh and, in a good light, the skyline of the Royal Mile with its many spires is clearly visible in great detail across the open stretch of water. Below the kirkyard wall is a superbly restored beehive doocot. There is another beehive doocot at Ravenscraig Castle but although many doocots have survived in Fife, few of them are beehive. If less visually interesting, the more common "lectern" ones do have an evocative name. Down at Hawkcraig Point there is a good view of the Inchcolm Abbey buildings but an even better one is from one of the many seats just beyond Aberdour Harbour. Also, the footpath from the Point to the Harbour is worth taking for its sheltered seats and varied views over the harbour and the Forth.

Either side of the Gothic west window of St Fillan's are organ pipes which occupy the space where, in the seventeenth century, Lord Morton had built a gallery for his family. In the eighteenth century another Earl of Morton enclosed the space below his loft to form a burial vault for his family. When the church was restored in 1926 the vault was cleared and the Mortons buried underground. Today their coffin plates are fixed to the wall underneath the west window and below the Leper Squint. Local tradition accepted not only that King Robert I, the Bruce, was a leper, but that after Bannockburn he came to Aberdour to give thanks for the great victory. Being a leper he did so through the Leper Squint in the west gable. The coffin plates of the Mortons are reminders of Scotland's violent history. The ruthless and greedy James Douglas, fourth Earl of Morton, was involved in the murder of Riccio, favourite of Mary Queen of Scots. The Earl was Regent during the early years of the reign of James and very powerful from 1572 to 1578. In December 1580 he was accused of involvement in the murder of Queen Mary's husband, Darnley. Execution followed in June 1581 by a "kiss" of the "Maiden", a crude kind of guillotine which he had introduced into Scotland. This now seems particularly evil within these old church walls where the subdued light encourages an awareness of these peaceful and harmonious understandings that Wordsworth wrote of above Tintern Abbey, "A presence that disturbs me with the joy/of elevated thoughts; a sense sublime/Of something far more deeply interfused . . .".

When the church was restored in 1926 by William Willamson, architect of Kirkcaldy and Kinghorn, the stained-glass windows in the chancel were made by Alexander Strachan, who helped to establish the stained-glass studio in Edinburgh College of Art. The west window on the south wall of the chancel is dedicated to the memory of Rev Robert Blair. Outside on the south wall of the kirk there is a memorial to Mr Blair erected by his sons some six years after their father had been buried in the kirkyard. The first words of the inscription, which are set either side of skull and crossbones, are "Mors Janua Vitæ" or "Death the Gate of Life", and the Latin inscription can be translated as, "Here lie the mortal remains of the Rev Robert Blair, a most faithful preacher of the Gospel at St

Andrews. Died Aug. 27, 1666 aged 72". The lettering remains readable but is showing signs of wear with the lower part of the border almost gone, as is the detailing on the skull.

Rev. Robert Blair was Professor of Moral Philosophy at Glasgow, chaplain to King Charles I and a famous churchman. Whilst a minister in St Andrews, Mr Blair, who had Covenanting beliefs, was expelled from St Andrews by Archbishop Sharp, which may explain the six-year delay in having his memorial erected. So it was that, for a few months only, Blair lived with friends at Couston Castle in the Parish of Aberdour. The castle, or house, faces Otterston Loch, near Otterston Castle which also decayed into a ruin, but Couston was restored in the 1980s by Ian Begg who has also done much good work in Edinburgh's Old Town. His firm's motto is "Ilkane at seeks finnds". Recently Ian Begg has collected for publication *The Drawings of Sydney Goodsir Smith: Poet.*

Rev Blair of Aberdour was the grandfather of Robert Blair who wrote one of the most morbid long poems ever penned. It is *The Grave*—published in 1743 and comprising 767 lines of blank verse on not only death but its effects on the bereaved. Some people do not find graveyards restful places—or perhaps they remind them of over-restful times to come. But, not unjustly, this son of the manse has been described as "the father of graveyard poetry." *The Grave* has the distinction of having been illustrated by William Blake. Blair, the poet, followed his grandfather and father into the ministry and from 1731 to his death in 1746 was at Athelstaneford in East Lothian. He was succeeded there by the dramatist John Home who was forced to resign following the kirk objecting to his play *Douglas.* To round up these biographical links to the tablet in Aberdour, the great-grandson of the man remembered by it became Lord President of the Court of Session.

Although extracts from *The Grave* are not printed in many modern anthologies of Scottish poetry, Robert Blair has featured surprisingly largely in some anthologies of English poetry; presumably because of a certain ghoulish power. These lines seem apt in relation to Blair's work but not to St Fillan's of Aberdour,

> See yonder hallowed fane, the pious work
> Of names once famed, now dubious or forgot,
> And buried midst the wreck of things which were:
> There lie interred the more illustrious dead.
> The wind is up: hark how it howls! Methinks
> Till now I never heard a sound so dreary,
> Doors creak, and windows clap, and night's foul bird,
> Rooked in the spire, screams loud. The gloomy aisles,
> Black-plaistered, and hung round with shreds of 'scutcheons
> And tattered coats of arms, send back the sound,
> Laden with heavier airs, from the low vaults,
> The mansions of the dead. Roused from their slumbers,
> In grim array the grisly spectres rise,
> Grin horribly, and obstinately sullen
> Pass and repass, hushed as the foot of night.
> Again the screech of owl shrieks—ungracious sound.
> I'll hear no more; it makes one's blood run chill.
> Quite round the pile, a row of reverend elms,
> Co-eval near with that, all ragged show,
> Long lashed by the rude winds; some rift half down
> Their branchless trunks, others so thin atop
> That scarce two crows could lodge in the same tree.

Strange things, the neighbours say, have happened here.
Wild shrieks have issued from the hollow tombs;
Dead men have come again, and walked about;
And the great bell has tolled unrung, untouched.
Such tales their cheer, at wake or gossiping,
When it draws near to witching time of night.

A 1626 Bible that had belonged to a grandson of the Bonnie Earl of Moray was given to St Fillan's Church by the Earl of Moray. The estates of the Moray family at Dalgety Bay were sold in the 1960s for the creation of what is a new town of private homes. This now stretches along the coast to St David's Bay. The opening of the Forth Road Bridge had made commuting to Edinburgh much easier. Whilst so much has changed around Dalgety, St David's and Donibristle, the once almost abandoned kirk of St Bridget still stands on a site that has an ecclesiastical history that goes back to at least 1178. This is one of the less obvious treasures of Fife. Many people know vaguely of it but it remains almost a secret place. It is now cared for by Historic Scotland on behalf of the Secretary of State for Scotland—for the people of Scotland. Although the western end of Inchcolm island can be seen from St Bridget's, the Abbey is out of sight behind Braefoot Point. At one time this mainland church must have belonged to the Abbey. This is another church consecrated by Bishop David Bernham; the date is 1244. The consecration of Burntisland's Parva Kingorne is dated 1243. The very wide and well-proportioned stairs on the east gable of the kirk may look odd, but they were added, after the Reformation, in the late-seventeenth century, to give access to a new gallery at the end of the nave. Another new gallery at the west end was entered through the interesting laird's loft.

This loft at the west end of the simple rectangle of the original thirteenth-century church was probably built about 1610 for Alexander Seton, Earl of Dunfermline. The loft is part of a larger building that includes a ground-level burial vault, stairtower with ten steps, and, beyond the loft with its large window into the church, a drawing, or retiring, room. This small drawing room has a fireplace. There are three windows, with the central one opposite the fireplace looking to the Pentland Hills across the Forth with Arthur's Seat just in view. Below the water laps gently in the bay. On one of the stones of the small drawing room someone has, in recent years, made fine-line carvings that may be attempts to imitate prehistoric symbols such as those in the Wemyss caves. The Dunfermline loft, or aisle, is a spacious area with two windows looking west and two sharing the view of the drawing room across the water. The floor of the body of the church is some twelve feet below the aisle. High overhead a bellcote tops the west gable; a most emotive survival from, probably, the eighteenth century. Southwards, the open and unusually bright churchyard extends to a wall with a drop to a path which in turn is supported by a wall some ten feet above the sandy, rocky and seaweed-strewn bay.

At ground level on the northern wall, beside the heavy, but open, wooden door of the stairtower, a similar door is locked to prevent entry to the burial vaults of the Earls of Dunfermline. Eastwards along that north wall are two other aisles; the ruined Fordell Aisle which was probably built in the early seventeenth century; as was the slab-roofed Inglis Aisle which was built by William Inglis of Otterston.

Inside the church there is a memorial to Janet Inglis, the Latin inscription of which has been very well cut in formal Roman capitals; also, the date, 1681, is cut in superb Arabic figures. On the outside of the west wall of the Dunfermline Aisle is another interesting monument dated 1685 and, the records show, to Robert Meikle. This large monument must be twelve feet tall with three angel's heads at the top of a curved pediment with two skulls at both bottom edges; the centre section carries the date 1685, with a garland enclosing a crest, and topped by an hourglass. Below this are two columns supporting a decorative frieze bearing flower heads. The central section lacks its inscribed panel and is open to the stone wall of the Aisle. The solid base carries a skull and cross bones.

There is a table stone dated 1665 of John Moubray of Cockairnie and, on the south wall of the kirk, there are plainer nineteenth-century memorials to the Moubray family of Otterston and Cockairnie. On the day I visited St Bridget's Church in February 1998 a great-great-grandson of Sir Robert Moubray, whose name appears on the memorial of his daughter who died in 1885, had come from Kent with his family to see the memorials of his ancestors. I learned from him that the Moubrays once had a monopoly on the ferry at South Queensferry. Otterston Castle has been demolished but Cockairnie House stands near Otterston Loch. Coming off the A921 St Bridget's is well signposted; a locked gate enforces a pedestrian approach to the church which can also be reached on the Fife Coastal Path.

Although an old family, the Setons only came into very grand titles through becoming important as administrators for the Crown. The fifth Lord Seton, Alexander Seton, became Chancellor of the Realm in 1605, became Lord Fyvie and died in 1622 at Pinkie, one of his three grand houses, as the Earl of Dunfermline. His sister Mary was one of the Queen's four Maries. The body of the first Earl of Dunfermline was brought to the vaults at St Bridget's. At the interment Archbishop Spottiswoode addressed what has been described as the "most distinguished gathering of nobles of Scotland ever held within a remote country church." Two more Earls were buried at Dalgety Bay but the fourth, and last, fought on the wrong side at Killiecrankie and ended his days, like the deposed King, at St Germain where he died. The Setons had lost an earldom; the Stewarts a crown.

The mansion of the Earls of Dunfermline at Dalgety Bay passed from the Setons to the Earl of Moray who already owned the less extensive Donibristle estate. The old house of Dalgety fell into ruin and Donibristle House was to be burned three times; the house that stands today has been converted into luxury flats. It was behind a green point east of St David's Bay, below Donibristle Castle, that James Stewart of Doune, the bonnie Earl of Moray of ballad fame, was killed by the sixth Earl of Huntly in 1592. The ballad is not history, at least as regarded by academic historians of the age of James VI, but its verses ring down the centuries,

> Ye Highlands, and ye Lawlands,
>   Oh where have you been?
> They have slain the Earl of Moray,
>   And they laid him on the green.
>
> "Now wae be to thee, Huntly!
>   And wherefore did you sae?
> I bade you bring him wi you,
>   But forbade you him to slay."
>
> He was a braw gallant,
>   And he rid at the ring;
> And the bonny Earl of Moray,
>   Oh he might have been a king!

Inverkeithing is a place that always surprises me. I see it most often from a train's window or looking over from the road from Dalgety and St David's Bays but, within a few yards of the Square on the High Street, there are several old buildings that can reveal much about Scottish architecture that is neither neo-classical nor Scottish baronial. The tower of the Parish Church exclaims vigorously to us that it is a genuine fourteenth-century structure. Across the street is the seventeenth-century town house of the Hendersons of Fordell which was a model for the nineteenth-century baronialists—crowstepped gables, corbelled turret and dormers set firmly into the top of the wall. Angled out of the High Street, and behind the Mercat Cross with its interesting arms of King Robert III and the Douglas family, is Bank Street. And here is another attractive house, Thomson's, with a three-storey stairtower and interesting inscriptions. The Town House, or Tolbooth, stands at the top of the steep brae of Townhall Street and is easily identified from a distance by its attractive pepperpot belfry.

Behind the remains of the Friary is a well-laid-out garden overlooking the bay and the harbour where many great ships have spent their last months in the breakers' yard. The topmost girders of the cantilevered railway bridge can be seen, although not, I think, the towers of the road bridge. The two bridges form a natural barrier for me and I do not know Fife westwards from Rosyth as well as I do the more easterly parts. Rosyth was created in 1903 to house the workers at the new Admiralty Dockyard, and belongs to the "garden city" concept that influenced the design of Welwyn Garden City and the new towns, including Glenrothes.

Charlestown is another variety of "model village" created by Charles, fifth Earl of Elgin, with the street plan shaping the initial letter of his name. This is an "estate" village of 1770 and these particular estate workers were not of the land but employed in the extraction of coal and limestone and in the very large limeworks which did not become economically unviable until the 1930s. Nearby Limekilns gave employment not only to those working in the limeworks but also in a surprisingly wide range of industries, including brewing and ropemaking. The Earl lived (and lives) at nearby Broomhall, a neo-classical mansion fashioned in the 1790s around an earlier building. The villages of Low and High Valleyfield and Low Torry housed hard-labouring mining communities. At Torryburn we can think of a delicate writer with a fondness for a velvet coat but who, in his own situation, also suffered physically and mentally.

Torryburn is the birthplace of Robert Louis Stevenson's childhood nurse, Alison Cunningham, who was born on 15th May 1822. The delicate child was eighteen months old when "Cummy", as the child was to call her, arrived in the Stevensons' home. When Stevenson published his *A Child's Garden of Verses* in 1885 he dedicated the book, "To Alison Cunningham. From her boy",

> For the long nights you lay awake
> And watched for my unworthy sake:
> For your most comfortable hand
> That led me through the uneven land:
> For all the story books you read:
> For all the pains you comforted:

Alison Cunningham told her charge the stories of the Old Testament and of Scottish covenanting history. For an imaginative child some of these may have been rather too vivid. In "Nuits Blanches" Stevenson wrote, "If anyone should know the pleasure and pain of a sleepless night, it should be I. I remember, so long ago, the sickly child that woke from his few hours' slumber with the sweat of the nightmare on his brow, to lie awake and listen and long for the first signs of life among the silent streets." And in an autobiographical piece Stevenson refers to some kind of hell that Alison Cunningham, good Calvinist that she was, had made him aware of,

> I had an extreme terror of Hell, implanted in me, I suppose, by my good nurse, which used to haunt me terribly on stormy nights, when the wind had broken loose and was going about the town like a bedlamite. I remember that the noises on such occasions always grouped themselves for me into the sound of a horseman, or rather a succession of horsemen, riding furiously past the bottom of the street and away up the hill into town: I think even now that I hear the terrible *howl* of his passage, and the clinking that I used to attribute to his bit and stirrups. On such nights I would lie awake and pray and cry, until I prayed and cried myself to sleep.

In a letter to Mrs Sitwell, from Swanston, in the autumn of 1874 Stevenson wrote,

> Last night it blew a fearful gale; I was kept awake about a couple of hours, and could not get to sleep for the horror of the wind's noise; the whole house shook; and, mind you, our house *is* a house, a great castle of jointed stone that would weigh up a street of English houses; so when it quakes, as it did last night, it means something. But the quaking was not what put me about; it was the horrible howl of the wind round the corner; the audible haunting of an incarnate anger about the house; the evil spirit that was abroad; and, above all, the shuddering silent pauses when the storm's heart stands dreadfully still for a moment. O how I hate a storm at night! They have been a great influence in my life, I am sure; for I can remember them so far back—long before I was six at least . . . And in these days the storm had for me a perfect impersonation, as durable and unvarying as any heathen deity. I always heard it as a horseman riding past with his cloak about his head, and somehow always carried away, and riding past again, and being baffled yet once more, *ad infinitum*, all night long.

These memories were used by Stevenson in "Stormy Nights", printed in *Poems 1869-1879*, but that is a prosey poem when set against the direct scariness that comes through in the fine poem, "Windy Nights", printed as the ninth poem of *A Child's Garden of Verses*,

> Whenever the moon and the stars are set,
>   Whenever the wind is high,
> All night long in the dark and wet,
>   A man goes riding by.
> Late in the night when the fires are out,
> Why does he gallop and gallop about?
>
> Whenever the trees are crying aloud,
>   And the ships are tossed at sea,
> By, on the highway, low and loud,
>   By at a gallop goes he.
> By at the gallop he goes, and then
> By he comes back at the gallop again.

Often today the mining communities of Fife await new opportunities. The uniqueness of Culross, pronounced Coorus, is in part due to so few opportunities coming to its inhabitants in the late-nineteenth century. I was in Culross on 1st August 1992 when the people celebrated 400 years of their village being a Royal Burgh. The heavy rain showers encouraged visits to historic buildings including the Town House, or Tolbooth, although the Palace was not then fully restored and was closed to the public. At a later date I visited this most interesting building which was built between 1597 and 1611 as the mansion of George Bruce (to become Sir George). It is a curious puzzle of a house and so a very interesting building. The complex structure apart, I remember the paintwork of the timber-lined walls, ceilings and beams.

In many ways the most enjoyable aspect of a visit to Culross is merely walking through the narrow streets. We can believe that we are in the late-seventeenth century. The earlier datestones came, probably without exception, from older buildings. We can take the "croun o the caussie" where superior burghers walked to avoid the draining water and mud of the lower parts of the narrow road. The base of the Mercat Cross is late sixteenth-century but the shaft and head are not that old. Uphill is the Abbey which has a history going back to 1217 when Malcolm, Earl of Fife, founded a Cistercian abbey. Many walls have been built here since then, and some have gone, but enough survived to become, in 1633, part of the Parish church which was restored in the early years of this century.

As I have said, Culross was far from prosperous during the late-nineteenth century but the industrial history of the royal burgh includes not only the mining of coal and the exporting of salt, but also 150 years of very profitable girdle making. The coming of the Carron Iron Works to Falkirk finished off the Culross hammermen. As a memorial verse lamented,

> My sledge and hammer lie declined
> My bellows too have lost their wind
> My fires extincted, my forge decayed
> My shovel in the dust is layed
> My coal is spent, my iron gone,
> My nails are drove, work is done
> My fire-dried corpse lies here at rest
> My sole, smokelike, soars to the blest.

Not all the old occupations left Culross in the eighteenth century. At the 400th Anniversary celebrations I met a horseman who was displaying a Clydesdale. Over eighty years old, he told me, half-joking, that he had been born in a stable and spent all his days in one. Having learnt as a boy the language of those who worked with heavy horses, I was pleased to hear again of breedles, bits, bellybaunds, nosebaunds and martingales; of brechams and rigwiddies and haims and traces. Very good use of Scots, first learned in the Culross area, can be seen in translations made by Bill Findlay, in collaboration with Martin Bowman, of plays by the Quebec playwright Michel Tremblay.

I like also to think of the many boats that sailed out of Culross. Indeed I indulge my imagination by picturing my wife's great-great-grandfather, Captain Joseph Murray, sitting in his old age, with his Norwegian wife, Christina, looking out over the Forth as he re-lived voyages out of this once important port.

Dunfermline,
Loch Leven, Leslie, Falkland
and Freuchie

DONALD BAN, brother of Malcolm III, Canmore, was the last Scottish King to be buried on Iona and from 1107 Dunfermline was the favoured burial place of the Kings of Scots. A list might include: Malcolm III, Canmore, and his Queen Margaret; their sons Edgar, Alexander I with his Queen, and David I with two Queens; Malcolm IV; Alexander III with his first wife Margaret, and their sons David and Alexander; Robert I, the Bruce, with his Queen Elizabeth and their daughter Matilda; and Annabella Drummond, wife of Robert III and mother of James I and the Duke of Rothesay who was possibly murdered in Falkland Palace. Rothesay was buried at Lindores Abbey.

For hundreds of years Dunfermline was one of the principal "capitals" of Scotland. Kings were born there: David II in 1323 and James I in 1394. Charles I was born in Dunfermline, as was his sister Elizabeth, second child of James VI whose Hanoverian descendants came to the throne of the United Kingdoms.

Dunfermline is also known for its associations with Queen and Saint Margaret who was the second wife of King Malcolm III. The Princess Margaret was a royal "Saxon" refugee who fled northwards following the victory of the Normans. The royal wedding took place about 1070 in Dunfermline in a small Celtic church which stood some 200 yards east of the royal wooden fortified tower in what is today Pittencrieff Park. The Queen soon replaced the church of her wedding with a building suitable for a princess of the royal house of Essex, and of the royal house of Hungary, who tended to adhere to Roman and not Celtic usage. The new church was completed by 1072 and when Margaret died in 1093 in Edinburgh Castle her body was brought back to her church in Dunfermline and buried in the nave before the High Altar.

The church of Queen Margaret was replaced by a great abbey established by her son David I in 1128 and its pillars were placed on the foundations of her church. The twelfth-century nave survives but not the choir which was completed by 1226. Three hundred years later King James I regretted his predecessor's grants to the church with his description of David as "a sair (costly) sanct for the crown". In 1249 Queen Margaret was canonised by Pope Innocent IV. A new shrine was built at the east end of the still developing abbey and on 19th June 1250, less than a year after the inauguration of the eleven-year-old Alexander III as King of Scots, her remains were carried in formal and royal ceremony to it. The bones of her less holy husband, Malcolm III, were also moved. Today the base of the walls of the saint's shrine, and the pillars that supported its roof, can be seen outside the east end of the Abbey Church, as can large blocks of well-cut stone which look as if they came from the shrine.

In 1818-19 the ruined parts of David I's great abbey were demolished and a new Parish Church was built onto the magnificent Scoto-Norman nave. When the choir of the old ruined church was being cleared the workers found what proved to be the tomb of King

Robert I, the Bruce. Such neglect is hard to envisage today but the Reformers had ruined much of the Abbey. Bruce would seem to have been not above average height. The breast-bone had been sawn through to allow the removal of his heart for its journey, with Good Sir James Douglas, to the war against the Moors in Spain. The heart was buried in Melrose. Today not only can we stand before the well-identified grave of the Bruce but we can also read his name carved in very large letters on the balustrade of the tower of the "new" Church. According to taste we may regard these letters as either vigorous or crude. In another hundred years they will have become interestingly vernacular! The Parish Church is open less often than the nave of the Abbey.

Without qualification, the nave of Dunfermline Abbey is magnificent. I like it best when not being used for a display. The roof is of timber but it is the great piers, or pillars, that make this space something very special. On a sunny day in March my eyes were drawn the full length of the Abbey to an area of startlingly pure red light on the farthest pillar. The same stained glass window threw a display of a mottled spectrum onto the next column and, almost within touching distance, a pillar was bright with direct sunlight that came in through an open door. Outside we can admire the vigorously ornate Norman stonework that surrounds that wooden door.

In a corner of the nave is the very large memorial to William Schaw (1550-1682) who, in 1583, was appointed Master of Works of King James VI's building operations. The eulogy, in Latin, on the memorial was written by Schaw's friend, Alexander Seton, Earl of Dunfermline, and Chancellor of the Kingdom, whose vault is at St Bridget's Church, Dalgety Bay. Outside in the kirkyard is a beautifully simple headstone that bears, in sharp lettering, the words, "The Burial Ground of John Miller, bookseller, 1812".

Close to the Abbey are the ruined walls of the Refectory. The fifteenth-century west window has survived to delight us with its very fine tracery. From alongside the Refectory, above Monastery Street, there is a good view of the two bridges over the Forth, with the Pentlands forming another backcloth, and the dark mass of Edinburgh Castle contrasting with the spire of St Giles and emphasising the shape and height of Arthur's Seat.

The view of the Refectory from Monastery Street is very dramatic, but the adjoining Palace is best seen from near the site of King Malcolm's Tower which is easily accessible from the Abbey side of Pittencrieff Glen. From the Abbey kirkyard a gate gives access to the garden of Abbot House. Some may prefer to approach this superbly restored building from the street. The garden must lift the spirits of even the weariest visitor. It is a herb garden in the formal style of the seventeenth century. A peacock suns itself in one of the flower beds and decorated fountains offer ideas as well as pleasing waters. Near the street entrance a plaque, with a scene in relief, informs that "Margaret, mother of William Wallace lies buried beneath a thorn tree in the grounds of Dunfermline Abbey." Below this peaceful garden lie the graves of pilgrims who came to the shrine of Saint Margaret and, deeper down, are medieval forges whose furnaces were last glowing before Bannockburn. The excellently restored Abbot House has been described as "a treasure house of Scottish history", and the displays reveal not only the hands of first-rate graphic designers but also that scholarly minds have been at work. The video is given a popular vehicle of a talking ghost but, again, the scholarship is impressive and the staff, who offer guidance, are very knowledgeable.

As with many libraries and educational ventures, we owe Dunfermline's Pittencrieff Park to the generosity of Andrew Carnegie, the great steel magnate of Pittsburg, USA, who was born in Dunfermline. He donated Pittencrieff Park to the citizens of Dunfermline in

1902 and, from the grand wrought-iron Louise Carnegie Memorial Gates, we can look along an avenue to a bronze statue of Carnegie that is enhanced by the subtle green of its patina. Pittencrieff House dates from the seventeenth century but Sir Robert Lorimer was commissioned to resconstruct it with interiors as a local history museum. In Pittencrieff we can climb above the ravine to stand on stones that can be linked to the great fortress of King Malcolm III, Canmore. These are the foundation stones of a much later tower but, as we look over the gorge of the park, see the tower of the Abbey, hear the chime of its musical clock, and envisage the great seaway of the Firth of Forth that is hidden by many trees, we can remember the old ballad, "Sir Patrick Spens" which begins,

> The king sits in Dumferline toune,
>   Drinkin the blude-reid wine:
> "O whar will I get guid sailor,
>   To sail this ship of mine?"

> Up and spak an eldern knicht,
>   Sat at the king's richt knee:
> "Sir Patrick Spens is the best sailor
>   That sails upon the sea."

This famous ballad ends with the haunting verse,

> Haf owre, haf owre to Aberdour,
>   It's fifty fadom deep
> And thair lies guid Sir Patrick Spens,
>   Wi the Scots lords at his feet.

The guid sailor is often regarded as a man who sailed out of Fife in the seventeenth century and was lost off Aberdour where he had walked the golden sands, but other versions of the ballad link him to the ship which sailed in 1281 to enable King Alexander III's daughter Margaret to marry the fourteen-year-old King Eric II of Norway.

Athough his work is less well-known to most visitors to Dunfermline than the old ballad, or Andrew Carnegie, a good case can be made for claiming Robert Henryson not only as Dunfermline's greatest poet but as the greatest of the Scottish literary tradition. We know very little of his life, but in 1462 Maister Henryson may have been teaching law in Glasgow University before settling in Dunfermline as a teacher who lived in the violent years of the reigns of James III (1460-88) and James IV (1488-1513). Henryson may have died in 1490 and he certainly missed the battle of Flodden in 1513 when James IV fatally led his army to a comprehensive defeat. Henryson's greatest long narrative poem is "The Testament of Cresseid" but I am in good company when I regard the Dunfermline poet's "Morall Fabillis" as being equally significant and more enjoyable.

Based on the fables of Aesop and very old tales of Reynard the Fox, the essential quality of the *Fabillis* is their humour, allied to profound understanding of the humanity in man. It is a poetry that does not undermine the essential animal qualities of the characters, whilst creating a tension between such qualities and those of humans. Through the homely language of "The Taill of the Uponlandis Mous and the Burges Mous", from which I have chosen an extract to represent the work of Henryson, is revealed to us a major poet's high characterisation which is rich in homely yet sophisticated humour. This is the voice of a medieval Scot writing in a language which still exists. It has tones and attitudes that ring true to our twentieth-century ears; the ring of an authentic Scots language that survives in a new form today in a Fife that has crossed many divides since the times of the great poet.

When they were lugit thus, thir sely mice,
The youngest sister into her butterie glide,
And brocht furth nuttis and peas insteid of spice;
Giff this wes gude fare, I do it on them beside. [leave for them to decide]
The burgess mous prunyit furth in pride,
And said, "Sister, is this your daily fude?"
"Why not", quod she. "Is not this meat richt gude?"

"Na, by my saul , I think it but ane scorn."
"Madame," quod she, "ye be the mair to blame.
My mother said, sister, when we were born,
That I and ye lay baith within ane wame;
I keep the ryte and custom of my dame,
And of my syre, levand in povertie,
For landis have we nane in propertie."

"My fair sister," quod she, "have me excusit;
This rude diet and I can not accord.
To tender meat my stoomak is ay usit,
For whlis I fare alsweill as ony lord.
Thir witherit peas and nuttis, or they be bord,
Will brek my teeth, and mak my wame full sklender,
Whilk usit wes before to meatis tender."

"Weil, weil, sister, quod the rural mous,
"Give it you please, sic thing as ye see here,
Baith meit and drink, harberie and house,
Sall be your awin, will ye remain all year.
Ye sall it have with blyth and hartlie cheer,
And that suld mak the maissis that are rude,
Amang freindis, richt tender, sweet and gude.

"What plesure is in the feastis delicate,
The whilks are given with a gloumand brou?
Ane gentill hart is better recreate
With blythe visage, than seethe to him ane cou.
Ane modicum is mair for til allow,
Sae that gude will be carver at the dais,
Than thrawin vult and mony spicit mais."

For all this merry exhortatioun
This burgess mous had littil will to sing,
But heavilie sho kest her browis doun
For all the dainties that she culd her bring.
Yet at last sho said, half in hething,
"Sister, this victual and your royal feast
May weill suffice for sic ane rural beast.

"Let be this hole and cum unto my place;
I sall you shaw be true experience,
My Gude Friday is better than nor your Pace;
My dish lickings is worth your hail expense.
I have housis aneuch of great defence;
Of cat, na fall trap I have na dreid."
"I grant," quod she; and on togither they yeid.

lugit: lodged   sely: harmless   prunyit, preened
wame: womb   Pase: Easter feast   aneuch: enough   yeid: went

There I leave the two sisters as they set out to the home of the town mouse, but the moral of this tale you may well guess.

We do not know for certain where Henryson died or, as some believe, that he is of the family that owned the estate of Fordell on which, east of Dunfermline and north of Dalgety Bay, was built the castle of that name. In the time of the great poet it was a James Henryson, Lord Justice Clerk, who lived at Fordell. He died, with his eldest son, on Flodden field. Fordell Castle is sixteenth century and, like the Hendersons' town house in Inverkeithing, exposes the heavy excesses of the Scottish baronial architects who took such buildings as their models.

The reputation of Fifers for being somewhat different from other folks has been dissipated somewhat since the bridges made the county more accessible to commuters from Edinburgh and also by the making of the new town of Glenrothes. Not that there is much wrong with some distinction of language, customs and views of the world. It is not clear to me if James Hogg's village of Balmaquapple is in Fife although the singer calls on "St Andrews, the god o' the Fife fo'ks" to save this great and wicked, and certainly most characterful, place which his imagination has created,

There's Cappie the cobbler, an' Tammie the tinman,
An' Dickie the brewer, an' Peter the skinman,
An' Geordie our deacon, for want of a better,
An' Bess, wha delights in the sins that beset her.
O, worthy St Andrew, we canna compel ye.
But ye ken as weel as a body can tell ye,
If these gang to heaven, we'll a' be sae shockit,
Your garret o' blue will but thinly be stockit.

Hogg's *The Queen's Wake* is set in the narrative context of a festival of poetry held in honour of Mary, Queen of Scots, and the Eighth Bard's poem, "The Witch of Fife" is set near Loch Leven. The bard is described by the narrator as he approaches to sing,

Mounted the bard of Fife on high,
Bushy his beard, and wild his eye:
His cheek was furrowed by the gale,
And his thin locks were long and pale.
Full hardy passed he through the throng,
Dragging on crutches, slow along,
His feeble and unhealthy frame,
And kindness welcomed as he came.

142

The poet of Loch Levenside is Michael Bruce who was born in Kinnesswood in 1746 and died too soon aged 21. In the 1950s I cycled down the steep, rough road that then went through Bruce's birthplace and it has remained in my memory as narrower and more rustic than in fact it was even then. The inn at Kinnesswood lingers in my memory as being rich in fishing lore. Bruce's cottage is now a museum. His most famous poem is "To the Cuckoo" which was stolen by the dead poet's friend John Logan but there is now no doubt that Bruce wrote this sad lyric which some Victorians regarded as the finest in the English language. It begins,

> Hail, beauteous stranger of the grove,
> Thou messenger of Spring.
> Now heaven repairs thy rural seat,
> And woods thy welcome sing.
>
> What time the daisy decks the green,
> Thy certain voice we hear.
> Hast thou a star to guide thy path,
> Or mark the rolling year?
>
> Delightful visitant, with thee
> I hail the time of flowers;
> And hear the sound of music sweet
> From birds among the bowers.
>
> The schoolboy, wandering through the wood,
> To pull the primrose gay,
> Starts the new voice of Spring to hear,
> And imitates thy lay.

Today the A911 road goes from Kinnesswood and Scotlandwell to Leslie and the new town of Glenrothes. The old burgh of Leslie, which has not yet been fully merged into Glenrothes, was known as Fettykil before the Leslie family became the local lairds, Earls of Rothes and famous for their involvement in the murder of Cardinal Beaton. Norman Leslie, leader of the murderers, was to die in Europe. His kinsmen Alexander Leslie, the Earl of Leven, and Sir David Leslie, Lord Newark, could be said to have added to the glories of the house of Leslie. Leslie House was built for John Leslie, Duke of Rothes and Chancellor of Scotland from 1667 to 1674. Additional titles of the Duke show other local names: John Leslie, Duke of Rothes, Marquis of Bambreich, Earl of Leslie and Lord Auchmuty. Mills at Tullis Russell, papermakers, are Auchmuty and Rothes.

The Earl, briefly Duke, of Rothes was the son of a Covenanter but he became an instrument of State charged to put down the Presbyterians who had taken to the fields and hills to worship by their own rules. Always a royalist, Rothes cruelly dealt with all who rose against his King. He marched south with Charles to the final defeat at Worcester and many years of captivity. He carried the sword of state at the coronation of Charles II at Scone and on the Restoration began his life of glorious splendours and sins of the flesh. To Sir Walter Scott in "Wandering Willie's Tale" this is the "dissolute Rothes", and historians of the kirk portray him as either drunk or ill. His wife, Lady Anne Lyndsay of the Byres, and daughter of the Earl of Lyndsay, remained faithful to her Presbyterian upbringing and Leslie House could be a safe one for her Covenanting friends so perhaps the Chancellor was not all hard heart. The Earl, who became a Duke only as he entered his last year, is reputed to have said, "My hawks will be out tonight, my lady, so you had better take care of your blackbirds".

The body of the Duke of Rothes was brought from Holyrood Palace, via Leith and Burntisland, to be placed, with trumpets sounding and a display of ducal ostentation, in the Leslie vault in Christ's Kirk on the Green. The original building has been replaced but this is a name that has sounded down the centuries not for great soldiers or noble autocrats but for a wild outdoor party as described in a poem—"Chrystis Kirk on the Green".

The author of the poem could be royal—King James I or King James V—or it could be by an unknown, but well-educated, man of Fife who may have gone about his daily work in Fettykil, Falkland or, who knows, Auchtermuchty. What we do know is that this is one of the most influential poems in the Scots language. The stanza was used by many poets including: Alan Ramsay, who added a good few verses to the early poem; Robert Fergusson in "Hallow Fair"; and Robert Burns in his "The Holy Fair". No guarantee can be given that the green by the kirk of Leslie was the site of this riotous poem but the tradition that this is so is very strong.

Was never in Scotland hard nor sene
Sic dansing nor deray,
Nother in Falkland on the grene,
Nor Peblis to the play,
As was of wooeris as I wene
At Chrystis Kirk on ane day.
Thair come our Kittie weschen clene
In hir new kirtill of gray,
  Full gay,
At Chrystis Kirk on the grene.

To dance the damisallis thame dicht
And lassis licht of laittis;
Thair gluvis war of the raffell richt
Thair schone war of the straitis;
Thair kirtillis war of the lincum licht
Weill prest with mony plaitis.
Thay war so nyce quehn men thame nicht
Thay squeild lyk ony gaitis,
  Ful loud,
At Chrystis kirk on the grene.

Off all thir madinis myld as mede
Was nane sa gymp as Gillie,
As ony rose hir rude was reid
Hir lyre was lyk the lillie;
Bot yallow yallow was hir heid,
And sche of luif so sillie,
Thoch all hir kin suld have bein deid
Sche wald have bot sweit Willie,
  Allane,
At Chrystis kirk on the grene.

As with all these poems of rustic merrymaking, it develops into a brawl,

144

Than Lowrie as ane lyoun lap,
And sone ane flane culd fedder;
He hecht to pers him at the pape
Thairon to wed ane wedder;
He hit him on the wambe ane wap
And it bust lyke ane bledder;
Bot lo! As fortoun was and hap,
His doublat was of ledder,
    And sauft him,
At Chrystis kirk on the grene.

The baff so boustuouslie abasit him,
To the erth he duschit doun;
The tother for dreid he preissit him
And fled out of the toun;
The wyffis come furth and up thay paisit him,
And fand lyff in the loun,
And with thre routis thay raisit him
And coverit him of swoune,
    Agane,
At Chrystis kirk on the grene.

And on through another ten verses to end,

Quhen all wes done, Dick with ane ax
Come furth to fell ane further,
Quod he, "quhair ar yon hangit smaikis
Richt now that hurt my brother?"
His wyf bad him gang hame gud glaikis
And sae did Meg his mother;
He turnit and gaif thame bath thair paikis,
For he durst stryk na uther,
    Men said,
At Chrystis kirk on the grene.

deray: wild revelry   wooeris: suitors   wene: imagine   kirtill: dress
damisallis thame dicht: maidens prepared themselves   laittis: manners
raffell: roe-deer skin   schone: shoes   straitis: morocco leather
lincum licht: Lincoln green   nyce: bashful   nicht: approached
gaitis: goats   gymp: slim   rude: cheek   lyre: skin   Thoch: Though
lap: leaped up   flane: arrow   hecht: promised   pape: nipple   wed: bet
wedder: castrated ram   wambe: belly   wap: blow   bledder: bladder
fortoun: chance   baff: biff   abasit: abashed   preissit: hastened
up thay paisit him: got him on his feet   loun: lad   routis: shouts
coverit: recovered   futher: heap   smaikis: wretches
gud glaikis: silly fellow   paikis: deserts

Leslie House was destroyed by fire in 1763 and only the west wing was rebuilt, in 1765-67. During the nineteenth century small additions were made to the house and the seventeenth Countess had much repair work done. It was an aunt of the seventeenth Countess who inherited but soon the nineteenth Earl was making more efforts to restore the house. In 1906 he commissioned Sir Robert Lorimer to make improvements but, apart from a bay window on the south gable and placing a coat of arms in the pediment's tympanon, little can be seen on the surface of the house. Debts remained a problem for the estate and in 1919 Captian Crundall of Berkshire moved in. In the same year the estate was sold in parts and Major R. S. Nairn, of the Kirkcaldy family that owned the linoleum company, bought the house and the land around it. He was to add Ballingal, Balgeddie and Collydean Farms to the north and Macedonia and South Parks to the south. Today these names appear as districts of Glenrothes. The New Town Development Corporation could buy land by compulsory order and the situation of Leslie House was to be altered by new housing. Major Nairn gave the house, and its immediate grounds, to the Church of Scotland for use as an Eventide Home which it still is today. The Nairn family also owned nearby Balgeddie House which became a hotel in the late 1960s under the ownership of James Crombie.

One of the first families to live in the Woodside area of Glenrothes was that of Mary and Eddie McGrory. I knew Mary and Eddie in the 1950s when they were living in one of the Carriston Cottages, near Markinch, but it was not until his later years that Eddie began to write poetry. I was pleased to write introductions to two of Eddie's collections of poems which he published to benefit local charities. Eddie was originally from Glasgow and so is Maureen Macnaughtan, who was born there in 1954, but her recent poetry shows the influence of her years in Glenrothes.

Gradually Leslie is being merged even more into Glenrothes, but the road over the Lomond Hills seems to be largely unchanged since I cycled round to Falkland in the 1950s. Falkland is a delight, with the gardens of the Palace one of my favourite places. The remains of the Palace that we see today belong to buildings that were erected by the Stewarts as a hunting lodge in the sixteenth century. There were two building phases; 1500 to 1513 and 1537 to 1541. The old castle, which was destroyed after the building of the new palace, was of the fourteenth century and replaced a castle destroyed by the English. Today the south section of the quadrangle is complete and there are good remains of the east quarter. The courtyard facade was the work of two French master masons and the columns and medallion busts give it a gentler, more romantic, quality than the vigorously constructed gatehouse which is the work of a mason who had built parts of the Palace of Holyroodhouse. Many visitors find the unique Royal Tennis Court, which James V had built, very interesting.

The Stewart monarchs haunt the old stones of Falkland Palace, with the story of the death of James V known to many Scottish children to whom the name Falkland means nothing. Certainly it meant nothing to me in a Lanarkshire primary school but the sadness of the dying king turning his face to the wall remains with me as told by a young teacher. The story is very well told by Robert Lyndsay of Pitscottie, the most literary of the early prose historians, who had the advantage of being born in Fife about 1532. Lyndsay was sympathetic to James V but he was a natural writer and liked telling a good story and he certainly did so when relating the last days and minutes of James V,

> He passit to Edinburgh and thair tairit viij dayis witht great dollour and lamentatioun of the tinsall and schame of his lieges quhilk was be misfortoun and evill goverment brocht to schame and dishonour quhilk pat the kingis grace in dispair that he could never recover his honour againe. This being done the king passit out of Hallieruidhouse to Falkland and thair became so heavie and so dolarous that he nether eit nor drank that had good degestioun, and so he became so vehement seik that no man had hope of his lyffe. Than he send for certane of his lordis baith speritual and temporall to have thair consall bot or they come he was nearhand strangled to death be the extreme melancollie.

146

. . .

Be this the post came out of Lythgow schawing to the king goode tydingis that the quene was deliverit. The king inquyrit "wither it was man or woman." The messenger said "it was ane fair douchter." The king ansuerit and said. "Adew, fair weill, it come witht ane 'lase, it will pase witht ane lase,' and so he recommendit himself to the marcie of Almightie god and spak ane lyttill then frome that tyme fourtht, bot turnit his bak into his lordis and his face into the wall. At this tyme David Bettoun cardinall of Scottland standing in presentis of the king, seing him begin to faill of his strength and naturall speiche held ane through of papir to his grace and caussit him subscryue the samin quhair the cardenall wrait that plessit him for his awin particular weill, thinkand to have autorietie and prehemenence in the goverment of the countrie bot we may knaw heirbe the kingis legacie was verie schort, ffor in this maner he depairtit as I sall now tell. He turnit him bak and luikit and beheld all his lordis about him and gaif ane lyttill smyle and lauchter, syne kissit his hand and offerit the samyn to all his lordis round about him and thairefter held upe his handis to god and yeildit the spreit. This nobill king depairtit in this manner as I have schawin to yow, at Falkland in his awin palice the xx day of the monetht of December in the yeir of god I^m v^o xlij yeiris and that verie quyetlie for few was at his depairting except the cardinall the erle of argyle the erle of rothus the lord askyne the lord Lyndsay the Doctour Mr Michall Dury schir David Lyndesay of the Mont Lyone herauld the laird of graunge andro wood of largow Normond leslie maister of rothus. The rest war bot his awin secreit serwandis. . . .

The worthy Lyndsay is over-generous to James V when he blames his many failings on the company the King kept in the later years of his reign. In his boyhood James had the advantage of the tutelage of the good Sir David Lyndsay. In his "The Dreme" Lyndsay remembers happy days with the young King, and a good relationship,

> Quhen thow wes young, I bure thee in myne arme
> Full tenderlie, tyll thow begouth to gang,
> And in thy bed oft happit thee full warme
> With lute in hand, syne, sweitlie to thee sang!
> Sum tyme, in dansing, feiralie I flang,
> And, sum tyme, on myne office takkend cure
> And, sum tyme, kyke ane feind, transfegurate;
> And, sum tyme, lyke the greislie gaist of gye:
> In divers formis, oftymes, disfigurate;
> And, sum tyme, dissagyist full pleasandlye.
> So, sen thy birth, I have continewalye
> Bebe occupyt, and aye to thy plesoure;
> And sum tyme, seware, coppare, and caruoure.

Lyndsay has given us a glimpse of these days at the hunting Palace of Falkland,

> Fare weill Falkland, the fortalice of Fife—
> Thy polite park under the Lomond low
> Sum tyme in thee I led ane busy life
> Thy fallow deer to see them raike in row.

William Dunbar must have come to Falkland with the court of King James IV and known the woods and the Palace, although the poetry suggests that the poet was very much a man of towns and the indoors of the court. He was the poet for grand occasions including, in "The Thrissel and the Rois", the marriage of King James to Princess Margaret Tudor on 8th August 1503. Today in a seventeenth-century cottage in Falkland there is Kynd Kittock's Kitchen which is a traditional Scottish tearoom. For many years Bert Dalrymple has owned this very good tearoom, but the founder was Lillias Forbes, poet, and she gave the establishment its name. When she opened the tearoom Lillias displayed on the walls works of art by Sydney Goodsir Smith, who wrote a poem entitled *Kynd Kittock's Land,* but the name comes not from Smith's work but from an equally rumbustious poem, "The Ballad of Kynd Kittok", possibly written by William Dunbar,

My Gudame wes a gay wif, bot scho wes ryght gend,
　　Scho duelt furth fer in to france, apon Falkland Fell;
Thay callit her Kynd Kittok, quhasa hir weill kend;
　　Scho wes like a caldrone cruke cler under kell;
Thay threpit that scho deit of thrist, and maid a gud end.
　　Efter hir dede, scho dredit nought in hevin for to duell,
And sa to hevin the hieway dreidles scho wend,
　　Yit scho wanderit and yeid by to ane elriche well.
　　　　Scho met thar, as I wene,
　　　　Ane ask ryand on a snaill,
　　　　And cryit, "Ourtane fallow, haill!"
　　　　And raid ane inche behind his taill,
　　　Till it wes neir evin.

Sa scho had hap to be horsit to hir herbry
　　Att ane ailhous neir hevin, it nyghtit thaim thare;
Scho deit of thrist in this warld, that gert hir be so dry,
　　Scho never eit, bot drank our mesur and mair.
Scho slepit quhill the morne at none, and rais airly;
　　And to the yettis of hevin fast can the wif fair,
And by Sanct Peter, in at the yet, scho stall prevely:
　　God lukit and saw hir lattin in and lewch his hert sair.
　　　　And thar, yeris seven
　　　　　Scho levit a gud life,
　　　　　And wes our Ladyis hen wif:
　　　　　And held Sanct Peter at strif'
　　　Ay quhill sch wes in hevin.

Scho lukit out on a day and thoght ryght lang
　　To se the ailhous beside, in till ane evill hour;
And out of hevin the hie gait cought the wif gaing
　　For to get hir ane fresche drink, the aill of hevin wes sour.
Scho come agine to hevinnis yet, quhen the bell rang,
　　Sanct Peter hat hir with a club, quhill a gret clour
Rais in her heid, becaus the wif yeid wrang.
　　Than to the ailhous agane scho ran the pycharis to pour,
　　　　And for to brew and baik.
　　　　　Frendis, I pray yow hertfully,
　　　　　Gif ye be thristy or dry,
　　　　　Drink with my Guddame, as ye ga by,
　　　Anys for my saik.

end: simple　elriche: elvish, fairy　herbry: shelter　nyghtit: benighted
yettis: gates　clour: bump　yeid: went　pycharis: pitchers

Lillias Forbes has written a Falkland poem that also dances along to a very good rhythm and says something about the character of the town and the social, religious and political views that have been influential in Falkland. It is entitled, "Nae Bield in Falkland",

Dinna bide in yon chaumer
Wi the wee, clorty winnock
At the tap o the hoose
Up the kypie stair
I tell ye, ye'll no ken yersel
Aince up in yon chaumer
An the door steekit efter ye.

Aiblins ye'll try a canny keek oot the pane
Dichtin the gless wi yer thoum
A'thing unco quaet—deil's wark doon the wynd
Syns, ower the causey, tae yer frichtit een
The gantin Palace wa', rowed in deid-licht,
The peelie mune blintin owre cauld stane,
Ower wally een o beast or hoodie craw
Or halie kists o kings—
Tak tent—ye'll catch them keekin at ye—back!

Nae warm bield beddin doon in yon chaumer
Ye may hap yer heid nicht lang atween the sheets
Stappin yer lugs tae the wun's wersh chunnerin,
They'll aye come for ye, loupin oot their kists
Een bleezin as het coals,
Corbies wi knablick nebs,
Stookie saunts o the kirk,
Queer wizzent carls an quines
An a hail smarrich o Stuarts.

Like Lillias, I like Falkland, the Lomond Hills and the Palace walls and gardens, but the Stewart monarchs who went hunting from the Palace were often nasty, greedy and vindictive men. The last of them to be properly resident in Scotland, James VI, always had his eyes set on the English throne and a cavalcade that would remove him to claim a richer crown in London. One of my earliest poems, "The Heid o Hecht", written in the early 1960s, is in part concerned with this aspect of James's ambitions,

The laverock rises owre blin waws
At ane wi the great North wund
At the heid o hecht. Here
The Stuarts huntit the reid deer
And I look doon at that sma grey toon
Wi its fremmit Freench-like Palace
Whaur aince kings walked wi thochts
O the saft wunds o the Sooth.

Saft wunds that cam lowin north
Bringin the bricht bird o simmer
That has but a glisk o that cauld ane

That moves baith gress and pine. There
By toom waws whaur aince kings sat
Wi braw suddron tapestries hidin
The grey stane that cam straucht
Frae the quarries o this hill.

Stanes and laverock risin heich
In the cauld wund that kens nae
Swallow, gowk, or that simmer swarm
O flees. And the muckle stanes are bare.
Nae claith or burnin wud that can
Gie and tak frae that cauld hunter oot
On the hill wi the laverock wha passes
Owre aw at the heid o hecht.

laverock: skylark   heid o hecht: top of the hill
fremmit: strange or foreign   lowin: glowing   glisk: glimpse
toom: empty   heich: high   suddron: southern
straucht: straight   gowk: cuckoo   muckle: large
claith: cloth   aw: all, everything

David, Duke of Rothesay, who was the presumed heir of King Robert III, is the "prince in the tower" of Scottish history with his uncle Robert, Duke of Albany, who was also Earl of Fife, cast as the instigator of the murder. The year was 1402, and the first act was the kidnapping of Rothesay, who was on his way to seek a safe haven in St Andrews Castle. He was kidnapped "between Nydie and Stratirum". The castle of Nydie stood on Strathkinness moor about two Scots miles west of Strathtyrum. Albany had control of St Andrews Castle and Rothesay may have been first rushed there and lowered into the Bottle Dungeon. Albany and the Earl of Douglas rode quickly to St Andrews and when Rothesay left there the group that took him to Falkland was led by these two powerful men. Their route would be that of today's B939 with much then undrained moorland on both the Strathkinness and Ceres sides. There was a castle at Struthers and the old road to Cupar, which passed Chance Inn, would be crossed that stormy and very wet night, but still the old tower of Falkland must have seemed a long way off to Rothesay with his known enemies around him. Falkland was then a place of enclosing woods and the Tower must have looked nightmarish under such dreadful and intimidating circumstances.

In his history, Wyntoun, who lived until 1422, made no accusations, and this may indicate that contemporary opinion accepted that this was a death by natural causes. Or, again, although Albany was dead, the historian may have had good reason to be cautious when he wrote of Rothesay,

Oure Lord, the Kingis eldest sone,
Suete, and vertuos, yong, and faire,
And his nerast lauchful ayre,
Honest, habill, and avenand, . . .
His cors til halowit sepulture,
In Lundoris his body lyis
His spirite in til Paradyis.

150

Later historians relished a tale of Rothesay's slow starvation in a dungeon in Falkland Tower. Sir Walter Scott made the most of traditional stories in *The Fair Maid of Perth* and added to them for dramatic effect,

> Rothesay's bed chamber in the Tower of Falkland was well adapted for the execution of such a horrible project. A small narrow staircase, scarce known to exist, opened from thence by a trap-door to the subterranean dungeons of the castle through a passage by which the feudal lord was wont to visit in private and in disguise those miserable regions. By this staircase, the villains conveyed the insensible Prince to the lowest dungeon of the castle, so deep in the bowels of the earth that no cries or groans, it was supposed, could possibly be heard, while the strength of the door and fastenings must for a long time have defied force, even if entrance could have been discovered.

The actual act of murder has been allocated not to knightly swords but to two so-called ruffians, John Selkirk and John Wright, of Falkland. Both men were on Albany's payroll which proves nothing, but in 1501 John Wright, sometime Constable of the Castle of Falkland, was convicted of treason in the reign of James I, Rothesay's younger brother. The death of Rothesay was accomplished by, tradition says, Easter Day 1402. The official line was that Rothesay had died of dysentery and the case against Albany lies unproven. It does, however, seem strange that Rothesay's funeral procession moved out of Falkland not to Dunfermline, where so many kings were buried, but to Lindores Abbey.

The narrow old streets of Falkland invite the casual stroller to remember the weavers as much as the royal personages or the superbly named Onesiphorus Tyndall Bruce. Professor John Bruce bought the Nuthill estate at Falkland in 1820 and so became Keeper of Falkland Place. He also bought the Myres estate near Auchtermuchty. Having no children, Bruce left his considerable wealth and lands to his already-wealthy niece Margaret Bruce who married Onesiphorus Tyndall; he took his wife's surname. Educated at Eton and Oxford, this English barrister joined his wife in continuing the many improvements made by Professor Bruce. They also demolished Nuthill House, to have a grand new House of Falkland built; this was the work of William Burn (1789-1870) who worked on some 200 mansions. The Tyndall Bruces also demolished the early-seventeenth-century Parish Church built by John Mylne, one of a dynasty who were masons to kings. The present building (1849-50) is the work of David Bryce (1803-76), a partner of William Burn before setting up his own practice. Bryce worked on over 100 Scottish country houses and took the Scottish Baronial style to almost laughable excesses.

An intriguing statute of Onesiphorus Tyndall Bruce stands in the church grounds. The interesting fountain in the wide street near the church was also paid for by the Tyndall Bruces who are buried in the vault of the church they had built. Like her uncle, Mrs Bruce was childless and the estate passed to a near relative and then to his son who, in 1887, sold it and Falkland House to the third Marquis of Bute who became the Hereditary Keeper of the Palace. About 1887 John Crichton Stuart began the restoration of the Palace and today both Palace and gardens are maintained by the National Trust for Scotland although they are still Crown Property.

Facing the Palace are Moncrieff House, dated 1610, and Hunting Lodge Hotel, with interesting panels incorporated into its front wall; one is dated 1607 although the building was considerably restored in the nineteenth century. Within sight of the Palace is the house known as Cameron which is thought to be where Alan and Margaret Cameron lived, as did their eldest son Richard (1648-80) who was to become one of the legendary names of the heroic Covenanting times, dying in battle at Airds Moss with his sword drawn against the men of Charles II under the command of Bruce of Earlshall, near Leuchars, known to Presbyterians as the "Fife Persecutor".

One of my favourite lanes in Falkland is the narrow, cobbled Sharp's Close which is still lined by weavers' cottages and runs from Brunton Street to Back Dykes. In the 1960s one of the houses in Brunton Street was owned by Kulgin Duval and Colin Hamilton, rare booksellers, who have in more recent years negotiated the sale of the archives of the poet Hugh MacDiarmid to the National Library of Scotland. Kulgin and Colin carefully restored their eighteenth-century house although, unless my memory is playing me false, I do not think the house was then harled. The larger Brunton House carries the arms, with a falcon, dated 1712, of the Simson family who were hereditary falconers to the Crown.

The old saying "Awa to Freuchie", which can be extended into the even older version "Awa to Freuchie and eat mice", has its roots in the practice of sending out-of-favour minor courtiers there from nearby Falkland; those with higher status tended to be sent to the block or the gallows. Today Freuchie is a rural retreat that entices those who look for tranquillity in the beautiful Eden valley.

One of the poems of my "Traivellin Man" sequence ends in Freuchie,

SPECIFICS
"I gaed to spend a week in Fife—
An unco week it proved to be—"   George Outram

I gaed to Fife for a tourin week.

I crossed the brig at Kincardine
and went as faur as I could at Newport. I sat wi miners
in Bowhill and wi fishermen in Crail.
I saw coal loadit at Methil and whisky in Markinch.
I watched the golfers at Lundin Links
and the electronic girls at Glenrothes. I saw trout leap
at Strathmiglo and an Englishman asked me the wey to
Auchtermuchty. I watched the lawyers perform in Cupar
and the shipbuilders in Burntisland. I walked the gress atween
the stanes o the cathedral of St Andrews and stood by
Mr Morris's grave. I pondered on Carnegie's
steel, the richt saintly Margaret's iron will, the warrior Bruce's
missin hairt, and the maisterly Henrysoun's
twa mice in richt royal Dunfermline.
I stood unner the auld railway brig at North Queensferry
and missed the smell o linoleum at Kirkcaldy. I tried for high tea
at Peat Inn and had dinner in Falkland near the Palace.
I was sent to Freuchie
and there I settled doon, for a rest.

Where are you from they ask me. I tell them
whaur I've juist been. No, they say,
you're "from Glasgow"

like the English say I'm "from Scotland"
and the French say "from England".

13

Strathmiglo, Auchtermuchty, Newburgh,
Collessie, Monimail, Fernie,
and the Mount

THE POEM BY George Outram from which I took the lines at the head of my poem "Specifics" is entitled "The Annuity", and is the best poem by this West of Scotland poet,

>I gaed to spend a week in Fife—
>An unco week it proved to be—
>For there I met a waesome wife
>Lamentin' her viduity.
>Her grief brak out sae fierce and fell,
>I thought her heart wad burst the shell;
>And—I was sae left tae mysel—
>I sell't her an annuity.
>
>The bargain lookit fair eneugh—
>She just was turned o' saxty-three:
>I couldna guessed she'd prove sae teugh,
>By human ingenuity.
>But years have come, and years have gane,
>And there she's yet as stieve's a stane—
>The limmer's growin' young again,
>Since she got her annuity.
>
>She's crined awa' to bane and skin,
>But that it seems is nought to me;
>She's like to live—although she's in
>The last stage o' tenuity.
>She munches wi' her wizened gums,
>An' stumps about on legs o' thrums
>But comes—as sure as Christmas comes—
>To ca' for her annuity.
>
>. . .
>
>I thought that grief might gar her quit—
>Her only son was lost at sea—
>But aff her wits behoved to flit,
>An' leave her in fatuity.
>She threeps, and threeps, he's living yet,
>For a' the tellin' she can get;
>But catch the doited runt forget
>To ca' for her annuity.

If there's a sough o' cholera
Or typhus—wha sae gleg as she?
She buys up baths, an' drugs, an' a',
In siccan superfluity.
She doesna need—she's fever proof—
The pest gaed owre her very roof;
She tauld me sae—an' then her loof
Held out for her annuity.

Ae day she fell—her arm she brak,—
A compound fracture as could be;
Nae leech the cure wad undertak,
Whate'er was the gratuity.
It's cured! She handles't like a flail—
It does as well in bits as hale;
But I'm a broken man mysel
Wi' her and her annuity.

unco: strange   stieve's: stout as   limmer: creature   crined: shrivelled
thrums: threadpaper   crack: chatter   hurkles: crouches   ingle: fire
gar: make   threeps: swears   gleg: spry   loof: hand

Human nature may not have changed so very much since Outram's fictional seller of annuities travelled through Fife, but many railway lines have been torn up and there are many new roads. There have been changes to the roads through the Howe of Fife but I doubt if a pre-1939 traveller would have difficulty in recognising those around Falkland.

North of Falkland is Strathmiglo and along the A91 to Cupar and St Andrews is Auchtermuchty. Strathmiglo has attracted many artists who have featured the octagonal steeple of the tolbooth. I associate Strathmiglo with very hot summer days in the 1950s and a bridge over the Eden on the Falkland road at which I often rested to cool down and watch the fat trout lean against the fast-flowing current. West of Strathmiglo is Gateside and the road out of Fife that goes up to Beinn Inn *en route* to Bridge of Earn and Perth. For all my youthful fitness, and many a rest, this was no mean climb for me on my old bike. And I got little rest in Perth. As I wrote in my poem "'The Hert o Scotland'",

Perth I reached efter a lang bike ride
and had to turn back as soon as I gote there
haein nae lichts.

The M90 complicates my memories of another route I took in the 1950s from Kinnesswood to Glenfarg and Bein Inn and back down to Gateside and Strathmiglo. Before Gateside a minor road branches off eastwards to twist and turn to join the road from Abernethy to Strathmiglo.

In Falkland, and throughout Scotland, the name of Richard Cameron lives as one of the Covenanting martyrs and for his name being given to a regiment of soldiers, the Cameronians, but in Strathmiglo the name of Jenny Nettles has lived on for a more private and intimate tragedy. To me she is a woman whose unhappiness needs no linking to events that may not be true to her biography. The story as told locally is not that which I associate with the song that was printed in David Herd's eighteenth-century collection of *Ancient and Modern Scottish Songs, Heroic Ballads, etc.*

The Strathmiglo version tells that in 1715 the beautiful Jenny attracted the attention of an officer in the army of Rob Roy Macgregor to whom she succumbed and who promised to marry her. The army marched out of Fife and the faithless Highland lover with it. The abandoned Jenny was found hanging on a roadside tree on the beautiful road that runs from Strathmiglo to Falkland where Rob Roy had his headquarters. As a suicide Jenny was denied burial in consecrated ground, and so she was buried, at night, in the middle of the moor south of Barrington and about a mile west of Kilgour. The details are exact and may be true to what happened to a woman in Strathmiglo. "A mile west of Kilgour" is almost directly below the summit of the West Lomond and on the edge of what I knew as Drumdreel Wood.

The version of the old song that I prefer has short, singing lines that emphasise the tragic loneliness of the abandoned Jenny who seems to be almost out of her mind as she holds the child that her ungrateful lover had denied was his. The end result is still suicide and again Jenny was denied a Christian burial, but her grave was not a "mile west of Kilgour" but between two lairds' lands at the foot of the Ochil hills. Thus do the primary facts of Jenny's life become a folk-tale that was related in various versions in several localities.

> Saw ye Jenny Nettles,
> Jenny Nettles, Jenny Nettles,
> Saw ye Jenny Nettles
> Coming frae the Market;
> Bag and Baggage on her Back,
> Her Fee and Bountith in her Lap;
> Bag and Baggage on her Back,
> And a Babie in her Oxter.
>
> I met ayont the Kairny,
> Jenny Nettles, Jenny Nettles,
> Singing till her Bairny,
> Robin Rattles' Bastard;
> To feel the Dool upo' the Stool,
> And ilka ane that mocks her,
> She round about seeks Robin out,
> To stap it in his Oxter.
>
> Fy, fy! Robin Rattle,
> Robin Rattle, Robin Rattle;
> Fy, fy! Robin Rattle,
> Use Jenny Nettles kindly:
> Score out the Blame, and shun the Shame,
> And without mair Debate o't,
> Take hame your Wain, make Jenny fain,
> The leal and leesome Gate o't.

In the early 1920s Hugh MacDiarmid was writing his great short lyrics in Scots and for one of them, "Empty Vessel", he took the tragedy of Jenny and her bairn and gave it a twentieth-century significance with a closing reference to Enstein's theory of relativity—

"The licht that bends owre a' thing". MacDiarmid begins this eight-line poem with an actual line from the Jenny Nettles folk song,

> I met ayont the cairney
> A lass wi' tousie hair
> Singin' till a bairnie
> That was nae langer there.

The River Eden flows from Strathmiglo to Dunshelt which lies between Falkland and Auchtermuchty. Dunshelt is an unspoiled village of low cottages many of which have a view of the full long slopes of both the East and West Lomonds. Again the views over the arable fields of the Howe make a peaceful contrast to the hills to both south and north.

Auchtermuchty is yet another old Fife Royal Burgh (charter in 1517 from King James V) with a good square tower—with almost obligatory balustrade parapet—to its Town Hall. When I was in Auchtermuchty in the early 1990s the village was being made over, dated and dirtied, by scenery artists for the filming of the TV programme "Dr Finlay's Casebook" which is another kind of tribute to days gone, to an escape into auld lang syne that has been over-popular in Scotland since the days of the kailyard novelists—J.M. Barrie, S. R. Crockett and "Ian MacLaren"—in the 1890s.

The most famous literary work to be set in Auchtermuchty is a comic masterpiece of the fifteenth or sixteenth century, "The Wyf of Auchtermuchty", who offers her husband the chance to do her work in the house and its outhouses whilst she does his ploughing, etc,

> In Auchtermuchty thair dwelt ane man,
> Ane husband, as I hard it tawld,
> Quha weill cowld tippill owt a can
> And nathir luvit hungir nor cawld,
> Quhill anis it fell upoun a day
> He yokkit his pleuch upoun the plane,
> Gif it be trew as I hard say,
> The day was fowll for wind and rane.
>
> He lowsit the pleuch at the landis end
> And draif his oxin hame at evin;
> Quehn he come in he lukit bend,
> And saw the wyf baith dry and clene
> And sittand at ane fyre beik and bawld
> With ane fat sowp, as I hard say.
> The man being verry weit and cauld,
> Betwene thay twa it was no play.
>
> Quoth he, "Quhair is my horssis corne?
> My ox hes nathir hay nor stray!
> Dame ye mon to the pleuch to-morne,
> I salbe hussy, gif I may."
> "Husband," quo scho, "content am I
> To tak the pleuch my day abowt,
> Sae ye will rowll baith calvis and ky
> And all the hous, baith in and owt.

156

husband: farmer   can: mug   yokkit: yoked   pleuch: plough   lowsit: unyoked
bend: into the next room   beik and bawld: well-stoked   fat sowp: thick soup
mon: must go   hussy: housewife   rowll: rule   ky: cattle

The outcome can be envisaged but it is well told in the poem.

The most famous resident of Auchtermuchty is Jimmy Shand whose band set a tone for large chunks of Scottish radio and country dancing for many decades and this ethos spilled into television with the very popular White Heather Club.

The oldest house in Auchtermuchty is known locally as MacDuff House. It stands just off the Cross diagonally over from the War Memorial. It took me some time to find the date, 1597, on this impressive solid, dark and quite massive building. The small white Arabic figures are almost hidden under the rhone or gutter. I liked the modern sculptures which sit in the interestingly varied garden of this historic house. There is a lectern doocot in the garden that may have stood here since the late seventeenth century. It could be that Mary Livingstone, one of the Maries of Mary, Queen of Scots, and the son of Lord Sempill were married in Auchtermuchty in this house. This is the couple libelled by John Knox when he suggested that they had to be hurriedly married to avoid a scandal.

Between Dunshelt and Auchtermuchty stand the complex structures of Myres Castle where Queen Mary is said to have frequently rested during boar hunts in the then marshy Howe. The original plain tower house of Myres was built in the early-sixteenth century but has undergone many additions since then. In its early years it was the property of John Scrymgeour who was involved in building Falkland Palace and the Palace of Holyroodhouse. This is another house and estate that became the property of Professor John Bruce, who had bought the Falkland estate and Falkland Palace. In the 1880s Myres Castle was sold to James Ogilvy Fairlie who continued the tradition of making alterations to the house. The admirably restrained Auchtermuchty War Memorial was designed by Reginald Fairlie of Myres Castle. The inverted rifle, cast in bronze, is very emotive against the stone of the Memorial.

Fairlie also showed restraint in his restoration work, including that on Leuchars Parish Church, although the many churches he designed show him to have an individual style. He worked as a young man for Sir Robert Lorimer before setting up his own practice in Edinburgh in 1909. St James Church, The Scores, St Andrews was one of his first commissions, carrying the date 1910. Standing on a cliff overlooking St Andrews Bay, the church has a tower that reminds me of the War Memorial in Auctermuchty. Inside the church there is a plaque to James Ogilvy Fairlie, of Myres, who died on 28 September 1916, his son Captain John Ogilvy Fairlie who "fell at the battle of Loos, 27th September 1915", and Jane Mary who died 5 July 1931 wife of A. J. Ogilvy Fairlie of Myres.

The younger Fairlie went on to design over thirty new churches, including the beautifully simple and well-proportioned Church of Our Lady Star of the Sea in Tayport which I have described as his masterpiece. Methil Parish Church, overlooking the sea from Wellesley Road, is another building that shows Fairlie's ability to create simplicity by balancing the tower with a pointed gable and smaller round tower. Reginald Fairlie, excellent architect, died in 1952.

The road from Auchtermuchty to Newburgh is a delight as it twists and turns through enclosing woods, enfolding hills, and over many a heich and howe. And then we get our first glimpse of the Tay. The village of Grange of Lindores sits high before the narrow twisting road goes under the railway bridge to Den of Lindores. The small wooden bus shelter carries a pleasing name board of matching wood. Several Fife villages have these shelters; I particularly remember that at Largoward. As Newburgh is approached the hills of Perthshire can be seen over the River Tay, and scenically this is a road for walking but, as so often these days, there is no footpath and, although a quiet road, its many corners and narrow stretches must make it a few miles of constant anxieties.

In Newburgh, Mason Street leads down to the Tay with pleasant riverside walks and seats from which to view the river and the low hills of Perthshire. Salmon fishing was important to Newburgh in the nineteenth century, and a linoleum factory provided employment from 1891 until 1978. The influence of the monks at nearby Lindores Abbey lasted much longer but ended with the Reformation. From perhaps the thirteenth century the monks encouraged fruit-growing, thatching and agricultural developments in general. We owe the Abbey to David, Earl of Huntingdon, who founded it in 1178 and whose infant sons were buried there. The Duke of Rothesay, who also lies buried here, could have been King of Scots but for murder, or dysentery. Earl David, who had two older brothers both of whom became King of Scots, was the father of Isabella who married Robert de Brus and whose great-grandson was King Robert the Bruce. We owe the destruction of the Abbey to the Reformers and to those who took its stones for their own new buildings.

Just as the stones of the Abbey found new uses, so one of the famous crosses of Newburgh, which dates from 700-1100 AD and could be the sanctuary stone of the MacDuffs, may also have had hammers put to it till only a mighty boulder remained. This is believed to have been the pedestal of the Cross. Sir Walter Scott claimed for Fife and Scotland the view from the MacDuff Cross as "one of the finest and noblest in the world." I have left it to others, younger or fitter than I, to climb up to the "Cross" to assess Scott's claim. In her most informative, *MacDuff, Thane of Fife,* 1997, Alison Chapman writes, of the great pedestal boulder, "Today it is almost obscured by long grass, but the atmosphere and mystery remain." The other ancient stone near Newburgh is the Mugdrum Cross, which takes its name from the house of that name and may be 1300 years old.

The most competent of the Jacobite Generals, Lord George Murray, lived high above the Tay at Mugdrum before the fateful years of 1745 and 1746. The outcome of the Battle of Culloden, on 16th April 1746, and the rout that followed, are generally seen as inevitable but, as Michael Lynch has written in his *Scotland: A New History,* "This was only Cumberland's first victory (and, as events would prove, also his last); Murray expected to do better in a return contest with Cumberland, and Lochiel was even as late as mid-May planning a summer campaign. Neither a defeat at Culloden nor a rout after it had been inevitable. What turned the tables was Charles's own decision to issue a *sauve qui peut* order." In the Highlands, it was "every man for himself" in the years that followed.

Between Newburgh and Den of Lindores is the ruined Denmylne Castle. This is an important building for Scottish historians and patriots. The property at Denmylne was owned by the Balfours from the early sixteenth century and in it lived Sir James Balfour who was, in the 1620s and 1630s, at the centre of an intellectual group of Royalists and Episcopalians. Balfour gathered Scottish manuscripts and, with Archbishop Spottiswoode, rediscovered the Declaration of Arbroath. It was only in the nineteenth century that patriots began to see the Declaration as what Professor Michael Lynch has aptly described as a "surrogate Scottish constitution". The most famous section has undoubtedly a fine ring to it even when translated from the original Latin, "For it is not glory, it is not riches, neither is it honours, but it is liberty alone that we fight and contend for, which no man will lose but with his life." *The Historical Works of Sir James Balfour* were published in 1824-25.

Four miles from Newburgh, off the Cupar road, is Glenduckie, which was in the Parish of Dunbog. At Glenduckie lived Graham Moffat (1866-1951) who wrote the kitchen comedy, *Bunty Pulls the Strings,* which was written in 1911 but not published until 1932. I learned of Moffat's associations with Newburgh from Mrs Birrell, who now lives at Lalathan above Kennoway, but whose mother used to have tea with Kate, sister of the playwright. In addition to this play, Glenduckie can claim a Hill with what may be an Iron Age dwelling.

From Newburgh the A913 joins a minor road that passes alongside Lindores Loch and hilly country to delightful Collessie. What was a hamlet with a small burn, large church and kirkyard, has expanded somewhat with the erection of a group of new houses on level ground below the church. Another piece of land was, in 1998, being offered as a site for four new houses. Across the way stands Collessie Mill House and, higher up, white farm houses are protected from northern gales by the surrounding hills.

Standing by the kirk wall, and looking over a very-well-maintained thatched house and the small burn to the long curve of the East and West Lomond hills, it is easy to see why more families should wish to live in Collessie. It must be a place that lowers the business executive's blood pressures and eases stress. The railway line from Ladybank to Newburgh and Perth merges into this pastoral landscape and few trains disturb the rural silence. On the bank scampering rabbits allowed me, that unseasonably warm February day of blue skies, to indulge the townsman's sentimental view of these bob-tailed burrowers. Inevitably, traffic can be heard, but to the north and east the landscape cannot be much changed since Sir James Melville enjoyed his retirement from the Court of King James VI and sat quietly at Halhill writing his memoirs and diaries.

Uphill from Collessie, past Halhill Farm, is the hamlet of Monimail, and nearby is Melville House which I have linked to the Melvilles at Raith, Kirkcaldy. As I have said in a previous chapter, Sir John Melville of Raith, who was named by John Knox, in relation to the suppressions of Cardinal Beaton, as "the faithful laird of Raith", was executed in 1548. Two of his sons are Sir Robert Melville of Murdocairney who became the first Lord Melville in 1616, and the courtier and diarist Sir James Melville of Halhill. The diarist of Halhill is one of the most notable prose writers of the sixteenth-seventeenth centuries. It was George, fourth Lord Melville, who in 1643 took Raith into the barony of Melville, and became Earl of Melville in 1690. The Earl, who died in 1707, outlived his son, the Lord Raith who built Raith House, and the next Earl was David Melville who also became Earl of Leven on the death of his mother, Katherine Leslie, grand-daughter of General Leslie.

The classically-styled Melville House was built between 1697 and 1703 for the first Earl by James Smith, who had built Raith House, Kirkcaldy. Melville House, once the home of earls, is now the residency of difficult boys. The local rumour in 1998 was that new accommodation was to be found for the boys.

The Earls of Leven and Melville remained at Melville House into this twentieth century and their memorials can be seen in Monimail Church. Nearer Melville House there is a Burial House of Melvilles in the old kirkyard of the earlier ruined church which was abandoned when the new one was built in the 1790s. The preserved Melville aisle of the old church carries a nicely decorative coronet monogram of one of the Earls of Melville. Others buried here include Bethune of Balfour, and Balfours of Fernie Castle. Also in Monimail old kirkyard is the Burial Ground of Sir Michael Barker Nairn, Bart., whose home was at nearby Rankeilour when he died. Other members of the Nairn family are buried here, including Sir Robert Spencer Nairn, Bart. Until I read the inscriptions on these memorials I was unaware that the Nairn family had received two baronetcies. This is a peaceful spot, with a low wall of polished granite enclosing an area of uninterrupted lawn, although I have been told that aconites do flower along the walls.

Near Melville House, and alongside the old kirkyard, a rough pathway leads to a tower. This is a fragment of a quadrangular building which was a palace of the Archbishops of St Andrews, with Archbishop Hamilton the last to live here. The tower has interesting portrait roundels similar to those on Falkland Palace, but it has lost some dignity in becoming part of one of the walls of what was the garden of Melville House. In 1998 the old tower was occupied by a community of artist-craftspeople, who have founded an educational trust and who work, teach and live in the various buildings. Atop the old tower there is a heart-warming and many-pointed golden sun—perhaps made of metal. Initially I assumed that this had been put there by the craftspeople, but they told me that it was erected, to celebrate a wedding, by one of the last Earls who lived at Melville House. Beyond the tower and over the green fields of the Howe, the Lomonds again show their elegant lines and slopes.

Retracing our steps from Melville House and Monimail Tower towards Collessie, we again pass the roadway to Halhill Farm. The courtier and diarist Sir James Melville owned the estate of Halhill from about 1575 till his death in 1617. Probably born in 1535, Sir James was a trusted adviser to Queen Mary and a diplomat during both the minority and the reign of James VI. He has given us shrewd insights into the nature of Queen Elizabeth of England, particularly when she declared her intention not to marry, "if I be not thereto necessitated by the Queen my sister's harsh behaviour to me". "I know the truth of that, madam", replied Melville, "you need not tell it me. Your Majesty thinks, if you were married, you would be but Queen of England; and now you are both King and Queen. I know your spirit cannot endure a commander."

Despite James VI's entreaties, the old Melville did not go south in 1603 but, much prefering Halhill, Collessie and Monimail to Whitehall, he retired to Halhill where he wrote his Memoirs which were discovered in Edinburgh long after his death. He died in Halhill in 1617 and was carried down the feared Coffin Road to be buried in Collessie kirkyard in the Melville tomb. The Coffin Road is said to have been walked only on final journeys from Halhill. I have failed to pinpoint either the exact site of Halhill or the route of the Coffin Road. Mr Andrew Barr, who farms Halhill and Monimail, told me that the tradition in his family is that a large standing stone marked the site of Halhill Castle, but experts have advised him that the stone is Pictish. I like to envisage Halhill as downhill from Robert Barr's farmhouse and so standing above the hamlet of Collessie beneath the sloping green hill. In his *Diary* in 1590 Melville wrote,

> About this tym his Maieste send for me, and at my commying to Falkland, wher the court remanit for the sommer seasoun, it plaisit his hynes to tell me, how that at his commyng out of Denmark he had promysed to the Quen and Consell ther, to place about the Quenis Maieste his bedfallow gud and discret company; quhilk he had left over lang ondone, till at lenth he advysed with him self that I wald be metest; willing me not to refuse the just calling of my prince. Wherein I mycht serve as in ane lawfull vocation; because they that sut for service in court or any office, dois it for ther awen proffit; bot they ar mair proffitable for princes, that ar socht and chosen for ther qualites.

The Melville, or Halhill, tomb built into the south wall of the kirkyard looks as if it has been roofless for a long time. Henry Rae-Arnot said some ninety years ago, "There is no lettering inside the Melville tomb". Outside the kirkyard, but on the south wall of the Melville tomb, is a long inscription with the date 1609. These words were probably written by the diarist, and certainly the inscription could be read by him as he walked about the kirktoun enjoying his years of retirement. We can also try to read it as we pass along the steep, traffic-free lane that runs alongside the kirk wall. For many minutes I stood trying to read the decorative old lettering, but time and weather have done their work and mostly I failed to make sense of these fine words. Thanks to Mr A. Maloco, who lives in Collessie, showing me a copy of the very rare and handsomely bound *Collessie Churchyard,* which was written early in this century by Henry Rae-Arnot, I can quote them. The inscription reminds me of that at St Fillan's, Aberdour, but is considerably more kirkyairdy,

1609

Ye loadin pilgrims passing langs this way,
Pans [pause] on your fall and your offences past.
Hou your frail flesh first formit of the clay
In dust mon be dissolvit at the last.
Repent, amend, on Christ the burden cast
Of your sad sinnes, who can your sauls refresh,
Syne raise from grave to gloir your grislie flesh
Defyle not Christ's kirk with your carrion,
A solemne sait for God's service prepard
For praier, preaching, and communion.
Your byrial should be in the kirkyaird.
On your uprysing set your great regard,
When saul and body joynes with joy to ring
In Heaven for ay with Christ our Head and King.

Beyond the Melville memorial, the kirk's wall, topped by a thick, dark green hedge—which I think may be yew—takes a long curve into a narrow lane on which stands what we like to call weavers' cottages. The road in front of them is not tarmac-ed or cobbled but laid with stone and leads only to the cottages. Downhill the immaculate thatched cottage can be seen and two others with good thatch face it. The old manse lines the other east wall of the kirkyard and it is an older building than the church which, as we can read on its northern wall, was built in "1839 by R. & R. Dickson. Arch". They also designed: Dunimarle Castle, near Culross; completed Balbirnie House, Markinch, to a design by their uncle, Richard Crichton; and built Kilconquhar Church to a design by Richard Crichton for Cockpen Church in the Lothians—which may be a poor excuse in a book on Fife for quoting the first verse of Lady Nairne's best song, "The Laird o' Cockpen",

The laird o' Cockpen, he's proud an' he's great,
His mind is ta'en up wi things o' the State;
He wanted a wife, his braw hoose to keep,
But favour wi' wooin' was fashious to seek.

The former manse, now The Glebe, dates from 1796, designed by John Stewart but extended in 1824 by Robert Hutchison. From Mr Maloco, retired architect and skilful craftsman of colourful traction engines, I learned that Collessie has the distinction of being the only Scottish village in which the Riot Act has been read twice. The villagers had opposed the demolition of the old church and when the new building was started in 1838 they crept out at night and undid the previous day's work. This they repeated till the authorities had the said Act read to them. Naethin dauntit the villagers continued their nightly sabotage till the Riot Act was again read to them.

In the churchyard of Collessie I was surprised, indeed startled, to find the very fine memorial of Sir William O. Hutchison, President of the Royal Scottish Academy. I knew that Sir William had died in 1970, but not of his family's position as landowners in the Howe of Fife. His large but simple memorial of pale cream sandstone is landscape in shape with very good relief lettering. Like that of the Nairn family uphill at Monimail, the Hutchison burial area is a simple lawn edged with a wall. The other plaque is that of Col. Harry Oliphant Hutchison (1833-1935).

Melville House stands as a testament to the wealth of the first Earl of Melville and the ability of his descendants to retain, into this century, the beautiful building that he had made. It is to be hoped that a suitable use will be found for it. Like Balbirnie House, Markinch, nearby Fernie Castle has been saved by its conversion into a superior hotel. Fernie has a tower that may have replaced a castle of the Earl of Fife, and it was certainly a seat of the Balfours of Mountquhanie, near Creich, whose descendants only sold up in 1965 when the property became Fernie Castle Hotel.

Sir James Melville of Halhill is an interesting prose writer, but finally a minor literary figure when placed beside Sir David Lyndsay of the Mount (c.1490-1555). There is continuing debate about the site of the old mansion of the Mount, but I like to think of it on the south side of the hill, thus having a good view of much of the Eden valley. Today the lands of the old Mount estate are crowned by the Hopetoun Monument which stands high above the A913 and what I regard as the "new" A92 and can be seen from many parts of the Howe of Fife. The monument was erected in 1826 in memory of Sir John Hope of Over Rankeilour who was a commander in Spain during the Peninsular Wars. Over Rankeilour is a late-eighteenth-century mansion and another building designed in the classical style. Today Over Rankeilour Farm houses the Scottish Deer Centre. As related above, nearby Rankeilour was bought by Sir Michael Barker Nairn but the mansion has been demolished. Sir Robert Spencer Nairn still has his home on the estate.

As we have seen, there are many Lyndsays around Kilconquhar and here in the Howe there were many other branches of the family. Sir David Lyndsay may have been succeeded as Lord Lyon King-of-Arms by a younger brother of the same name—except that he was of Rathillet. The Earls of Crawford claimed back Rathillet but by 1635 it was owned by James Halkerstoun whose heir was David Halkerstoun or Hackstoun or Hackston. It is this younger Hackston who, as one of the murderers of Archbishop Sharp, has conferred some fame on a property that was once owned by the great poet's namesake brother.

Sir David Lyndsay of the Mount is the last of the great auld makars, the heir to Henryson, Dunbar, and Douglas. He is also the great popular predecessor of Robert Burns. Before Burns, Lyndsay was the poet read by the ordinary literate people of Scotland. In *Marmion* Sir Walter Scott could write,

> Still is thy name in high account
> And still thy verse has charms,
> Sir David Lyndsay of the Mount.
> Lord Lion King-at-Arms

The flash of that satiric rage
Which, bursting on the early stage,
Branded the vices of the age,
And broke the keys of Rome.

Lyndsay was certainly a satirist of the highest level. He was of the Protestant side, but to see his poetry in such simplistic terms is to under-estimate it—he is the intellectual asking questions of a wider range beyond theology. His attacks on the Old Church helped to create a climate of opinion on moral as well as theological attitudes that enabled the Reformation to take Scotland into new political and economic attitudes and structures.

Perhaps because he had known him since he was a boy, and been kindly taught by Lyndsay, James V seems to have accepted the poet's satirical work with surprising benevolence, despite its encompassing the idea of serving leadership, an attitude which had been seen, uniquely for that time, in Barbour's epic *Bruce*. This attitude in Lyndsay's poetry is perhaps exemplified by the words, "what is a king bot ane officer". It has been said that James V was "the poor man's king" and, for reasons of power and politics, the Stewart kings did present themselves as kings of the people rather than of the territorially competitive nobles. This is the voice that is heard in the poetry of Scotland and which is a stubborn "democratic" base in the history of the Scots, despite all the power of a few noble families and Anglicised lairds in both highlands and lowlands.

The idea of James V as the "gaberlunzie king" who mixed incognito with his people as "the guid man o Ballengeich" made him in my childhood, and perhaps still today, a favourite with Scottish schoolchildren. Later I was told by the worldly-wise that this was a lecherous king seeking village lassies. Unlike Robert Lyndsay of Pitscottie, recent historians have dealt harshly with James V; Gordon Donaldson, for example, writing, "Perhaps James is not to be judged by Scottish standards. He was, after all, half a Tudor by birth and perhaps a Tudor rather than a Stewart in character. He combined in his own person the acquisitiveness of his grandfather, Henry VII, the lust and ruthlessness of his uncle, Henry VIII, and the unrelenting cruelty of his cousin, Bloody Mary." The paradoxes of James V's life will never be resolved, any more than those of the Scots literary tradition with its delight in the formal offset by a passion for the seemingly uncontrolled; or again, what I have referred to above as its "democratic base" offset by a desire for authoritarianly-imposed discipline. This is to be seen in the post-Reformation stance of the individual Scot who demanded the right to speak to his God face to face but accepted the disciplines—the law and logic—of Calvinism.

Today Sir David Lyndsay is best known for his play *Ane Satyre of the Thrie Estatis* which was revived at the second Edinburgh Festival in August 1948. Other productions have followed at regular intervals and it is strange to reflect that the 1948 production could have been the first since Sunday 12th August 1554. This took place before Marie de Lorraine, Queen-Regent, on the Playfield at Greenside below the Calton Hill in Edinburgh. A version of the play had been performed in Linlithgow in the Banqueting Hall of the Palace before James V and Marie de Lorraine, together with the Lords Spiritual and Temporal, at the Feast of the Epiphany, 6th January 1540. This version is described as an "Interlude". An extended version of Lyndsay's masterpiece was performed on the dramatist's home ground—on the Castlehill, Cupar. The date was 7th June 1552. For that day Cupar was the literary capital of Scotland. We may hear a "Proclamatioun"

Richt famous pepill, ye sall understand
How that ane prince rycht wyiss and vigilent
Is schortly for to cum in to this land
And purpossis to hald ane parliament.
His Thre Estaitis thairto hes done consent,
In Cowpar toun in to thair best array
With support of the Lord omnipotent,
And thairto hes affixt ane certane day.

. . .

Faill nocht to be upone the castell hill
Besyd the place quhair we purpoiss to play.
With gude stark wyne your flacconis see ye fill,
And hald your self the myrieast that ye may.
Be not displeisit quhatevir we sing or say,
Amang sad mater howbeid we sumtyme relyie;
We sall begin at sevin houris of the day,
So ye keip tryist—forsuth, we sall nocht felyie.

purpossis: intends   hes done consent: have given consent
stark: strong   flacconis: flagons   the myrieast that ye may: in the merriest state possible
howbeid: although   keip tryist: keep the tryst/be there   felyie: fail.

Rather than quote speeches from the great play, I have taken another extract from "The Dreme of Schir David Lyndsay" in which the poet explains that he had been a servant to the young King James V to whom he told stories with educational aims. The "Dreme" is presented as such a story. The poet is asleep in a cave and Dame Remembrance takes him to see hell and purgatory and gives him a glimpse of heaven and Eden. Then he is shown that Scotland is a ruin underneath its prosperous surface. Onto this stage, as in the *Thrie Estatis*, steps John the Common Weill of Scotland who exposes the greed and falseness and pride and sloth that the land has sunk into. So, part of "The Compleynt of the Comoun Weill of Scotland",

My tender friendis ar all put to the flycht;
For polecey is fled agane in France.
My Syster, Justice, almaist haith tynt hir sycht,
That scho can nocht hald evinly the ballance.
Plane wrang is plane capitane of Ordinance,
The quhilk debarris Laute and reassoun,
And small remeid is found for oppin treassoun.

In to the south, allace, I was neir slane
Over all the land I culd fynd no releiff;
Almoist betwix the Mers and Lowmabane
I culde nocht knaw ane leill man be ane theif
To schaw thare reif, thift, murthour, and mischeif,
And vecious workis, it wald infect the air:
And, als, langsum to me for tyll declair.

tynt: lost   Ordinance: Authority   Laute: Loyalty   leill: loyal
be: from   langsum: tedious

14

Cupar, Pitscottie, Pitlessie and Kirkton of Cults, Kingskettle and the Howe of Fife, Markinch and Star, and Balgonie

THE OLD BURGH of Cupar is a mixture of the formal and informal. The vigour of the tower of the Old Parish Church, the spire of the Duncan Institute and the narrow wynds contribute to the latter; the neo-classical design of St Catherine Street to the former. In 1810 James Gillespie Graham provided the general plan for St Catherine Street although Robert Hutchison designed the "classical" County Buildings and Town House which are currently undergoing cleaning and repair. Gillespie Graham also designed a neo-classical building for a prison in Cupar. Originally it was planned to build it where the War Memorial now stands at the end of similarly neo-classical St Catherine Street, but it ended up across the river. The building became the premises of William Watt, nurseryman and seed merchant, and that name can still be seen on the building which, as Watts of Cupar, now houses a bar, restaurant and function suite.

It was in Cupar, just before the First World War, that Hugh MacDiarmid, or Christopher Murray Grieve to give him his real name, met his first wife, Margaret (Peggy) Skinner, then aged sixteen and working as a copyholder in the proof-reading department of the Innes group of newspapers. Grieve was working for the group and writing for three papers: *Fife Herald, Fife Coast Chronicle* and *St Andrews Citizen.* Peggy Skinner and Christopher Grieve were married in Edinburgh in June 1918. By then Peggy was in the Women's Auxiliary Army Corps and working as a secretary to the Colonel of the Black Watch at Queen's Barracks, Perth. Her home address was given as 31 Durie Street, Methil; her father, David Skinner, had left Cupar to work as a colliery surface overseer. A few years later Christopher and Peggy Grieve were living in Montrose and it was there that Grieve began to write as "Hugh MacDiarmid" and to produce some of the greatest poetry of this century.

Uphill from Cupar is the village of Pitscottie where Robert Lyndsay, great chronicler of Scotland's history, lived. For his novels, Sir Walter Scott very productively plundered the work of the man he called "Auld Pitscottie". The full title of Lyndsay's book as printed by the Scottish Text Society between 1899 and 1911 is *The Historie and Cronicles of Scotland. From the Slauchter of King James the First to the Ane thousande fyve hundreith threi scoir fyftein yeir.* In a short Preface it is said that the work was written and collected "by ane Robert Lindesay of Pitscottie." There have been doubters who cannot accept that this tenant farmer was the author of this important work. There always are such snobbish sceptics when important works of earlier times are written by those who did not achieve national fame in areas other than that of their writings. We need think only of Shakespeare. Or of our knowledge of William Dunbar's life compared with that of Gavin Douglas who was the son of a warrior earl.

This great Fife writer was born about 1532 and probably died soon after 1578, and certainly before 1592 when his son, Christopher, "lawfull heir to the late Robert Lyndsay of Pitscottie" married Christian Scott, daughter of William Scott, an uncle of William Scott of Abbotshall and so a relative of the Scotts of Balwearie.

The large nineteenth-century farmhouse which now stands at Easter Pitscottie may have replaced the building in which the historian lived as a tenant but no-one is now certain where his house stood. The old house was a typical well-built farmhouse of its time—once "a countrie house of strae and reed". It would have crow-stepped gables and a high-ridged roof of large and heavy grey slates or slabs. The old house may have been demolished in 1821 during the tenancy of David Lee whose family had been at Easter Pitscottie for many generations, and indeed were to be there for many more. The last Mr Lee at Pitscottie died only recently having reached a very great age—into his nineties. Since 1969 the Kay family have been at Easter Pitscottie but soon there will be new owners.

The village of Pitscottie sits on the Ceres burn just before it goes into the gorge known as Dura Den which became famous for the fossil fish of its sandstone beds. There are five roads out of Pitscottie: to St Andrews; to Ceres; to Kemback and Dairsie; to Cupar; and to Peat Inn. Easter Pitscottie farmhouse sits some three hundred yards along the Cupar road. To reach it the burn has to be crossed by a fine-looking bridge and the farmhouse is protected to the rear by a steep slope and by a line of evergreen trees. The land behind Easter Pitscottie farmhouse is a gently sloping continuation of the Hill of Tarvit. Beyond the entrance to the farm, and its extensive modern buildings, the Cupar road climbs up to allow a view eastwards, and over Dura Den, to what looked to me like the spire of Dairsie Church and the roofs of the newly-restored Castle, but above the Den sits the hamlet of Kemback. Quickly the road goes downhill to the entrance to the avenue of Dura House, and soon the rooftops of Cupar can be seen, as can the elegant column of the Hopetoun Monument. The steep sloping land south of Pitscottie will be greener, and the land more cultivated, than in Auld Pitscottie's time, but what would surprise him more would be the new houses that face the entrance to Easter Pitscottie. A fine new wooden pedestrian bridge allows owners of these mint-new houses to cross the fast-flowing burn.

Robert Lyndsay would be known by the land he farmed, to distinguish him from the many other Lyndsays. It seems that he was a tenant on property owned by Scott of Balwearie whose barony of Strathmiglo included the lands and mills of Pitscottie. The Scotts had acquired Pitscottie when they were forfeited by Sir John Melville of Raith and the Melvilles do not seem to have regained this part of their old properties until after the historian's death, although the forfeiture was rescinded by Parliament in 1563.

The historian was a younger son of the small laird William Lyndsay of Pyotstoun and his mother Isabella Logan. The name Pyotstoun remains in use as Pyeston farm above Star, near Markinch. The historian's grandfather is Patrick, fourth Lord Lyndsay of the Byres who was granted the Mains of Kirkforthar which, then as now, adjoined Pyotstoun. The castle of Lyndsay of the Byres was the wonderfully named Ochterutherstruther which name came to Fife from an older Lyndsay estate in East Lothian. Shortened to "Struthers," this great castle features in Sir David Lyndsay of the Mount's poem "Squire Meldrum". As a distant kinsman of the poet, who died about 1553, Pitscottie could have met him at Struthers Castle, and I shall return to Squire Meldrum later. We may see from a road map that the name Struthers is still in use.

Pitscottie draws on his family's history for good stories in his *Chronicles*. It was his great-uncle David, Lord Lyndsay of the Byres, who loaned King James III the great stallion which was to bolt and make possible the King's murder at Beaton's Mill, not far from Bannockburn. It was the chronicler's grandfather, Patrick, who defended his older

166

brother, Lord David, following the accession of King James IV, and was rewarded with the lands of Kirforthar. His cousin, the sixth Lord Lyndsay of the Byres, was a stout supporter of John Knox who opposed Mary, and provided Pitscottie with the story of his part in the siege of Edinburgh Castle. Pitscottie also, as already related, chronicled the execution of the captain of the Castle, Kirkcaldy of Grange. A hundred years ago the tomb of Pitscottie's cousin, Patrick, sixth Lyndsay of the Byres, who died in 1589, could still be identified in Ceres kirkyard but not that of the historian.

Auld Pitscottie Lyndsay cannot always be relied upon for historical accuracy but he could write very well and his work deserves to live because it is literature. He does have some advantages over later historians who go to the documents as he could speak to some of his authorities who could have spoken to their grandfathers who could have told of events before their time. Showing no consistent regard for capital letters, Lyndsay names the following as some of his authorities,

> Patrick lord lyndesay of the byres [Pitscottie's grandfather] Schir William Scot of balwirrie knicht [Pitscottie's "landlord" and also his kinsman by marriage] Schir Androw Wood of Largo knicht (King James IV's sea captain] Maister Johne Mair doctour of theologie quha wret his cronickill heirupone and alsua schir david lyndesay of the mount allias lyoun herauld king of armes [Pitscottie's cousin] with Androw wood of largo principall and familiar servand to King James the fyft [a son of the above captain] Androw fernie of that ilk ane nobill man of recent memorie [he owned an estate near Falkland] Schir William bruce of erleshall knicht wha hes wrettin verrie justlie all the deidis sen flowdane field [the builder of Earshall, by Leuchars].

These are mostly men of action and political intrigue who were, like the more private Lyndsay of Pitscottie, partial to the politics of their time, as are all historians. It is, however, a worthy roll-call of Pitscottie's Fife neighbours and kinsfolk, plus John Mair (or Major) Provost of St Salvator's College, St Andrews, who had published his history in 1521 and died in Pitscottie's lifetime—in 1550. To that list we can add Hector Boece (or Boyce) as Pitscottie described his work as "the historie and cronickillis of Scotland quhilk was left onwrettin be the last translature to wit maister boes and maister Johne ballentyne."

It seems that Robert Lyndsay of Pitscottie was not keen to have his work published whilst Morton was in power, but he need not have worried as it did not become publicly available until 1778. For two centuries Scottish history, as told by Pitscottie, has permeated through other writers and many primary school teachers into the minds of the people of Scotland. His stories live because he was a great writer of Scots prose. His phrases have been repeated by many who did not know where they came from. Sometimes Pitscottie may have been repeating phrases given to him by others, including Sir David Lyndsay of the Mount, but even if this were so they live because he could tell a good story.

The death of James II lives in Pitscottie's phrase that the monarch's interest in guns made him, "more curious than became a king" and the result was that because of "ane piece of ane misframed gunne, his thigh bone was dung in two". There is the famous confrontation of King James V with Johnnie Armstrong, the Border reiver who, about to be hanged, uttered his final defiant words, "I am bot ane foole to seik grace at ane graceless face." The most famous words used by Pitscottie are in his description of the scene at King James V's Falkland death bed; these must have been repeated verbally a hundred thousand times, but certainly they are worthy of a second printing in this book, "And so he recommendit himself to the marcie of Almighty God, and spak ane little then from that time forth, bot turnit his back into his lordis and his face into the wall."

In Lyndsay of Pitscottie's day the tower on the crest of Tarvit Hill, if it was there at all, would have been lower. Also, it was not known as Scotstarvit until bought by Sir John Scot in 1611. Today, travelling on the A916 from Kennoway, as the picturesque hamlet of Chance Inn comes into sight there is also a good view of the tall and elegant walls of tower of Scotstarvit set above the green slopes and against the skyline. A few moments later the tower can be composed into a landscape that also includes, to the west of Craigrothie, the monument on Hill of Tarvit.

The mansion of the Hopes at Craighall, south of Ceres, has both come and gone since Lyndsay of Pitscottie's time. It was built in the early seventeenth century and the remnant demolished in the 1950s. Hill of Tarvit mansion has a history that dates back to the end of the seventeenth century and, like Craighall, the original house may have been built to a design by Sir William Bruce. Additions were made in the nineteenth century but the earlier structures are now hidden. What we see today is a mansion house and garden created in 1906 by Sir Robert Lorimer for F. B. Sharp, a Dundee industrialist, who had a collection of very fine French, Chippendale and also vernacular furniture. The house is now in the care of the National Trust for Scotland and visitors to it can also see Sharp's Chinese porcelain and bronzes. Here also are paintings by Ramsay and Raeburn.

Struthers is south of Craigrothie on the A916 and the old castle of the Lyndsays of the Barns stood beyond the farmhouse close to what was a farm track when I was there in the 1950s. I remember Struthers Barns as being off the other side of the road. Sir David Lyndsay has his heroic Squire Meldrum die at Struthers Castle. Although Lyndsay works within the mediaeval romance tradition, he does so with an awareness that he is using an old and dying tradition. His *The historie of ane nobil and vailyeand squyer William Meldrum, umwhyle Laird of Cleische and Bynnis* remains very readable. The poem is based on a real-life noble Squire who, in 1513, fought with the Scottish army in France and had a passionate love-affair with Marion Lawson, widow of John Haldane of Gleneagles. Lack of a Papal Dispensation prevented their marriage but the heroic Meldrum fought to defeat her enemies. A jealous rival, "a cruel knicht", of course, ambushed Meldrum,

> And come behind him cowartly,
> And hackit on his hochs and theis
> Till that he fell upon his knees.
> Yet when his shanks were shorn in sunder,
> Upon his knees he wrocht great wonder.
> Sweipand his sword round about.
> Not havand of the death na doubt
> Durst nane approach within his bounds.
> Till that his cruel mortal wounds
> Bled sa, that he did swap in swoun;
> Perforce behuvit him then fall doun.
> And when he lay upon the ground
> They gave him mony cruel wound,
> That men on far micht hear the knocks,
> Like butchers hackand on their stocks.
> And finally without remede
> They left him lyand there for dead . . .

The hero survived, but his lady was forced to leave him and, unmarried, he turned to be a caring surgeon. The poem ends,

> And when he did decline to age
> He faillit never of his courage.
> Of ancient stories for to tell,
> Abone all other he did precel,
> Sa that everilk creature
> To hear him speak they took pleasure.
> Bot all his deeds honorable
> For to descrive I am not able.
> Of every man he was commendit,
> And as he leivit, sa he endit,
> Pleasandly, till he micht endure,
> Till dolent death come to his door
> And cruelly, with his mortal dart,
> He strake the squire through the heart.
> His saul with joy angelical
> Past to the heaven imperial.
> Thus at the Struther into Fife
> This noble squire lost his life.

Back in Cupar we may remember again the day when Sir David Lyndsay's *Thrie Estatis* was performed on Castlehill. Today the hill is topped by a quadrangle of various buildings but if we go round behind these to the car park we can see that this is indeed a high-standing motte which could have provided a fine setting for such a stirring work.

Out of Cupar goes the long straight road that passes Springfield road end, Pitlessie and Kettlebridge to join the A92 as it comes south from the Tay Bridge and on to Glenrothes. These are flat lands and, in the 1950s, the stretch of road from near Kingskettle to the edge of Cupar was used for a ten mile sprint race by cyclists, five miles there and five miles back. There were also, if I remember correctly, races as long as 100 miles and, indeed, a twenty-four hour race. I remember Dave Wallace from Kirkcaldy as a strong contender at all distances.

As we come along the A914 we can see up on the sloping fields the Cults & Pitlessie Lime Works—which now make bricks as well as processing lime. The Works belong to the Cochrane family and are currently being run by Julian Cochrane, brother of Lord Cochrane whose home is at Crawford Priory. Many Cochranes are buried in Cults kirkyard in Kirkton of Cults. Amongst them is Thomas H. A. E. Cochrane, first Baron Cochrane of Cults who died in 1951. He was the second son of the eleventh Earl of Dundonald and related by marriage to George, sixth Earl of Glasgow. The remains of Crawford Priory stand off the Cupar road. These complex buildings were built around Crawford Lodge which was erected by the twenty-first Earl of Crawford in 1758. It was the Earl's sister, and the heir to his estate but not the title, Lady Mary Lindsay Crawford, who instigated the building of a Gothick Hall and also had the older building made into a "Priory". Lady Mary's heir was the fourth Earl of Glasgow, and his heirs made further alterations, but the interior was to decline into dereliction.

Kirkton of Cults lies about a mile to the south-east of Pitlessie village and the kirk is a striking feature in these acres of good farmland. The village of Pitlessie, with its fast-flowing burn and twisting and turning streets, is of another idyllic-looking world that truly does not require to be enhanced by envisaging David Wilkie's painting of "Pitlessie Fair", but I do think of Wilkie's work each time I pass Pitlessie. Also, when I think of Wilkie, I remember not Wilkie's kinsman Professor Wilkie who encouraged the poet Robert Fergusson, but Robert Lyndsay who wrote his history in a farmhouse near Pitscottie. Both Wilkie and Lindsay have qualities in their work that have deep roots in rural Fife.

Wilkie was born in the manse of Cults in 1785 and went to school in Pitlessie, Kettle and Cupar. He was born in a manse that was, even in 1785, in poor condition, and his youth was spent in a new manse built in 1796. This building, Kirkton House, still stands but is in private ownership. Today's Cults Parish Church, by the Cults Burn, was built in 1793 but it stands on a site where there has been a church for some 800 years. Again we have a dedication by Bishop David Bernham; the date is 1234. The small Session House, by the kirk gate, was shown to me by Mrs Garland, the Session Clerk of Cults, and her enthusiasm for this small room did, as she has written, give me a "glimpse of the last century". The belfry is a classic country kirk structure with a bell that, with my inner ear, I could "hear" sounding out, every Sunday, over the Howe and echoing up to the Hill of Tarvit monument. The bell is inscribed, "John Meikle, Edinburgh, fecit for the Kirk at Cults, 1699". So David Wilkie would have heard that bell many a time.

The interior of the church silences unnecessary words. The general impression is of lightness but the boxed pews remain a rich, deep oak colour. There is also stained glass, and a window with coloured surrounds but clear panes. This window offers a view of a landscape of pastoral and arable acres, trees and green-faced hills that is as far removed from the stereotyped view of a cold and grim Calvinist Scotland as is the interior of the kirk. Either side of that well-proportioned window are tablets in memory of members of the Wilkie family. On the facing wall, either side of the pulpit, are the plaques in memory of Sir David Wikie and his parents, Rev David Wilkie and Isabella Lister. The monuments are fine, that of Wilkie's parents being (1833) by Sir Francis Chantrey (1789-1841) and that of the artist by Samuel Joseph (1791-1850), made about 1841. In Pitlessie the name of Wilkie's mother lives on in Lister Place and in Lister House from which can be seen Pitlessie Mill where the Listers lived. In Lister House lives Elder Garland whose family have been joiners in Pitlessie for three generations, and who restored the kirk pews and the old wall brackets, turning lamps for them and renewing the shades. David Wilkie would have appreciated such fine craftsmanship. Dignified memorials of the Garland family are in the kirkyard.

In 1799 the young Wilkie left for Edinburgh to study at the Trustees Academy. He was aged 19 when he came back to Fife in 1804 and immediately produced two major works, "Pitlessie Fair" and a portrait of the Chalmers-Bethune family. Both works are masterpieces but the portrait, although of a rural man, wife and daughter, rises above any narrow parochialism, or provincialism. The painting of the fair is also a great work but, unjustly, it is difficult to look at it without remembering the countless sentimental scenes of Scottish rural life that came later. Wilkie's strength is that he was a social realist whose works are given significance by his skill as a painter of portraits that enhance his visual narrative. This takes him beyond mere illustration and out of rural sentimentality.

When exhibiting "Pitlessie Fair" in London in 1812, Wilkie said that the people he painted at the fair "are portraits of the inhabitants of a small village in Scotland, where the Fair is held annually, and near to where the picture was painted." Included in the picture are portraits of the painter's father, Rev David Wilkie, and several members of his family. So we cannot deny the authenticity or suggest that Wilkie did not know village life. The young Wilkie also knew that the pomposity of artists has to be pricked and so he painted a dog with its leg lifted over the artist's signature. There is great craftsmanship, and the composition of a later narrative masterpiece, "The Letter of Introduction", painted in 1813, has a hint of what F. C. B. Cadell achieved much later, but there is also in Wilkie's best work a suggestion of earthiness and a humour that comments on the artist as well as the subjects. Fame was to come to Sir David Wilkie but he is perhaps best remembered for his family portrait of William Chalmers-Bethune, his wife Isabella Morrison and their daughter Isabella which has only recently become widely known although an early work.

A feature of this part of the Howe of Fife is the tower of Kettle church and the village of Kingskettle remains well worth a visit. Ladybank owes a lot to the coming of the railway and lacks the true Fife old-village atmosphere. I think of Kettlebridge as a small village of one street, and a garage, lying at the foot of a long hill down which I allowed my bike to speed; in reality it always had more width than that. Together these villages, with Freuchie and the river Eden and the views to the Lomond Hills, make the flat lands of the Howe of Fife an ever-varying delight. There are fewer men and women working the lands of the Howe, and the gear and tackle has been revolutionised, yet our sense of the rightness of these lands and those who live on them remains comparable to the lands and people of Gerard Manley Hopkins' "Pied Beauty",

> Landscape plotted and pierced—fold, fallow and plough;
> And all trades, their gear and tackle trim.

Near Kingskettle is the steep brae known as Kettlehill that continues to Kennoway, Star and Markinch. At the top of the hill the road continues to meet the road from Cults & Pitlessie Lime Works and Coaltown of Burnturk to go past Rameldry, Milldeans, the edge of Drummy Wood and the Star road-end to go down to Kennoway.

My memories of the country roads around Kennoway and Markinch are mostly of warm summer days in the 1950s but I do clearly remember a winter that was cold beyond any of recent years. One cold day was memorable enough to me for it to become the subject of a poem that tells of a walk across the fields from Teuchat Head farm, near Kennoway, to Carriston farm which sits above Star village. In these days Carriston House was more enclosed by trees through which its lights shone rather eerily. I named the poem "Thochts" and, for me, it is more about youthful courting days than the extreme cold,

> Only three miles but seemin like ten.
>
> You and I oot for a Sunday walk in oor courtin days
> and takin the straucht wey hame across the fields
> frae Teuchat Head.
> Frozen stubble haurd and ruttit aneath oor feet
> and bravely walked through. The quait December air
> enclosin stillness aw aroond but for the crunch o frost
> agin the earth. Hand in haund we lean furrit
> and think only o the end o this walk
> and escape frae that cauld,
> we thocht. Haunds sculptured lumps withoot feelin
> and noses cauld ayont onie pain.
> The nicht is closin in fast for aw the brichtenin hoar
> and aheid the sma lichts o Burnside show we've faur to gae.

But soon doon by the watterman's cottage
and the tall windaes of Carriston House oor next goal
bricht owre the reservoir unseen ahint its bank
but felt in a cheynge o air. Noo roond by the loch's faur edge
and large doocot agin the Western sky. And Lomond Hill
a white Matterhorn aw day noo a distant greyness
and ither warld. We think o the sma cottage
and blazin fire, and escape frae this cauld,
we thocht.

Noo I mind the walk frae Teuchat Head to hame
and you oot walkin wi me.

The name Carriston is very old, being known as Caraldstone in the 1550s when David Balfour was the laird. His daughter and heir married John Seton, a son of Lord Seton and Elizabeth Hay, a daughter of John, Lord Yester. The Setons were at Carriston till near the end of the eighteenth century and they with other lairds attracted a popular rhyme,

Cariston and Pyetstone,
Kirkforthar and Drum,
Are four o' the maist curst lairds
That ever spak wi' tongue.

At that time there were Lyndsays at Pyetstone and Kirkforthar, kinsfolk to the historian Robert Lyndsay of Pitscottie and a Lundie was at Drum. Drum Farm sits near the woods known as Drummy and there are also Milldeans Wood and Kirkforthar Wood. When I saw these densely planted trees in 1997 I assumed, unthinkingly, that they were those that I had run through in the 1950s. Of course, that was nonsense and there could have been two fellings and two plantings since then. At the end of the road through these enclosing conifer woods, a steep brae leads down to join the A914 west of Kettlebridge. The view of the Howe of Fife from the top of that hill is literally eye-opening and breath stopping. The Lomond hills should dominate and, especially in winter, they are certainly strikingly Alpine. Below them, however is the long, low strath with a diversity of farmlands, each with its variously-sized fields and unnameable, and uncountable, tones of green and brown; small villages and hamlets, every one with its distinctive cluster of buildings; a diversity that equals, and balances in its broad sweep, the dramatic but simple lines of the hills; a varied but harmonious landscape that awaits a twentieth-century Cézanne.

The Balfours of Balbirnie, Markinch, were to acquire Pyeston and Kirkforthar and Kirkforthar Feus. I know of at least three generations of the Lathangie family at Pyeston. I rather think that Ballenkirk remained outside the Balfour estate and until the 1950s there was a succession of Lawsons at neighbouring Carriston; their restrained headstones ("Tom of Carriston" for example) line a wall in the old Northall cemetery on the edge of Markinch below the railway bridge at the foot of Cuinin Hill. There have been two owners at Carriston since Tom Lawson sold up, and the house, steading and land appear to be in exceptionally good order as tended and worked by Matthew Jack and his family.

From Northall cemetery, a track goes up and round the Cuinin Hill to reach the Kennoway road above Star village. At the top of the track there lived, in the 1950s, a group of travelling people. They seemed to be camped there all year and there was a second group camped within singing distance across the Kennoway road. Not infrequently

I came up that track late at night, summer and winter, and twenty years later I wrote "The Unkent",

> Late at nicht we come owre the Cuinin Hill
> through the trees closin in, and oot by the tinkers' camp
> wi daurk bulbous tents and tethered horses.
> We walk very quaitly close thegither but fast
> at the soond o their howlin and wailin that's mebbe
> singin. And the stirrin o horses.
>
> The stars are bricht in a daurk black sky
> and the moon castin lang hidin shadows. Feelin
> the nip in the air and that singin gettin nearer
> we set aff into a slaw tip-toe run
> haund and haund past their tents. Quicker and
> quicker but as quaitly as we can wi quick looks back
> owre oor shooders. The singin cheynges key
> as we turn onto the main road
> and the soond o oor feet loud as drums
> but there's nae thocht o stoppin wi the deil at oor heels.
> Weill past noo, we laugh and are aff into a happy run thegither
> doon into Star village wi its daurk windaes
> and the neighin o grey mare aside North Dalginch fairm,
> and soos gruntin in Bellfield's styes close to the road.
> A stoat or weasel's quick across the road
> and hoolets cry in the nicht air.
>
> But what we ken
> —at haund!

In the summer of 1958, having spent six months never out of central London, I climbed with my wife the 450 foot Cuinin to look over to the Lomonds and the fields around Star and Kennoway. The air was so clear and the silence so complete to our Londonised ears that the memory of that silence remains uniquely with us. And when we returned to the hill in the early 1900s the quiet and calm rural scene looked untouched by change. That was a false impression as, although the silence remained unbroken and the traffic on the roads minimal, the village of Star had become, in a small way, a place for discerning commuters to Glenrothes and elsewhere.

It has been suggested that the name Star derives from the boggy area, thick with sedge, to the west of the village towards Kirkforthar. Certainly the name is quite unconnected to any heavenly star, whether of Markinch or Kennoway. Star Moss is not only extensive but, within limits, well known. There was an old saying that may have a biographical root, "If I don't get on wi my wark, I'll stick in the Star Moss like Willie Lan's mither." When I was in Collessie kirkyard I noted a headstone of a David Wallace, who was from Letham but had died in Star in 1876, aged 62 years, so perhaps the village had not been as isolated as I thought in the 1950s. When I knew Star then, the village, like the cottages of the surrounding farms, lacked mains electricity and there was a well by the roadside for the few houses that lacked piped water. There was then a single road through Star. As today, it went up and down hill; and twisted and turned, the first track being made, I presume, to reach each new group of cottages. The result is that claims have been made for Star to be known as the longest village in Scotland.

The popular novelist Annie S. Swan (1859-1943) lived in Star schoolhouse for some years when her husband, John Burnett Smith, was the teacher. From her back windows Mrs Smith would have a good view over Star Moss and the lands of Kirkforthar to the Lomonds. For such low hills East and West Lomond present striking slopes and peaks to many points of the compass, although the view of them from above Star is particularly alpine, as is that from the road that leads to Kettlehill. One of my "Walking in Fife" poems is "Winter Peak",

> You couldna believe your een
> kennin it every day frae anither side.
>
> Me walking you oot on a bricht December day
> wi snaw to be struggled through to the Milldeans Road
> and alang the straucht stretch to Rameldry
> and the clear view to the West.
> There as if by magic lantern or carpet it rose
> as we steppt clear o the trees. It lookt baith distant
> and as if we could touch it in the dry clean air.
> Its outline sae sherp and risin white to the blue sky.
> A seemin Alpine giant wi knife-edge ridges and shadowed face
> suggestin baith heicht and depth.
> A real Matterhorn set doun in pastoral Fife.
>
> You couldna believe your een
> and held me close at the wunner o it,
> and nae words to speak . . .

The old Pictish capital of Fife may have been Markinch and it has been suggested that the name Dalginch goes back to that distant time. There were caves at Markinch and there is a tradition that their walls bore ancient art works similar to those at Wemyss. The Markinch caves were closed in 1929. The name Dalginch lives on in North Dalginch farm, which I mention in "The Unkent", and Dalginch farm sits off the Kennoway road above Star. I remember Dalginch as another Balfour property, as I do also Treaton which stands well back from the Kennoway road and was, and may still be, sheltered by the plantings known as Treaton Strips, a fine and simple-seeming name. Another Balbirnie property off the Kennoway Road was Newtonhall.

Newtonhall is of interest because of its possible associations with John Lamont, an interesting seventeenth-century diarist. When *The Chronicle of Fife; Being the Diary of John Lamont of Newton, from 1649 to 1672* was first published in 1810, it was said that the author was "John Lamont of Newton, in the Parish of Kennoway" but the John Lamont who was at Newton may have been another man, a skipper in Largo who came to Newton in 1695. The diarist was almost certainly the Factor on the Lundin estate. The main Lundin estate was in the area of today's Lundin Links and Largo but there were also Lundins at Auchtermainie which lies above Kennoway to the north and west of Baintown and near Lalathan. It was through marrying Isobel, daughter of the Earl of Rothes, that Robert Lundin, son of William Lundin of Lundin, acquired the lands of Auchtermairnie. The strength of the case for Lamont being the Lundin factor was put by And. S. Cunningham who quoted an entry which certainly shows the diarist's familiarity with the Lundin estate,

> 1563, May—I planted some elme trees in the garden yeard of Lundie, on the south quarter, nearest the dovecoat, and before I October 1654 they were hyger than ane ordinar man, and many of them some what great also; som eof them being thrie inche about, neare the roote. At the same time, also, I had some younge firrs up out of the seide; they be both neare thegreather, in that same place.

The Balfours of Balbirnie were to own not only Newtonhall but also part of Auchtermairnie. I believe that And. S. Cunningham was a partner in Purves & Cunningham, publishers in Leven of *Leven Advertiser and Wemyss Gazette* which was published every Thursday morning. It cost in 1906 "One Halfpenny" and in addition to normal local and district news printed, weekly, "Historical and other Special Notes". Mr Cunningham was quite prolific as a writer on Fife, his works including, *Romantic Culross, Inverkeithing and the Naval Base, Rambles in the Parishes of Scoonie and Wemyss* and *Kennoway and the Fringes of Markinch.*

The Balbirnie estate goes back at least to a John de Balbrennie of the time of King Robert I, the Bruce. The Balfours were lairds of all the Balbirnie estate from 1642 until 1969 when they sold Balbirnie House and grounds to Glenrothes Development Corporation. The Corporation restored the house and it is now a privately-owned country house hotel while the grounds are now a country park, owned by Fife Council. The Balfours did not begin altering the old estate house until 1777; they used good local sandstone of a pleasing fawn colour for these extensions. It was General Robert Balfour who, in 1815, created the present building which absorbed parts of the earlier structures but quite transformed the house. The new east-facing entrance, with its high Ionic portico, is particularly successful and, of the extensive alterations and additions to the interior, the saloon, or long gallery, is very attractive despite its dimensions being 68 feet long by 15 feet wide. The surrounding park was excellently landscaped in the late 1770s, and again in 1815, with the sloping acres of the wooded park enhanced by Balbirnie Burn. The plantings of rhododendrons are amongst the best in the country and the very tall monkey-puzzle trees, or Chilean pines, make a dramatic statement half way up the steep bank. There is a viewing point which gives a splendid panoramic view westwards to the Lomonds and the rolling agricultural lands. It was in 1770 that a young Mr Ballingal, aged 20, was appointed Agent to the Balfour estate. He was succeeded by his son and grandson and so the same family not only looked after but recorded the affairs of the estate until 1916.

The work of the Balfours in creating and maintaining Balbirnie Park has been excellently continued and extended by the Local Authority. What is new is Balbirnie Park Golf Club for which the sloping pastures above and around the house have been excellently landscaped. The current professional at Balbirnie, George Scott, is a grandson of the composer Francis George Scott who set to music lyrics by Hugh MacDiarmid. George's father, another George, taught English at Bell Baxter School in Cupar and his aunt is the poet Lillias Forbes. At the Balfarg end of Balbirnie Park is a prehistoric Stone Circle which was excavated during work on widening the A92 and moved to its present position where information is also given on the nearby great "henge monument" which has also been preserved and partly reconstructed for visitors to Balfarg.

Alan Bold, poet and general man of letters, died as I was reading the proofs of this book. Alan lived for many years in a cottage almost on the banks of Balbirnie Burn. Amongst his works are a biography of Hugh MacDiarmid, a selection of MacDiarmid's letters and of his poetry and prose. He was also an authority on Robert Burns and contributed weekly book reviews to both *The Scotsman* and the *Glasgow Herald*.

Hereabouts also lives John Bett, the actor, who, as a very young man, wrote a poem for Hugh MacDiarmid which I printed in a volume entitled *Poems Addressed to Hugh MacDiarmid* which was published for presentation to MacDiarmid on his seventy-fifth birthday—11th August 1967. John's poem is set in a bus on a journey from the poet's Brownsbank Cottage and begins,

> Afternoon steals by
> in a slow, Scottish drizzle,
> sunlight left behind in Brownsbank.
> The bus shaking, rattling,
> jogs the brain
> cutting out the memory.
> Was my landscape always rain?
> Did I really see the sun?
> The window of vision is blurred
> with the slow drops of monotony.

But the poem has a cheerful and optimistic ending,

> Look
> the rain has stopped
> and the grey mist is dancing.

Not many of those who now walk in Balbirnie Park can remember when red squirrels could be seen climbing the great beech trees. Also, no-one to whom I now mention the *aurora borealis* that I saw in the middle 1950s on dark winter nights when cycling between Markinch and Star village has ever heard of these displays. Looking up at them, with the lights of my bicycle switched off, I risked falling into a ditch on many of these black, rural late nights. On many of these clear nights the northern lights were vague and elusive white movements across the black sky but on a very few occasions there could be some colour in them.

Near the East Lodge of Balbirnie Park, on the Markinch to Star road, stands the Stob Cross. In the 1950s I assumed that this was a Pictish stone but experts now suggest that is a Sanctuary Cross which indicated the boundary of a sanctuary associated with a Culdee church. It could be that the Cross originally stood at the entrance to a predecessor to St Drostan's Church in Markinch. The Earl of Leven at Balgonie Castle had the mound on which the Cross stands repaired in 1790 and the plinth is of the nineteenth century.

The tower of the kirk of St Drostan is a magnificent landmark from vantage points many a mile around Markinch. It also looks most impressive from the High Street. St Drostan would have established his church in the sixth century, but the tower is a perfect example of its kind and dates from 1243. A low pyramidal stone coping topped by a rod and weathercock was removed in 1807 and the spire was also altered somewhat, but we can only stand and admire the proportions of the tower and its beautiful, simple and honest

176

masonry. Like St Rule's Tower in St Andrews, St Drostan's has two-light windows which add interest to the clean lines of the tower. In 1637 the clock, or knock, on the tower has its first recorded mention, "The minister and William Boswell ordained to give the General's lady thanks for bringing the Knocke to balgoney". I would guess that the General is Sir Alexander Leslie, First Earl of Leven, who had previously been Lord Balgonie, and whose Balgonie Castle, at Milton of Balgonie, stands on the south bank of the river Leven by the Windygates road.

A much later General who has close associations with St Drostan's Church is General Robert Balfour of Balbirnie who died in 1837 and was buried in St Drostan's. Other Balfours are buried in Northall cemetery which dates from 1853. There is a more modern St Drostan's cemetery high above the old burgh on the Milton of Balgonie road. The copse of trees that grew within its walls has been felled but there is a fine prospect of the Lomonds and the sea.

The castle of Balgonie has been excellently restored and its outlines, whilst not as dramatic as those of Ravenscraig, look not only very well balanced from across the fields but almost homely. The earliest known owners at Balgonie are members of the Sibbald family. There was a Duncan Sibbald at Balgonie in 1246. The Great Tower was built by a Sibbald about 1360 and is sixty-five feet high to the parapets. Other parts of the castle were built by Sir Robert Lundin towards the end of the fifteenth century. There were Lundins at Balgonie until early in the seventeenth century when it was sold to sons of Sir John Boswell of Balmuto, Auchtertool. It seems that in 1634 John, Earl of Rothes, bought the barony of Balgonie but quickly sold it, in 1635, to his cousin General Sir Alexander Leslie, Earl of Leven, who further developed the castle and laid out gardens down to the river Leven. In 1824 David, eighth Earl of Leven, sold the estate to Sir James Balfour of Whittinghame, grandfather of A. J. Balfour who was Prime Minister from 1902 to 1905 and became the first Earl of Balfour. This Balfour family owned Balgonie Castle until 1950, and they still own Balgonie Estates Limited, as they do the Newton Don Estate, Kelso. As early as the 1840s Balgonie was slipping into ruination, but the real destruction came when an increased number of vandals moved seriously in on the Castle in the 1960s.

Details of these destructions are given by Stuart G. C. Morris of Balgonie in his *Balgonie Castle: a Brief Profile*. One example gives a hint of what was destroyed, "The gap between the Tower and Hall House was filled in by a Scale and Platt Tower in 1666. This Great Stair was built by John Mylne of Balfarg, seventh Hereditary King's Master Mason, by order of John, Earl (later Duke) of Rothes, Guardian of the infant Margaret, Countess of Leven. The entire staircase was destroyed by vandals in the 1960s."

Saviours were at hand. In 1971 the Balfour estate sold the Castle to David Maxwell from Edinburgh. He began work on restoring the Tower. Fife County Council bought the north and east wings with the idea of restoring them for use as a museum and for educational use. These plans came to nothing and in 1985 the Morris family bought the whole castle. As Stuart Morris has written of his family, "We were the first people to live in the castle since 1824, when we moved in November, of what was the second coldest winter this century. Wet, green walls intensified the cold which, inside, reached -7C for a whole week." The Morris family have been working on the castle from that year to this and all who wish to see the wonders they have achieved can visit the castle all the year round between 10am and 5pm. Also, the Chapel is available for weddings and Christenings and the Great Hall for receptions. Unlike earlier Barons of Balgonie, R. S. Morris is a creative craftsman; a master leather carver and heraldric artist. Also, The Lady of Balgonie is a tapestry weaver who specialises in weaving panels of architectural subjects.

Looking from Balgonie Castle to where Balfour House once stood and where a portrait of the beautiful Mary Beaton may have hung to look down on many a famous visitor, I am reminded not so much of Field Marshall Sir Alexander Leslie, who became an earl in 1641, but of Rev John Pinkerton who, like the second Earl of Leven, was remembered by a plaque placed on a wall of St Drostan's, Parish Church of Markinch. Mr Pinkerton's plaque informed that, "After having spent a very cheerful evening at *Balfour House* with Mr Bethune and his *Family*, he was found in the morning in his bed room in a Chair by the Fire place with one stocking in his hand *Quite Dead*."

15

Kennoway and via Ceres
to Magus Muir and Strathkinness
(THE MURDER OF ARCHBISHOP SHARP)
and Markinch to Ceres
and Many a Hamlet

BEYOND Balgonie Castle and Milton of Balgonie lies Windygates and uphill eastwards is Kennoway. Despite being surrounded by modern industrial structures, the hill on which the Maiden Castle of Kennoway sat remains unmistakable as the village is approached from Windygates. As previously indicated, the Maiden has been a contender for the destination of MacDuff, the Thane of Fife, when he fled from Macbeth. The unspoiled country roads above Kennoway remain less-well-known than the Howe below them.

In 1998 I came to Kennoway on the Kirkcaldy to Dundee bus (no.41) and alighted at Bonnybank out of Kennoway on the Cupar road (A916). A short distance uphill from Bonnybank is Baintown and there a signpost indicates the Public Path to Porters' Brae via Balgriebank. To begin with, this is a farm road that briefly gives a glimpse of the Lomonds to the west but, as it climbs steeply up to the farm, the attraction of this high road is the view to the south and east. We have yet another profile of the slopes of Largo Law and Ruddons Point, near Earlsferry, is an eye-catching feature, as is the great curve of Largo Bay, with the red roofs of new houses prominent in the green acres below the Law. Further out are the steeples of the villages of the East Neuk and the May Isle is prominent. Inchkeith and other smaller islands also enliven the waters of the Forth and, as so often from east Fife, over the Firth, Berwick Law seems to rise closer than I believe it should do, and Edinburgh's Arthur's Seat surprises by the angle at which it is seen. It is said that in times past the local sailors could recite a rhyme to remind them of the route from Queensferry to the Tay,

> Inchcolm, Inchkeith,
> The twa Mickeries and Craigleith,
> The lofty Bass and the Isle of May,
> Round the Carr and in the Tay.

Landbound above Kennoway, the steepness of the climb to Balgriebank does not lessen until well beyond the farm's barns. A right-of-way arrow indicates a way past the intimidating farm gate which is topped by barbed-wire. In early March 1998 this tree-lined path was above the snow line which is not surprising even for short-lived snow as we are near Bighty Farm, which once claimed to have the "highest hairst (harvest) stane" in Fife", although others have spoken of a "hearthstone". Today Bighty (pronounced Bichty) is a ruin. At the hilltop the path seems to head for a ploughed field but the helpful Right of Way Society's arrow indicates that the route turns right and into a fine wood. A roofless building on the southern skyline could be Bighty. As the path begins to go downhill, the evergreen wood is lined by what is almost a formal avenue of beeches and other hardwoods. The Lomonds must lie straight ahead but the trees obscure any view. A southwards break in the trees does allow Arthur's Seat to make an unexpected appearance as, soon, does a delightful, low-lying village which it took me a few minutes to recognise as Star. In a few more minutes the vehicular road is reached and the East Lomond presents its snow-covered slopes for admiration. A sign indicates that the Public Path I had come along goes to Bonnybank by Balgriebank. We are at the top of Sailor's Brae which goes down past Star road end to Burnturk 2¼ miles away, with Freuchie 4 miles. One of the other two roads goes down to Cults 3 miles, and Cupar 6, and it is 1½. miles down the third road to Kennoway. This is an excellent viewpoint. Far below, the fields of Carriston, Ballenkirk, Pyeston and North Mains present a pattern of brilliant greens set off by the rich browns of newly-ploughed acres. Far to the west, below the hills over the Tay, a very large white building suggested to me that the village behind it is Auchtermuchty.

My route that day was back down to Kennoway past Langside farm and a quarry that had grown considerably since I last saw it some decades ago. The old village of Kennoway may take its name from a St Kenneth of Canlie who established a Culdee Church here in the seventh century. The Parish Church, on the Cupar road, was built in 1849-50 to replace the old kirk in Causeway which had a 1619 datestone. Until recent times "modern" Kennoway was a village of weavers, but coal miners came from Ayrshire in the 1930s and also after the Second World War, when it was intended to create a new mining town.

The old Swan Hotel has seen busier times, not least in stagecoach days, as Kennoway is on the main road from Newport and Cupar to Windygates and was an important stage on the route to Pettycur ferry. The coaches came along the Causeway which twists along behind today's main road. The most interesting buildings in Kennoway are reached via the road behind the Swan to the Causeway where the old Church of 1619 stood. The Church has gone, and a plumber has his modern business premises on its site. These premises are backed by the high wall that encloses the kirkyard, which stands off Dead Wynd—almost more apt than Anstruther's Burial Brae! In 1998 those wishing to see the old churchyard could get the keys from a helpful lady in nearby Forbes House. Close by is Seton House, with a very-well-restored stone buttress, and also Seith House. Seton House carries an inscription "Depressus Extollor" and the date 1877, but this is an extension to an older, late-eighteenth-century house. A modern double garage at Seath House has an old armorial stone with a date that looks like 1719.

Both Forbes House and Seton House have been designated as nineteenth-century buildings which replaced an earlier building in which Archbishop James Sharp spent the night before he was murdered en route to St Andrews. In Kennoway, in 1998, I was told that the relevant building is Seath house, which may have also belonged to a Seton. In recent times, Seton House has been said to have been the home of Captain Seton, and claims have been made for it having belonged to the family of Mary Seton, one of the four Maries of Mary, Queen of Scots. When I stood by Seton House, which has a complicated walled garden, two fine bearded goats came rushing down a garden path to greet me.

Robert Wodrow (1679-1734), historian of the Covenanters, said that the Archbishop "Came to Captain Seton's house in Kennoway, where he lodged all night." The old seventeenth-century Seton House was photographed and was described in 1906 by And. S. Cunningham as,

> a seventeenth-century two-storey building, typical of the "town houses" of the Scottish gentry of the period. Gaunt and worn with age, the building is a melancholy link with the past. As one mounts the outside stair, he is assured by the tenant that the west room is "the very room in which the Bishop slept," and attention is called to the wood panelling and

the fine old mantlepieces of both apartments. Externally the stringed windows, the crow-stepped gables, and ornate chimney-heads are the only features of the building. A little further down the "Causey" there is another quaint house which is also associated with the name of the Setons, and what gives this old building an air of importance is the fact that a coat of arms is sculpted above the main entrance, the date being 1712. Tradition does not tell us what event in national or local history the stone was placed above the door to commemorate. Writing in May 1793, the Rev. Patrick Wright says, "that a woman died fourteen years ago who remembered to have seen Archbishop Sharp at the manse of Kennoway the day before he was murdered."

James Sharp was born in Banff Castle in 1613 and educated at the University of Aberdeen. He married Helen Moncrieff of Randerston and they had a son, Sir William Sharp of Scotscraig, and four daughters. Two of their daughters married into north-east Fife families that have featured in this book; the eldest daughter's husband was Erskine of Cambo, and the second's Cunninghame of Barns. The Earl of Rothes influenced James Sharp's appointment as a professor in St Andrews and the Earl of Crawford presented him as minister to the Parish Church of Crail. He was imprisoned in London by Cromwell but talked his way to freedom. As spokesman for the Presybyterian cause to King Charles II, Sharp betrayed those for whom he spoke and was rewarded by being created Archbishop of St Andrews in 1661. He is a man who has been treated to many harsh words on his nature and personality as well as on his Episcopal views; schemer, greedy, devious, are three of the kinder ones. The new Archbishop was consecrated in Westminster Abbey, London. Times had indeed changed! The Archbishop made a regal journey across Fife to St Andrews. On 15th April he dined at Abbotshall before travelling on to Leslie House. The Earl of Rothes was organising the procession to St Andrews, and he rode on the right hand of the Archbishop with the Earl of Kellie on the left. In addition to the Earl, the Leslies were represented by David, Earl of Newark, and the second Earl of Leven, like his father an Alexander Leslie. To Presbyterians Sharp was a Judas; to David Forrest, minister of Kilconquhar, he was the "greatest knave that ever was in the Kirk of Scotland", which is a very high achievement!

The time had come for illegal conventicles, and for Rothes' wife, Lady Anne Lyndsay, to act as a protector of many a man in not only Leslie but in Markinch and Falkland and across the Howe of Fife. To the Presbyterians Rothes was dissolute, and Oliver Cromwell remarked of James Sharp, "that gentleman, after the Scotch way, should be called Sharp of that ilk." Both men had betrayed the reformed kirk when they rejected Presbyterianism for Episcopacy. Rothes died in his bed of ill health; Sharp by a roadside at Magus Muir near Strathkinness from where the towers and steeples of St Andrews can be seen.

Like the stories of the early Celtic saints, that of the murder of Archbishop Sharp has several versions, some more elaborate than others, but the essential details do not differ. I give a version taken from several sources. As always, both sets of historians—Episcopalians and Reformers—have had their political agenda—as I find have I. There is a good deal of sense in the daft-sounding statement that all narrative history is fiction. Intellectually my sympathies lie with neither of these two sets of religious killers, but I find myself favouring the Reformers whilst being appalled by their murderous act.

The Archbishop took a ferry over the Forth on the afternoon of 2nd May 1679 and stayed overnight at Captain Seton's house in Kennoway. The historian of the Covenanters, Robert Wodrow, recorded that, "if any body came to Kennoway enquiring about him, as the printed accounts by the Prelatick party say, I am assured it was none of the people who fell in with him tomorrow." The following morning the Archbishop took the St Andrews road in grand style but without a guard—in a luxurious coach-and-six which may have been the same vehicle in which he made his ceremonial entry into St Andrews sixteen years earlier. With him were his daughter and four servants with coachman and postillion. The Archbishop's first stop was at Ceres, or as Wodrow says, "Took Ceres in his way, stopped there, and smoked pipe with the Episcopal incumbent." There are those who believe that Sharp set out from the Melville manse in Anstruther.

It was chance that a party of Covenanters crossed Sharp's route that day as they were out looking not for him but for William Carmichael, a Sheriff Clerk, his vindictive agent. Again the leaders are Fife lairds, David Hackston and his brother-in-law John Balfour. Other chroniclers have said that James Russell was the leader. Of the other seven said to be there that day we also know the names of William Dingwall and Andrew Guilline. David Hackston was laird of Rathillet, near Kilmany, and his father was laird of nearby Hill Cairnie on the Cupar road. John Balfour was laird of Kinloch, at Collessie, and may have been related to the old family of Burleigh. Kinloch House is very early eighteenth century with not only Scots baronial additions but extensions by Sir Robert Lorimer. It could be that the steading at Rathillet includes the building where Hackston lived. Today it is a Balfour of the Balbirnie line who lives at Little Kinloch House with his father, a first cousin of the Earl of Balfour and the head of the Balfour families at Kirkforthar. The simplicity of Kilmany kirk encourages more peaceful thoughts than those associated with Archbishop Sharp and David Hackston. When Thomas Chalmers was minister at quiet Kilmany the kirk was filled to overflowing by those who came from far and near to hear him preach.

It is said to have been a boy up to neither mischief nor good purpose who told the party of Covenanters that the Archbishop's coach was coming to Blebo. Having taken a democratic decision to murder the Archbishop, say the covenanting historians, they waited at Magus Muir. Since Hackston had a personal grudge against Sharp he gave command of the group to Balfour and stood aside whilst the murder took place. Riding at speed they fired into the coach and forced it to stop. An apparently uninjured Sharp was forced out onto the road. It took the assassins more than half an hour to kill him with his daughter looking on and appealing for her father's life to be spared. The words used by James Melville in murdering Cardinal Beaton are said to have been used by Balfour as the attack on Sharp proceeded. Some have suggested that Hackston and Guilline wished to allow the praying, or begging, man to live but that they were over-ruled by Russell. We shall never know for certain what was thought or said near the long-gone village of Magus Muir as Archbishop Sharp was murdered "in the full sunlight of midday".

The murderers fled westwards to Rutherglen to join other militant and extremist Covenanters. They had a notable success on 29th May in fighting off John Graham of Claverhouse ("Bloody Clavers") at an armed conventicle at Drumclog, near Strathaven, but they were routed by an English royal force under James, Duke of Monmouth and illegitimate son of Charles II, at the battle of Bothwell Brig. The "Killing Times" of the 1680s had come for the indomitable Covenanters. Imprisonment, banishment, torture by the "boot", torture by the thumbscrew, and death by rope and gun continued through these years till William and Mary came to the throne in 1688. The conforming Episcopalians were replaced by those who had been "outed" from their manses in 1662. This time of yet more violence is known in kirk histories as the "Rabbling".

After his heroic minutes at Bothwell a wounded Balfour disappears into the shadows of legend as a crazed figure on wild moors and soaring rock faces; almost a King Lear of the Fife lairds. Sir Walter Scott invented a history for Balfour in *Old Mortality* where he appears under the name of Burley,

> Burley, only altered from what he had been formerly by the addition of a grisly beard, stood in the midst of the cave with his clasped Bible in one hand and his drawn sword in the other. His figure, dimly ruddied in the red light of the red charcoal, seems that of a fiend in the lurid atmosphere of Pandemonium.

David Hackston's history is known. He is another who was at Drumclog and he also fought with great courage at Bothwell Brig, commanding a troop of horse, and escaping into hiding. He joined the persuasive Richard Cameron, once of Falkland, and was taken at Airds Moss, in Ayrshire, on 22nd June 1680. His captor was Bruce of Earlshall, near Leuchars, ("The Bloody Bruce", the "Fife Persecutor"). Cameron was lucky; he died on Airds Moor. Hackston was taken to Edinburgh where, on his journey to Parliament Close, Cameron's head was carried on a halberd before him. A brave man, and never having wavered in his beliefs, Hackston was to be mutilated before he was hanged at Edinburgh Cross. His head was placed on Edinburgh's Netherbow and his limbs were displayed in St Andrews, Glasgow, Leith and Burntisland. One of Hackston's hands was buried in Cupar churchyard.

Following Cameron's death, Donald Cargill, another leader of the strict Covenanters, continued the struggle against the laws of King Charles II. Having excommunicated the King and his brother James, Cargill was taken prisoner at Covington Mill, Lanarkshire, on 12th July 1681 and executed in Edinburgh on 27th July. Andrew Pitulloch and Lawrence Hay were two of his three followers who were executed on 13th July for "denying lawful authority, calling the king a tyrant, and thinking it lawful to kill him." Tradition has it that Laurence Hay was a weaver from Kilconquhar and Andrew Pitulloch a farmworker from Largo. Their heads were sent to Cupar to be displayed with Hackston's hand. When I was in Cupar in 1997 most of the kirkyard gates were locked but I found a double gate in Ashlar Lane that could be opened. The headstone is not far in from the wall bordering the Lane. The headstone in Cupar kirkyard carries two heads, an open right hand and this inscription,

> Here lies Interred the Heads of LAURce HAY
> and ANDREW PITULLOCH who
> suffered martyrdom at Edinr July 13 1681
> for adhering to the word of God, & Scotlands
> covenanted work of Reformation, and also
> one of the Hands of DAVID HACKSTON
> of Rathillot who was most cruelly murdered
> at Edinr July 30th 1680
> for the same cause

On the reverse is inscribed,

> 1680
> Our persecutors fill'd with rage
> their brutish fury to aswage
> took heads & hands of martyrs off

That they might be the peoples scoff,
They Hackstons body cutt asunder
And set it up a worlds wonder
In several places to proclaim
these monsters gloryd in their shame.
        Re Erected   July 13 1792.

The modern stone mixture that has been laid in the walled area of the grave has broken into fragments but the words on this headstone remain readable. Also, the rough-hewn stone of the two large, water-filled bowls at the corners of the burial ground have retained edges that do credit to the mason who chiselled these emotive vessels.

The road at Magus Muir where the Archbishop was murdered no longer exists. The site of the murder is now within a wood and the memorial erected to mark it is reached by a narrow path. Within a few yards of this memorial is another marking the graves of five Covenanters who were symbolically brought to Magus Muir to be hanged and to "expiate and appease the Archbishop's ghost". When I visited the memorials in 1998 I took, from St Andrews, the no. 64 bus which runs to Springfield via Strathkinness, Pitscottie, Ceres and Cupar. From St Andrews this bus takes a minor road past Mount Melville and Craigtoun Country Park to a crossroads indicating Peat Inn to the left and Starthkinness to the right. Half way down that steep brae, that downhill joins the low-lying B939, a sign indicates a Public Footpath to Monuments. Travellers by car can take the B939 out of St Andrews and turn left at the Strathkinness crossroads.

There are in fact two paths that form a circular route to and from the monuments. The right-hand one tends to be boggier but it is surrounded by a less dense wood. It allows the Archbishop's memorial to be approached first. I prefer to take the left-hand path which goes through the wood and round to a stone wall edging a cultivated field. When I was there in February 1998 the crop seemed to be swedes or turnips although historians like to describe the place where the Covenanters were hanged as having become a cornfield. There is a gate in the wall to allow access to the short path to the burial place of the hanged Covenanters. The main path continues round a few yards to the place of Archbishop Sharp's murder, marked by a memorial which provides an ideological contrast to the nearby graves of the Covenanters. The rugged stones of this pyramid must rise to 12 feet and the sides of it are 8 feet across. The mortar is beginning to crumble and will soon need renewing. The light-coloured slab with the inscription contrasts with the heavy and vigorously cut old reddish-brown stones into which it is set. I suspected the slab to be man-made but the green colouring it had acquired prevented me from making a proper examination. The relief lettering was damaged and some of this looked like vandalism, especially the letters that form the Archbishop's name. The formal inscription is in Latin: "Near this place James Sharp Archbishop of St Andrews was murdered by savage enemies in the presence and despite the prayers of his daughter A.D. 1679". The scale of the pyramid is now wrong for this site by a woodland path. Also, it lacks space and its site does not allow us a prospect that could confer dignity. A smaller cairn with an inscribed tablet would be much better in the wood.

The burial ground of the Covenanters surprised me by its sizeable area which is surrounded by a 2-foot high stone wall topped by iron railings that show only a little rusting. The memorial stone stands in the centre of this area. The narrow path continues, allowing the poem on the back of the stone to be read. Both inscriptions are in reasonable order but the lettering is beginning to wear.

This was an exposed and treeless moor when the murder took place, although there may have been a long-gone hamlet named Magus Muir. Today, when out of the wood and by the graves in the field, the B939 to Pitscottie and Cupar can be seen beyond the long slope of the field and parts of Strathkinness village are visible on the slopes of its small hill. Looking straight over the gravestone, and across the fields of greens, a large farm, sheltered by a scattering of trees, seems isolated within these expansive acres. Despite these sightings of farm and road and village, I felt wary at that place. This had more to do with the dangers, supposed more than real perhaps, of our late-twentieth-century world, than with this wood being the scene of a slow and bloody murder. Standing by the Archbishop's pyramid, I was startled by an unexpected noise. It was a frisky spaniel and its young owner appeared seconds later to show concern at my fright. But this is a lonely path through an enclosing wood and I would recommend that two or more is good company here.

The five Covenanters hanged at Magus Muir were probably nowhere near that spot when the Archbishop was murdered but examples had to be made. These men were amongst the prisoners taken after the defeat of the Covenanting force at Bothwell Brig. They had refused to swear to be of good behaviour and were brought to trial. They refused even to admit that the killing of the Archbishop was murder and the government's court found them guilty of murder "after the fact". They were brought to Magus Muir in chains which were still on them when they were hanged. The date was 25th November 1679 and, as the inscription on the stone informs, "Here lies Thos Brown, James Wood, Andrew Sword, John Weddell & John Clyde who suffered martyrdom on Magus Moor for their adherence to the Word of God and Scotland's Covenanted Work of Reformation".

The stone marking the site of their execution has been renewed several times but the words which I read in 1998 on the other face of the stone are,

> 'Cause we at Bothwel did appear
> Perjurious Oths refus'd to swear
> 'Cause we Christ's Cause would not condemn
> We were sentenc'd to Death by Men
> Who Rag'd againsy us in such fury
> Our dead bodies they did not bury;
> But upon Poles did hing us high
> Triumph's of Babel's Victory.
> Our Lives we fear'd not to the Death.
> But consatant prov'd to the last breath.
> Renewed 1872

I have not been to the other Covenanting memorial near Magus Muir but it is close to Claremont Farm, and to "a small wood by a stream", where was placed the tombstone of Andrew Guilline who was, unlike the five men who were symbolically brought to Magus Muir to be hanged, involved in the murder.

In what is now known as the Sharp Aisle of the Parish Church of Holy Trinity, South Street, St Andrews, there is a very different monument to the memory of Archbishop James Sharp. Archbishop Sharp's funeral took place on 16th May 1679, thirteen days after the murder, in the Parish Church of the Holy Trinity, with the Bishop of Edinburgh, John Paterson, preaching at the funeral service. This Parish Church, or Toun Kirk, has a history that goes back to the twelfth century but the old church was not consecrated until 1246, by

Bishop David Bernham. In 1410 land in the centre of the town was given by Sir David Lyndsay of the Byres, an ancestor of the Earls of Lindsay, to enable a new church to be built. This was completed in 1412. With the Reformation came John Knox who preached in the Parish Church in June 1559. When Episcopacy came, Archbishop Spottiswoode used Holy Trinity as his "cathedral" and, when Charles II attempted to impose an extended Episcopacy, Archbishop Sharp was to use the church similarly. In 1899 plans were advanced for a restoration of the Church and Peter MacGregor Chalmers was given the most important commission of his illustrious career in church work. The church was near enough remade and re-dedicated in 1909. The great east and west windows, of 1914, have stained glass by Douglas Strachan. In 1926 a chime of fifteen bells was installed in the old tower in memory of Dr Playfair who had been very involved in having the church restored and in having the Playfair Aisle built. It is this church's bell that I listen for as I walk the streets and wynds of St Andrews. The church is often open to the public in the summer months but in the winter of 1997-98 it was open only on Saturdays from 10 am to noon and at the times of Sunday services. In 1998 when I visited Holy Trinity the Sharp Memorial was clad in scaffolding but this repair work should soon be completed.

The Sharp monument is very grand. It may have been made in the Netherlands and is certainly of black and white Greek and Italian marble and shows realistically, in bas-relief, the Archbishop's murder. It was commissioned by his son, Sir William Sharp, and is said to have been completed remarkably quickly; the Archbishop's murder and the battle at Bothwell Brig took place in mid June and the memorial may have been in place by December 1679. The monument is so high that the roof had to be raised to get it into what was then a communion aisle. The Latin inscription, in formal capitals, was written by Andrew Bruce, Bishop of Dunkeld. It is a terrible narrative, describing how he was,

> slaughtered in a terrible manner, having fallen on his knees that he might yet pray for his own people; he was pierced through by very many wounds of pistols, swords and daggers, by nine forsworn parricides excited by fanatical rage in the full sunlight of midday in the vicinity of his own metropolitan city in spite of the tears and protests of his most dear first-born daughter, and of his domestic servants, who had been wounded; on the third day of May, 1679, 61 years of age.

Strathkinness is a true hilltop village. The view over the wood with the memorials reveals that moorland still tops Drumcarrow Craig. The view northwards is to Guardbridge and the estuary of the Eden. I strained my eyes to see the tower of Earlshall but decided it must be hidden in the trees of its leafy garden. To the east the towers and spires of St Andrews look, as they also do from near Leuchars, tiny and toylike against the great vista of sea and sky. Even the largest aircraft on the runway of RAF Leuchars looks as if it belongs in a child's story book. From Strathkinness a minor road goes westwards 2¾ miles to Dairsie Bridge. My preferred route back to Cupar is the B940 via Pitscottie and Ceres. Viewed from a no.64 bus from St Andrews this is a route of scenic surprises.

For those who have no wish to walk the woodland paths, a long-range view of the Covenanters' monument can be got from the B940. On a bright day its railings are silhouetted against the sky. Passing below Blebo Craigs on a high summer day, which must resemble that on which the murderers met the idling boy, it is difficult to envisage this pleasant land of hill and pasture, of grand houses and sheltering trees, as the ground for so much hatred—both by Sharp's soldiers and the men of the Covenant. Then, suddenly, an open glen gives a full view of the spires and towers of Cupar and, high above the old

186

burgh, of the Hopetoun Monument on Mount Hill. The proud County Town of Fife could be mistaken for a small town in the Borders with sheltering hills and wooded acres. The hamlet of Pitscottie, and the site of Lyndsay of Pitscottie's farmhouse, can be missed if concentration lapses into admiration of some line of trees against the folding lands. At the Bidgend side of Ceres a sign informs that Hill of Travit lies one mile into these tree-clad slopes, as does Scotstarvit Tower where Drummond of Hawthornden may have written his "Polemino-Middinia".

In Ceres there is a work of art that I am eager to see each time I visit the "prettiest village in Fife". This is the piece of sculpture entitled "Provost" and nobody, surely, can deny that it is a delightfully rustic figure of a proper jolly civic dignitary or churchman; and hardly less sophisticated than a tribal totem pole out of North America or an Easter Island figure. The setting in which "The Provost" sits, looking along Main Street, is said to be a seventeenth-century fireplace. The village green is central to Ceres and the seventeenth-century bridge never fails to charm.

If I had to choose one inland Fife walk I think it would be from Markinch to Ceres. The route goes through Star and uphill past the farms of Carriston and Ballenkirk to Milldeans. The hamlet of Coaltown of Burnturk is at the road junction where one road goes down Kettlehill to join the Cupar road. It is the other road that my poem describes. It goes round to an unexpected hairpin bend that offers a surprise view of what could be a lush paddock and small layered hillsides. A little detour is necessary to visit Paradise Farm and the main route is to the well-set-up hamlet of Chance Inn which nestles below the main Cupar road like an idealised Naismith landscape rather than a Wilkie realistic social-narrative scene. The road branches at Craigrothie to Ceres and to Cupar with the latter passing Scotstarvit Tower and Hill of Tarvit.

This is a "walk" which I took many times in the 1950s, admittedly alone! Poetic licence was taken to give the poem dramatic form. It begins,

> You wantit a lang and truly rural walk.
>
> I reeled aff Mill Deans to Coaltown of Burnturk
> to Claybrigs to Cults and Pitlessie Lime Warks
> to Paradise Farm and Chance Inn and finally
> Ceres famed aw owre Fife. The maist rural walk in Fife I said
> endin up in its prettiest village. You made
> me tak you to prove me a deceiver and found three cottages
> lackin aw mod cons at Mill Deans, seeven cottages
> at Coaltown of Burnturk wi the only coal that for their grates.
> And Claybrigs truly an ideal fairm wi pure spring watter
> at its gates. The Lime Warks gied a blot it's true
> but David Wilkie was born at Cults and made Pitlessie
> Fair famous to become limner to the King.
> I near made Paradise at its fairm
> but you wantit to push on to the Chance Inn. A disappointment
> to find a wee hamlet o cottages but still raisin up
> imaginins o the auld coachin days.
> And to Ceres needin nae words wi famous green
> and brig and Bannockburn gemms played there still.

I have not been in Ceres on Bannockburn Day, but I like to think that some time during these celebrations there must be an opportunity for a rendering of the very old song that is best known in a version by Alexander Montgomerie. Robert Burns wrote "Scots Wha Hae" to the same tune and certainly "The Nicht is Near Gone" can be seen as a patriotic song, but it is more truly a sparkling and sprightly poem with which to welcome a bright new day of which, with its low rainfall, Fife has many,

> Hay! Now the day dawis;
> The jolie Cock crawis;
> Now shroudis the shawis,
>   Throw Natur anone.
> The thissell-cock cryis
> On lovers wha lyis,
> Now skaillis the skyis:
>   The nicht is near gone.
>
> The fieldis owerflowis
> With gowans that growis,
> Quhair lilies lyk low is,
>   Als rid as the rone.
> The turtill that trew is,
> With notes that renewis,
> Hir pairtie persewis:
>   The nicht is near gone.

shawis: groves   thissell-cock: mistle-thrush cock
skaillis: clears   gowans: daisies
low: a blaze   rid: red   rone: rowan berry
turtill: dove   pairtie: partner

Index

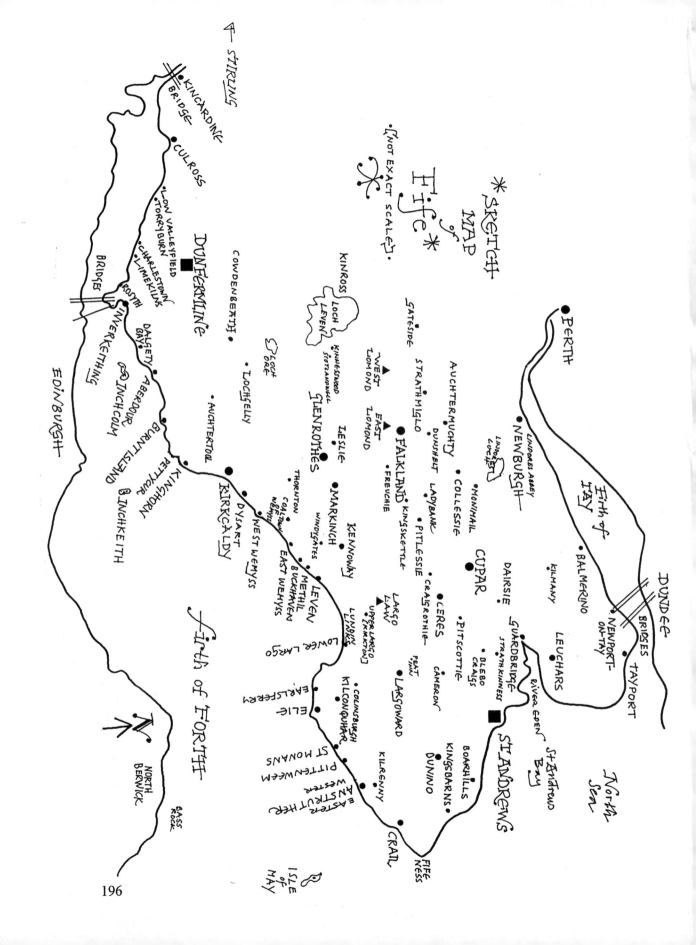

SKETCH MAP of Fife [Not exact scale.]

196